HISTORIC HOUSES

OF

SOUTH CAROLINA

BY

HARRIETTE KERSHAW LEIDING

WITH 100 ILLUSTRATIONS
FROM DRAWINGS BY ALFRED HUTTY, PHOTOGRAPHS
AND PRINTS

PHILADELPHIA AND LONDON
J. B. LIPPINCOTT COMPANY
1921

PRINTED BY J. B. LIPPINCOTT COMPANY
AT THE WASHINGTON SQUARE PRESS
PHILADELPHIA, U. S. A.

To

H. G. L.

THE BEST FRIEND
A WIFE EVER HAD

"No fire has touched them, and no flood;
They stand to-day where first they stood;
Places that knew them know them still,
Their doors swing wide, and on each sill,
In sweet confusion, wilting flowers
By noon, by night mark children's hours.
And closer still, like friends well tried,
The trees crowd up on every side,
Folding the roof-tree and the walls.
Each year their gracious shadow falls
Larger and larger; every spring
'Neath southern window some new thing
Lifts up its head and adds its grace
To sweeten the old Homestead place.
From every window to the skies
Women and men lift steadfast eyes,
Coming and going day by day,
Leading the life they must, or may . . . .
The world is full of open doors;
Step lightly in on friendly floors;
And throw thy rusty keys away
To locks which strange hands lock to-day."

FOREWORD

"The Almighty gives dreams to some and realities to others." The dream of the English Empire builders was to discover, and found a new civilization in the South, and it was out of the reality of the lives of the men and women who came and carried out the business of the dreams that South Carolina was formed, her homes erected, her fields tilled, and her civilization carried forward and outward; for it is a fact that from Colonial times South Carolina has been furnishing other South Atlantic States with the backbone of their civilization, although it is not generally known that she was one of the great emigrant States.

If South Carolina is to be judged by the aphorism that "A State is the product of its people," then this little section of land, which has stood for so much that is admirable, is indeed a great State. Little as it is known, South Carolina, geographically isolated in her early days, left to work out her own destiny in the following days of the development until the Revolutionary days surrounded by enemies on all sides (except to the Northward), has not only held its own but has led the Southeast in many agricultural, manufacturing and mining pursuits, led the Union in the yield per acre of corn, oats and cotton, and stands second in cotton manufacturing in the entire Union.

From the standpoint of inate ability, bravery, chivalry, purity of character and unselfish patriotism, the sons and daughters of Carolina are the equals of any on the American Continent and today represent the finest type of American citizen; yet it is difficult to try and tell the story of this people of mixed races, several religions, various customs and the modifications of these various differentations by climate, occupation, wars and the physical conformation of the land on the face of which they lived, and moved, and had their being.

It is an interesting peep into the past to envisage the homes in which these pioneer peoples and their descendants dwelt. These homes were the expression of their individualities modified by their occupations and means. The social, political and economic significance of these empire builders stands revealed in the homes they builded as well as the taste that prompted the style. Means were found for overcoming distances, securing material, and workmen were either developed or imported to carry out the design of the desired habitation, while the landscape gardeners were employed to decorate and embellish the neighboring grounds. All of these factors enter into the kind of house and the type of architecture found in lowland and highland of South Carolina.

Undoubtedly it is the sense of a story behind things that leads to the writing about the homes of olden times and about the inhabitants thereof by one set of people, and the reading of story of these houses by another set. Nor need we be afraid of being classed amongst those who have, as Rupert Hughes expressed it, '' Kicked themselves upstairs into that dreary attic where the critics go who are what Horace called ' the praisers of the past,' '' if we seek the human story of the individual homes and their builders.

If social life reflects the taste and is the measure of grandeur in the life of these dead and gone Carolinians, we can reconstruct for ourselves a picture of those yesteryears which lie forgotten in men's memories, but which nevertheless hold precisely the same human elements as our own existence of life and love, fun and flirtations, women's fears and women's tears, and the laughter of little children, all of which are held together in the scheme of things by men and their deep desires and ambitions.

Strong-minded persons are apt to think fashion a fickle jade and a trivial thing--yet in Carolina, indigo culture was introduced in order to dye the home-woven silks of milady and it is even whispered that gentlemen were partial to blue, the product of their staple indigo, yet indigo eventually rivalled rice and yielded to cotton only after the Revolutionary War, and became a standard of barter in foreign commerce

So interwoven are social life, agricultural interests, industrial evolution with commercial interests, that it is said " The lady of a Southern planter will lay out the whole annual produce of a rice plantation in silver and gold, muslins, lace veils and new liveries, carry a hogshead of tobacco on her head and trail a bale of Sea-Island cotton at her heels, while a lady of Boston or Salem, will wrap herself up in the net proceeds of a cargo of whale oil, and tie on her hat with a quintal of cod-fish." Thus it is that the beautiful old houses in South Carolina grew as the external expression of a certain ease, grace and dignity of life led by the landed gentry.

Near the coast the spacious verandas came in response to the need for coolness, and shadowy retreats from the brilliant sunshine of this sub-tropical climate, tall ceilings, large windows, and lattice jalousie blinds were borrowed from the neighboring Spanish Indies, while formal gardens and gateways came over in the inner consciousness of the Cavalier stock that settled low- country Carolina and found expression in manner fitting the locality.

Although the first settlers had confined themselves to the neighborhood of Charleston, the fact that Georgia was being settled (1732-34) protected the Western frontier of the State and gave a feeling of security hitherto unknown, so that the interior of the State received many immigrants; Germans, Scotch (after the battle of Culloden), and on Braddock's defeat, refugees from Pennsylvania and Virginia came and settled in the Piedmont sections of the State. Besides these various additions to the State, Irish Protestants, Swiss Colonists, German Redemptionists, Welsh Colonists from Pennsylvania, all went to the making up of the total populations and were added to the original English settlers, Cavaliers and gentlemen adventurers as well as the French Huguenot refugees.

Thus it is seen that various considerations enter into the discussion of the homes of such a mixed people. The homes of the Bacon and Rice aristocracy, situated in the low country, conformed to the English Manor type, being later modified to suit the climatic conditions, and becoming as Birge Harrison delightfully puts it, " infected by the spirit of the West Indian houses as though blown across from the West Indies," while the homes of the people in the middle lands of the State were builded and furnished to suit another set of people and to meet other needs, while the homes in highland counties conformed to yet another set of standards and conditions. So that the houses of Carolina the Province, Carolina the Royal Ward, when Kings George the First and Second, were said to be " Nursing Fathers " to the infant colony, or the homes of Carolina the devastated, by foreign or civil strife, all have different meanings and designs, but a spirit of high Romance permeates the entire history of the State, its people and their homes.

The present volume has been undertaken as a loving tribute to South Carolina, who gave to the writer the three beings most dear to her on earth; and, because the history of the houses in South Carolina is the history of the homes of kindred and friends, this effort has been made to give to the world a glimpse of the wonderful men and women of the state and the homes they builded.

It has been deemed best, incidentally, to mention a few of the first provincial laws in order that the reader may obtain some idea of the manner of life contemplated by those in authority in primitive Carolina. This is necessary because the history of the colony and its various settlements unwinds itself like a golden thread from the gleaming web of the history of the mother city, Charleston, until the outer threads are far from the center, yet connected by invisible and intangible bonds.

The houses in the upper part of South Carolina were erected at a later date than those in the low country, and so have been included in this volume with briefer mention, the oldest houses naturally being found along the rivers in the lower part of the state.

x

FOREWORD

My thanks are due to Misses Lillian Yates, Mary Von Kolnitz and Elsie Kirkland for their efficient and loving help. My thanks are also due to the many friends and the owners of properties throughout the state who so kindly responded to letters written to secure information. I have consulted all of the standard sources of information available, and have scanned the De Saussure records (the originals of which are owned by my aunt, Miss Isabelle De Saussure) and have in addition had priceless aid and information given me by my mother, Susan Boone De Saussure and my father, Reverend John Kershaw, D.D.

HARRIETTE KERSHAW LEIDING

CHARLESTON, S. C.
MARCH 1, 1920

CONTENTS

LIST OF ILLUSTRATIONS

LIST OF ILLUSTRATIONS

    xvi

LIST OF ILLUSTRATIONS

HISTORIC HOUSES
OF
SOUTH CAROLINA

NOTES FROM SOUTH CAROLINA ALMANAC 1765

BERKLEY COUNTY TAKES IN THE OLD PARISHES OF
1. St. Philip's Parish, Charleston
2. St. Michaels, Charleston
3. Christ Church
4. St. Thomas and St. Dennis.
5. St. John's
6. St. George (Dorchester)
7. St. James (Goose Creek)
8. St. Andrews (West side Ashley River)
County Town—Charleston

CRAVEN COUNTY TAKES IN THE OLD PARISHES OF
1. St. James Santee
2. St. Stephen
3. Prince George
4. Prince Frederick
5. St. Marks
County Town—Georgetown

COLLETON COUNTY CONTAINS PARISHES OF
1. St. Paul
2. St. Peter
3. St. Bartholomew
County Town—Jacksonborough

GRANVILLE COUNTY CONTAINS THE OLD PARISHES OF
1. St. Helena
2. St. Peter
3. Purrysburg, (see Peter Purry)
4. Prince William
County Town—Beaufort

CHAPTER I
OLD CHARLESTON AND SOUTH CAROLINA

LD houses resemble children in that their characters are greatly affected by environment and parentage. In dealing with the South Carolina homes it must be remembered that the state was settled in layers, so to speak, the homes of the sea-coast people being constructed to suit the ideas of people from sea-port towns in the old world, while those of the middle and upper parts of the state were built to meet the requirements of people who had drifted into the interior, or come in from other settlements.

It is amusing to read one of the early historical writers, Oldmixon, who describes Carolina as "lying parallel with the Land of Canaan," which would seem to imply the use of tents, and some of the primitive log-cabins erected by the first settlers were scarcely more than this. A more substantial type of primitive house was built of mud and clay—such a house is said to exist in Williamsburg county, near Kingstree. Another primitive house of a later period was constructed of a native cement composed of lime and oyster shell—called "Tabby"—an example of which is found on Fripp's Island, near Beaufort. The native marls of South Carolina also furnished materials with which the first settlers builded their homes. The remains of such a house are found on Fairlawn Barony on Cooper river.

Numerous descriptions of the colony were printed and sent out in order to induce immigration, many of which are included in B. R. Carroll's Historical collection. Some of these were printed in London "and to be sold by Mrs. Grover, in Pelican Court, in Little Britain, 1682." A small description and a map of South Carolina was published by Mr. Richard Blome, and printed for Dorman Newman, in the year 1678. Yet an-

1

other map of Carolina was printed by order of the Lords Proprietors "newly published in one large Sheet of Paper, a very spacious Map of Carolina with its Rivers, Harbor's Plantations, and other Accommodations, from the latest Survey, and best Informations, with a large and particular Description of the Entrances into Ashly and Cooper Rivers; this Map to be Sold for Is. by Joel Gascoyne, near Wapping Old Stairs, and Robert Green in Budge Row, London, 1682."

It will thus be seen that Charleston is the mother of the state, and a perusal of the Acts of Assembly published in Grimke's Digest will strengthen this belief. The first lawmakers of the colony were religious men, as is shown by their first law, which provided for the observation of the Lord's Day. Having taken this step they proceeded to the "suppressing of idle, drunken and swearing persons inhabiting within this state." Having thus provided for the just and the unjust our forefathers proceeded to the laying out of highways, and so successfully did they accomplish this latter task that the roadway system of South Carolina to-day occupies in large measure the highway system as laid out by our progenitors. One of the first provisions after this was "settling the militia." Then realizing that all these things would cost money they passed an Act for "raising a tax of £400 or the value thereof."

One class of settlers that came to South Carolina and built fine homes was of the Cavalier stock of England. Many Acts were passed to encourage immigration, among them "an Act to suspend prosecution for foreign debts." Another was for "making Aliens free of this part of the country," and "for granting liberty of conscience to all protestants."

Among the early laws permanency of building was provided for; the residences of Charleston were to be constructed of brick, but this was later repealed. Along with permanency of building came the desire for preservation of record, and an early Act provides for the registering of births, marriages and deaths in the colony. Philanthropic and educational enterprises were nurtured, rewards given to inventors of agricultural machines, and in every way possible a fine type of

2

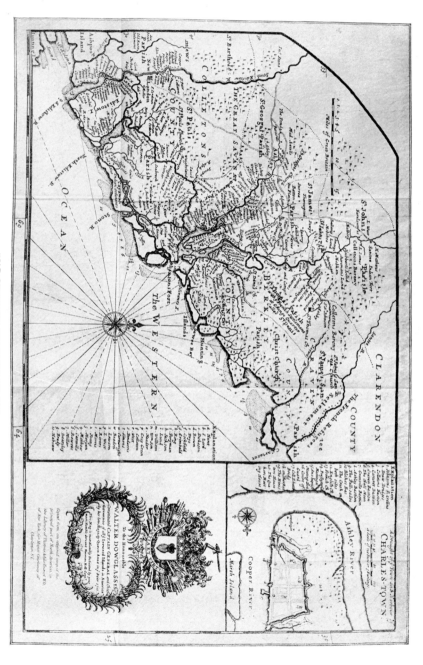

MAP OF SOUTH CAROLINA OF 1715

civilization established. One of the earliest Acts provides for a Provincial Library.

Mr. Langdon Cheves writes of the buildings erected in early days, saying: "Fine old Colonial brick houses probably did not exist in the up country; were few in the middle country and were comparatively rare anywhere. Most of the fine brick houses were built between the years 1710 and 1760, and in the neighborhood of Charleston. After 1760 the tradition of stone and brick houses faded, masons became scarce, and saw mills developed, then wooden houses on brick basements were built."

Concerning the topography of "Charles Town" (the name of the chief city was changed to Charleston by act of Assembly in 1783), although the first settlement was on the western bank of Ashley River the Council journal of date 21st February, 167½, says:

"Mr. Henry Hughes came this day before the Grand Councill and voluntarily surrendered up the one halfe of his land nere a place upon the Ashley River knowne by the name of Oyster Poynt, to be employed in and towards the enlarging of a Towne and common of pasture there intended. . . ."

The natural advantages of Oyster Point had not escaped even the first Governor, for Secretary Dalton tells us that "there is a place between Ashley River and Wando River, about 600 acres, left vacant for a town and fort, by the direction of the old Governor Coll. Sayle, for that it commands both rivers: it is, as it were, a key to open and shut this settlement into safety or danger."

THE HISTORIC HOUSES OF CHARLESTON

There are only two or three buildings which are discussed in this present volume, as the subject has been thoroughly covered from an architectural standpoint in the "Dwelling Houses of Charleston." But it is not out of place to say that in Charleston one sees over and over again houses on the old San Domingo model, of a three or four story structure, one room deep, that tower tall and narrow, as though turning a shoulder to the world. However, a balcony door let in the

3

façade gives a hint of welcome and provides access to the verandas which stretch the entire length of the houses. The advantage of this arrangement is that the house faces the walled-in garden, while not being set too far back from the city street. One writer says that "the arrangement of rooms in these houses is much like that of the average English house in that the drawing room (or with-drawing rooms) parlor and dining room are all on the second floor, while the library suite and breakfast room are found on the ground floor. On the third floor, which affords needed light and air, are the large, spacious bed rooms."

In 1706 the building of wooden frame houses in the town had been declared to be a nuisance and prohibited, later it was represented that bricks were not always to be had but at such excessive rates as prevented the building up of waste places, and the act was repealed. Houses were allowed to be built of wood, provided the hearths and chimneys were of brick and stone. McCrady says in his "History of South Carolina Under Proprietary Government" that "until 1717 there were few houses at Charles Town out side the fortifications . . . In that year the fortifications on the West, North and South sides were dismanteled and demolished to enlarge the town, which now began to spread out on the North across the creek, which ran where the market now stands, and on the West beyond what is now Meeting Street. There are but three buildings in the City of Charleston of which there are any historical authorities for believing that they were built during the Proprietary Government." These are supposed to be found on the lower part of Church Street, just below Tradd. None of these houses are very large. In this present volume the presentation of Charleston houses is confined to several very well known establishments of a much later date.

THE MILES BREWTON HOUSE

In " The Dwelling Houses of Charleston " Miss Alice Huger Smith and her father have given the history of many of the most significant houses in the City, but it has been felt that in a book (such as the present one) supposed to be dealing with

THE MILES BREWTON HOUSE, CHARLESTON

Showing old coach house and slave quarters

the historic houses of South Carolina, some mention must be made of a few of the Charleston places. The first discussion will be the Miles Brewton house, now in the possession of Miss Mary P. Frost and her sisters, Miss Susan P. Frost and Miss Rebecca Motte Frost.

Miss Mary Pringle Frost has written an attractive little booklet called the "Meaning of a House" in which she says: "My sister, Susan Frost, and I feel that this house should be known and loved by the community and that it should enter into the life of the community—it should live side by side with smaller houses in its love for what is true and friendly. A house needs friends: it needs interchange of human thought: it is a human habitation. What would a habitation be without an inhabitant? It would be lonely; its spirit would faint."

> "O floors that felt our life-long tread
> Windows whence babes peeped at their stars
> Thresholds whence passed away our dead
> O'er which our brides came from afar!"

The South Carolina Gazette and County Journal, August 22, 1769, gives the names of the men concerned in the designing and building of the Brewton house, now best known as the Pringle house, and occupied by the Misses Frost:

"Ezra Waite, Civil Architect, House-builder in general, and Carver, from London, Has finished the Architecture, conducted the execution thereof, viz.: in the joiner way, all tabernacle frames (but that in the dining room excepted), and carved all the said work in the four principal rooms, and also calculated, adjusted, and draw'd at large for to work by, the Ionick entablature, and carved the same in front and round the eaves, of Miles Brewton, Esquire's House on White-Point for Mr. Moncrieff.—If on inspection of the above mentioned work, and twenty seven years experience, both in theory and practice, in noblemen and gentlemen's seats, be sufficient to recommend; he flatters himself to give satisfaction to any gentleman, either by plans, sections, elevations, or executions, at his house in King Street, next door to Mr. Wainwright's, where architecture is taught by a peculiar method never published in any book extant.

N. B. As Miles Brewton Esquire's dining room is of a new construction with respect to the finishing of windows and doorways it has been industriously propagated by some (believed to be Mr. Kinsey Burden, a carpenter) that the said Waite did not do the architecture, and conduct the execution thereof. Therefore the said Waite begs leave to do himself justice in this public manner, and assure all gentlemen, that he the said Waite, did construct every individual part and drawed the same at large for the joiner to work by, and conducted the execution therof. Any man that can prove to the countrary, the said Waite promises to pay him One Hundred Guineas, as witness my hand, this 22nd day of August, 1769.''

"EZRA WAITE.''

The Pringle house is one of the oldest houses in Charleston and known as one of the best preserved and most elegant specimens of Colonial architecture in the country. Miles Brewton, for whom the house was built, and his whole family were lost at sea. The house then passed to his two sisters, of whom Mrs. Rebecca Motte was one. She was living in it at the time of the occupation of the city by the British. It was seized and used by Lord Rawdon and Col. Nesbit Balfour, Commandant of Charleston. An interesting item concerning Rebecca Motte is that a tablet has been erected to her memory in the vestibule of St. Philip's Church, by the Rebecca Motte Chapter of the Daughters of the American Revolution. The marble of the tablet erected to her memory was the top of a ''pier Table'' in her home. The first tablet erected to Mrs. Rebecca Motte's memory was also a marble which had served as the top of a pier table in her country home, and it was also set up in St. Philip's Church but was destroyed in the burning of the first Church on the present site, on February 15th, 1836.

There are traces of Lord Rawdon's occupancy still visible in the Miles Brewton house, for the portrait so valued of Mr. Brewton bears the mark of a sword thrust through it by one of his officers, and the marble mantel in one of the parlors has a slight sketch made by some sharp instrument, of a burly Englishman, with the swords of Sir H. Clinton above it. It was in this room that Lord Rawdon gave audience to the little sons of Col. Isaac Hayne, who came with a relative to plead for their father's life.

At that time and for long years after, the garden at the

back of the house went down to Legare Street, and Lord Rawdon is said to have cut a wooden gate in the high brick wall
that surrounded the premises, that he might have easy access
through the garden wall to another colonial house in Legare
Street, where his suite resided.

The house itself has been altered but very little since it was
built in 1765, thus preserving its former glory. It is a three
story brick building, with double piazzas each supported by
impressive stone pillars. Like most of the houses of this date
the wide hall has two large rooms on either side. On the third
floor is to be found the long drawing-room that reaches across
the front of the house. The beautiful and artistic carvings and
panelings of this old home are of great importance and reflect
the character of its builder, Miles Brewton.

HEYWARD HOUSE

Judge Thomas Heyward's house on the west side of
Church Street, just north of Tradd, was at one time considered one of the most splendid homes in Charleston. Although
not so large, nor the enrichments so profuse, this old home has
many features in common with the Brewton house. Formerly
double verandas adorned this three story brick structure. In
the rear is a long brick building where McLane opened his
famous billiard parlor and bar about 1830. The Heyward
house rises to fame, however, in being the place selected to
house President Washington during his visit to Charleston,
that being the most prominent event in the annals of the city.

The President had journeyed by land, stopping at Georgetown, South Carolina, and arrived opposite the city at what
is now Mt. Pleasant, on the 2nd day of May, 1791. A committee consisting of Hon. John Bee Holmes, Recorder, in his
official robes, General C. C. Pinckney, and Edward Rutledge,
Esq., had crossed the river to meet him, and accompanied him
in a barge rowed by the twelve American captains of vessels
then in port, and commanded by Captain Cochran. A flotilla
of boats of all sizes and kinds, filled with ladies and gentlemen,
and two bands of music, attended him over. As he approached
the town a salute of artillery was fired. The following extract

7

is taken from a paper giving an account of the proceedings of the City Council in anticipation of the President's arrival:

"The Intendant and Committee appointed to make the necessary arrangements for the reception and entertainment of George Washington, Esquire, President of the United States, on his arrival in Charleston, recommended that the house of Thomas Heyward, Esq., in Church Street, at present in occupation of Mrs. Rebecca Jamieson, be taken for the use of the President during his residence in this city, together with the furniture, for which the sum of £60 be paid, it being the lowest rate at which the said house can be procured."

The President spent a week in Charleston, there was a series of balls, dinners, breakfasts and other entertainments, and every attention that hospitality, public and private, could devise was shown him. One of the handsomest entertainments given in his honor was a splendid concert and ball at the "Exchange,"' on which occasion the ladies wore bandeaux of white ribbon interwoven in their hair, with Washington's portrait and the words "long live the President" painted on them. The late Mr. Charles Fraser says: "Every hand that could hold a pencil, professional or amateur, was enlisted to furnish them."

The week spent in the old Heyward home by our first President is not the only honor of which this dwelling boasts. It may well be proud of its first owner, Judge Thomas Heyward, a grandson of Captain Thomas Heyward, who served in the British Colonial Army. When the Indians surrendered the occupation of their lands beyond the Combee River, Captain Heyward acquired a portion of these lands and thenceforth his descendants became residents of that part of the province.

In March, 1775, the Provincial Congress enlisted two regiments, and Judge Thomas Heyward was appointed Captain of the first company. A year later he was chosen, with ten other men, to report a form of government for the colonies. Judge Heyward's name appears among the Signers of the Declaration of Independence, an honor which was conferred upon only prominent men of his generation.

The Heyward family was one of the first to give much

8

JUDGE HEYWARD'S MANSION, CHURCH STREET, CHARLESTON, AS IT WAS WHEN PRESIDENT WASHINGTON WAS THERE ENTERTAINED IN 1791

From an old print

attention to the cultivation of rice, owning large bodies of land adapted to cultivation of this grain, by the success of which they amassed considerable fortune.

The State of South Carolina has erected a monument over the grave of Judge Heyward in Jasper County and his body lies buried in a plot on the plantation that belonged to him in the Revolutionary days.

RUTLEDGE HOUSE

The square brick house on Broad Street, now owned and occupied by Mr. R. G. Rhett, was at one time the home of Dictator Rutledge. It is set upon a tall brick foundation with three additional stories above. The main entrance is in the form of a portico, which is reached on either side by a double flight of marble steps, protected by an ingenious extension of the portico. The whole façade of the building is very handsome and is adorned by this portico on the first two stories and a veranda extending across the face of the house on the second floor. All of this iron work was added to the house about 1850, when it was owned and occupied by William S. Gadsden, father of Norman P. and grandfather of Messrs. William and Dwight Gadsden.

The inside of this interesting home is finished with hardwood floors and walls, which latter are adorned with rare paintings. The rooms to the right upon entering are connected and are used as reception rooms, while the corresponding rooms to the left are used as dining and breakfast rooms, the household offices being downstairs in the basement. Up stairs a magnificent ball room occupies the entire front of this establishment, while the wings are used as guest rooms and private sitting rooms. The third floor is given over to sleeping apartments.

Mrs. Rhett (*née* Blanche Salley) has seen to it that this splendid mansion has received the dignified furnishings due such a historic house. In addition to the many Rhett heirlooms of furniture, paintings, silver, cut glass, etc., she has so arranged that their full artistic possibilities are utilized, and has produced a home of dignity and delight.

9

John Rutledge was the son of a physician, John Rutledge, who came to South Carolina about 1730, and Sarah Hext. The young John and his brothers, Edward and Hugh, were sent to England to receive an education. They all became lawyers in Charleston. John and Edward were members of the Continental Congress at Philadelphia in 1774 and also in 1775. After a battle fought in the harbor during the Revolution on the 12th of November, John Rutledge was made a member of the Council of Safety. He was soon afterwards chosen as first president of the separate and independent State of South Carolina, and was called "Dictator," being allowed absolute authority in his efforts for the safety of the State.

Some of the Revolutionary scenes which took place in and near the home of the "Dictator" are told in the Diary of Captain Barnard Elliott:

"(Gen'l Orders,) 28 March, Parole, Aera. Ordered, that Col. Robert's regiment of artillery and all the militia now in Chas. Town under the command of Col. Pinckney do, at 11 o'clock this morning, draw up two deep in Broad Street, on the side opposite St. Michael's Church. The regiment of artillery with two field pieces on the right, in order to receive the Hon'ble John Rutledge, Esq., constitutionally appointed by the Hon'ble the Legislature as President and Commander-in-Chief of the same, with the honors due that station. Ordered that should there not be room enough for the militia under Col. Pinckney in Broad Street from the State House to the Exchange, then that the remainder draw up on the Bay two deep as before, with their backs to the houses extending themselves from Guerard's corner on their left as far along the Bay as may be, in that manner. Col. Robert's regiment to fire 13 guns when President's appointment has been read, at Rutledge House. Two sentries to be placed at President's door."

OTHER HOUSES

East of the Rutledge house on Broad Street stands a substantial building of the same type, said to have been erected by a Mr. Bellinger as a copy of a house in England. It is stated that Mr. Bellinger never lived in this house and it is perhaps best known as the residence of Bishop Nor-

10

"DICTATOR" RUTLEDGE'S HOME, BROAD STREET
CHARLESTON
Now R. G. Rhett residence

THE PAUL HOUSE, BROAD AND CHURCH STREETS, CHARLESTON
From a print
Another house said to be Dictator Rutledge's

throp a kinsman of the Bellingers. It is now used as the Episcopal Residence.

The old Izard house stands next east of the Bellinger house. It is said to have been erected previous to 1757 and has escaped all the great fires, standing to-day a monument of colonial days. This house was for many years the residence of Judge George Bryan, the son of Judge George S. Bryan, the son of Jonathan Bryan, who was a son of George Bryan, Judge of Supreme Court of Pennsylvania, and who was a delegate to the First Colonial Congress in 1765. On the maternal side the Bryans are connected with the Lathams, Dwights, Johnsons and Broughtons.

To the west of the Rutledge house stood St. Andrew's Hall, which for many years was the favorite place for fashionable assemblies and public meetings. It was the home of St. Andrew's Society, founded in 1729 by Scotch immigrants. Historically it is famous as the meeting place of the State Convention which, December 20th, 1860, there passed the Ordinance of Secession, the act which inaugurated the great War of Secession. When General LaFayette visited the city, arriving March 14th, 1825, he was assigned, being the guest of the city, to St. Andrew's Hall, as his residence.

A house sometimes spoken of as the Rutledge house, but better known as the "Paul House," is a colonial brick structure at the southwest corner of Broad and Church Streets. Although the first floor has been altered into business offices, the upstairs is essentially the same as it was in the olden days. Its interior is finished as are all the early Georgian houses, with rooms of panelled wood and possesses high decorated cornices and wainscoating. In this old house is found the characteristic "Beufet" near the mantelpiece. It is desirable that this house should be kept intact on account of its purity of style, and as a relic of Colonial days.

CHAPTER II

ON COOPER RIVER FROM CHARLESTON TO THE "TEE"

BELVIDERE AND ITS NEIGHBORS

COOPER RIVER

HE handsome estate called Belvidere, now in possession of the Charleston Country Club, and formerly the residence of three Colonial Governors, Craven, Johnson and Glen, and of two wealthy families, the Manigaults and Shubricks, is situated on the west side of the Cooper River, north of Charleston, on what is vulgarly called The Neck. The present house was built about the end of the 18th or beginning of the 19th century. This home of the Shubrick family has a long and interesting history, of which space does not permit more than a brief mention, connected with Magnolia Umbra and the Cartaret Tract, which lies adjacent to the south where the old Powder-Horn buildings now are; the former site of "Exmount."

The Shubrick family were wealthy English merchants and shipowners who bought the site before the Revolutionary War, building thereon and calling the place Belvidere. General William Moultrie mentions this spot in his memoirs by saying that at the evacuation of Charleston, "The American Army was kept at Shubrick's farm until the British embarked, to avoid collision between the troops."

Just after the Revolution, one Sunday when the family were returning from church, they saw a smoke in the distance, and on reaching the farm (then three miles out from town) they found the house burned to the ground. The *City Gazette and Daily Advertiser,* in March, 1796, says: "Belvidere, the

12

elegant seat of Thomas Shubrick, Esq., three miles from this city, was yesterday morning destroyed by fire. We are informed that all the furniture except what was in the lower story was consumed.''

Tradition has it that this first house was set on fire to cover traces of theft by a negro slave girl who was infatuated with the handsome English gardener. He instigated the theft of the family jewels, which he duly received, fled the country, and left the unfortunate negress to face all consequences. In her frantic endeavor to hide one crime she committed another, and added arson to theft. She is said to have confessed to both of these crimes at her trial, and for them she was hung. Some say her ghost haunts the long double avenue where she was wont to meet her accomplice and quondam lover.

The present establishment, and second house to occupy this spot, is a square wooden structure set on a brick basement five feet in height. From this ascends the house which has two stories and an attic. The house proper contains eight rooms, exclusive of basement offices and attic rooms. Beside the main building two tower-like wings project on the north and south corners of the house; these are entirely independent, and partake of the nature of ''block-houses,'' evidently erected as defences against Indians. The only visible connection these two flanking buildings have with the main mansion is found in the substantial brick wall connecting all their basements, which wall forms a sheltering parapet.

Belvidere house faces westward, but has an open lawn not only to the rear on the east, but to the north and south also, where small formal flower gardens lie in the enclosures formed by the block-houses, after the manner of old fashioned wall-gardens.

The approach to this staunchly constructed house is through a magnificent double avenue of venerable oaks lining the semi-circular driveway. Directly in front of the house is a grassy sward, bisected by a formal pathway leading up to the stone steps and flagstone terrace. This latter forms a rather unusual entrance for a southern home, but affords a delightful promenade from which a scene of rare beauty is enjoyed.

13

This is particularly true on an autumn afternoon when the western sky is ablaze with crimson and gold. Then the trunks of the great oaks of the avenue show purple-black against the flaming sky, while their gnarled branches make perfect gothic arches for a leafy roof, through the interstices of which pours a mellow haze. In the pathway forming an aisle to this cathedral of the out-of-doors, the last faint rays of daylight meet and mingle with quivering lances of light from the "Sublime, Sweet Evening Star."

The stone terrace gives direct access, through an arched door with carved lintels and intricate fan-lights, to a front hall. From out of this hall open four doors, one of which gives access to the large rear room, one to the side hall containing the stairways, and one on each side to two delightful airy rooms, on the north and south respectively, with high ceilings and open fireplaces. The chimneys of Belvidere are so placed as to afford warmth to four rooms at one time, front and rear on each of the stories.

Just inside of the front door are to be found latticed jalousie blinds, lending an air of enchantment to the otherwise plain hall, and producing a mysterious atmosphere as though some dark-eyed beauty might here secretly look forth at a booted and spurred cavalier as he clattered up the avenue on his coal-black charger while the plume from his bonnet waved gaily in the breeze. A "Romeo Balcony" over the front entrance adds to, rather than detracts from, the air of discreet romancing which the whole house produces. This curved balcony, with the exception of five well placed windows with solid wooden shutters, forms the only break in the straight, plain exterior of the house.

Occupying the rear of the house both up and down stairs are two beautifully proportioned rooms which are quite unusually large and command an unobstructed view of the whole Belvidere tract to the south, east and north. Further afield the view is wonderful, including glimpses of the city and harbor, Cooper and Wando Rivers, Daniel's Island, and the mainland beyond in Christ Church Parish. This large room downstairs was evidently the state dining-room, and the corresponding apartment upstairs was the ballroom. On the lower main floor a flat-roofed piazza forms an agreeable and dignified finish to the rear exterior, across the whole width of which it extends and from which the same unbroken panorama as seen from the dining and ball rooms can be enjoyed.

Some of the special interior architectural features are the stairway with its mahogany balustrade and newel post, the large arched window on the landing, and the half-window found on the stairway leading to the attic. These excite the admiration of visitors to Belvidere, and bespeak refinement of taste, and abundant means in securing the correct execution of detail.

Perfect simplicity occurs again in the Adam design found in the decoration of this house. This is true of the ornamentation over the doors of the large ballroom and decoration of the mantelpiece. The scenes over the doors are pastoral in subject, representing a shepherd piping to his sheep, or wooing in rustic style. The mantel is decorated in a way quite out of the ordinary, with a sea-weed and sea-shell motif, the use of which may be ascribed to sentiment owing to the fact that the sons of Mr. and Mrs. Thomas Shubrick were all gallant sailors.

Capt. Templer Shubrick, one of the sons, distinguished himself in the war with the Barbary pirates, and was sent home with dispatches telling of victory. He sailed on the Sloop-of-war "Hornet" which foundered at sea and was never again heard of. Another son, Capt. Edward Rutledge Shubrick, also died at sea, and the officers and sailors of his ship, the frigate "Columbia," asked the privilege of erecting his monument, which now stands in the eastern cemetery of St. Philip's Church.

It was the father of these young men, Thomas Shubrick, who built the house. He was a daring soldier of the Revolution and for his patriotism his estate was sequestered by the British. His wife was a famous beauty, Miss Sarah Motte, who was selected, because of her beauty of face and form and charm of mind and manner, to sit opposite to President Washington at a dinner given to him upon the occasion of his visit to Charleston in 1791.

15

In spite of his estates having been sequestered, Thomas Shubrick must have either retained or regained Belvidere, advertising for a miller in 1806 or 1807. The property was inherited by Capt. Templer Shubrick, and after his tragic death his widow returned to her northern home, leaving the estate in trust for her son Edmund, then an infant. The property was later acquired by Capt. Edward Rutledge about the year 1834, and according to a deed of marriage settlement Capt. Rutledge gave it as a wedding gift to his daughter, Harriet Horry Rutledge, who married St. Julien Ravenel in 1851. By various processes the property passed through the hands of a Mr. Brewster, the Magnolia Cemetery Company, and Mr. C. O. Witte. From the latter was purchased the present portion constituting the Country Club and containing the mansion house called Belvidere.

THE RAT TRAP

Across the Broad Path from "Belvedere," according to Judge H. A. M. Smith, and situated on the Ashley river, was a plantation known as The Rat Trap, later changed to Dr. Harris' Hayfield Farm.

Near Belvidere lay, says the same authority, the Burnham Grant, some acres of which were west of the Broad Path, and some east; upon the portion lying east was found Cochran's Ship Yard, on Ship Yard Creek, the name then given Long Point Creek. This tract was afterwards broken up into small farms, and passed into the hands of various persons of note, Mr. Joel Poinsette acquiring one portion which was separated from Belvidere by Shubrick Avenue.

THE FOUR MILE HOUSE

Proceeding to the north, on the Broad Path is found an interesting edifice by the roadside. It is commonly called the Four Mile House, for many years a noted road-house or tavern for travelers on the road to and from Charleston. This inn was kept, about the year 1812, by a man named Fischer, and his wife, who robbed and murdered many persons who put up at this ancient hostelry. These two were finally brought to

"BELVIDERE," THE OLD SHUBRICK HOME, NOW THE CHARLESTON COUNTRY CLUB HOUSE

trial for the murder of one of several travelers who mysteriously disappeared after taking shelter at their inn, and were convicted and hung. An account of their trial, etc., may be had from reading "The Dungeon and the Gallows," by John Blake White, published in the "Charleston Book" (1845). Mrs. Fischer was said to have been a beautiful woman, who expected to be spared on this account; accordingly she dressed for the hanging in her wedding finery, but all of her arts availed naught, and she, with her partner, suffered the penalty of the Law at Charleston's "Tyburn Hill," then just north of the present Line Street.

BELMONT

Near the Four Mile House, north of the lands known as McLaughlin's Grant, and east of the public road, was Belmont, the country seat for many years of Chief Justice Charles Pinckney and his descendants, which appears in an old deed as being on "Cupar" River.

The late Mrs. St. Julien Ravenel, a descendant of Eliza Lucas Pinckney, describes the house as "a delightful residence, a large brick house, standing, as most of the country houses did, a few hundred yards from the water's edge, on a semi-circular headland making out into a bold creek, a branch of the Cooper River."

Quotations from a letter of Mrs. Pinckney state that "The Enemy" was at Belmont in 1780, and "destroyed everything in the house." Also Garden, in his anecdotes, states that Colonel Montcrief, of the British Army, destroyed certain oak trees of remarkable beauty which had been planted by Mrs. Pinckney's deceased husband. Apparently the house was destroyed sometime between 1780 and 1785.

STROMBOLI

A grant to John Pendarvis and the next to John Ladson seem to have been the last grants of land which crossed the neck from river to river. Upon one of these grants was founded Stromboli, north of Belmont on Long Point Creek, and east of the public road.

Some time before 1719, 158 acres of this land became vested in Thomas Elliott (Eleott), and his will (1731) mentions a house there, it being his residence.

Some portion of these last grants passed to John Clement, who established Clement's Ferry; 15 acres of this tract Clement apparently called Dover, and 15 acres on the other side of the Cooper River bore the name of Calais. On these were the respective landings for the ferry, the signs for which read "From Dover to Calais."

In 1817 Adam Tunno acquired the ferry tract containing 65 acres, a few days later Dover and Calais (15 acres each) were sold to Gordon and Spring. Later the portion called Dover was returned to the ferry tract which had been sold by Tunno to Nathaniel Heyward, who devised it to his daughter Elizabeth (wife of Charles Manigault) and the whole tract became part of the Manigault farm known as Marshlands, conveyed by Dr. Gabriel Manigault in 1880 to Mrs. Cecelia Lawton, who conveyed the part containing the residence to the Government. This is now embraced in the Navy Yard reservation.

MARSHLAND AND ITS NEIGHBORS

About four miles above Belvidere, on the same side of the Cooper River, stands a fine old house, which, according to Mrs. Cecelia Lawton, one of the later owners of Marshlands, was built by John Ball, one of the numerous Balls, and later acquired by Nathaniel Heyward, who devised it to his daughter, Elizabeth, along with the ferry tract that he had purchased from Tunno, which was included in the Manigault farm, better known as Marshlands.

There are many Balls of one family, and to add to the confusion attendant upon properly placing a Ball in town or county there are in South Carolina two families of this name absolutely unconnected by ties of blood. Representing the smaller family is Mr. Wm. Ball, Editor of *The State,* published at Columbia, S. C.

A clever relation of the "Big Ball" connection, Miss Caroline Moreland, has a delightful way of distinguishing the inter-

18

locking branches of the larger family. She differentiates them by bestowing titles derived from the names of the streets upon which they now reside, as for instance, the "Presidential" Balls, who reside on President Street, and the "Kingly" and "Queenly" Balls, who live on King and Queen Streets respectively. According to her method of nomenclature the "Bully" Balls belong on Bull Street in the old house, and the "New" Balls have their habitation in a new house on New Street. Nor does she omit that charming branch of the family, the Jack Balls, who live on Pitt Street.

Marshlands has been incorporated in the Navy Yard reserve. The building itself is a four story structure including its attic and a brick basement that is unusually high from the ground. At the time that it was built it was a dwelling of great magnificence, with fine examples of hand-carved woodwork inside, and mahogany doors and finishings, the front elevation showing a structure of about the same period as Belvidere. The tall gabled house, whose windows once overlooked a broad domain and commanded a view of the waters of the Cooper River, is now used as an office building. If houses have thoughts then this old place, modeled after the residence of an English country gentleman, must sometimes hark back to the good old days when family life went on within its walls.

In the southwest room upstairs is found in a closet by the chimney place a secret passage. It seems that in former days many colonial residences boasted of these inclosures, sometimes said to have been used as retreats in times of danger, and as methods of escape during Indian attacks. In some old houses these secret stairways were called "Chambermaid stairs"; the most modern building containing a set is that at Cote Bas, farther up on the Cooper River, built about 1850. Underground passages are found in the remains of Yeamans Hall, Goose Creek, and in the structure still standing at Mulberry on Cooper River, and at Fenwick Castle on John's Island. Some authorities dispute this fact, but others admit the presence of these underground passages, one of which the writer has traversed.

In the Navy Yard the Headquarters Building was erected upon the site of the old Turnbull mansion, the original stone steps of which are yet to be found leading directly to the magnificent avenue of oaks marking the walk to the river landing. Near Marshlands to the north were the plantations "Retreat" and "Palmettoes," adjoining Goose Creek.

QUARTER HOUSE

West of Marshlands over on the State road just below the turn where it divides into two branches, there stands a brick pillar marking the entrance of the old race course of the old Jockey Club's property. McCrady's "History of South Carolina Under Proprietary Government" (page 345) says that in 1707 "The neck of land between the Cooper and Ashley Rivers, about six miles in length was well settled. One passed about this time in riding up the road which Archdale described as so beautiful, the plantations of Mathews, Green, Starkey, Gray, Grimball, Dickerson and Izard on the Cooper; and further up those of Sir John Yeamans, Landgrave Bellinger, Colonel Gibbs, Mr. Schenkingh, Colonel Moore and Colonel Quarry."

Bearing out the truth of Mr. McCrady's statement in the light of later research Judge Henry A. M. Smith, in Vol. XIX *South Carolina Historical Magazine,* traces the titles of land grants from Charleston neck north to Yeamans Hall. In this article Stock Prior was described as a part of the Christopher Smith property, later known as "Izard's Quarter House plantation."

On Stock Prior the Broad Path, or country road from Charleston, made a fork; the right hand road at this fork went northwardly to St. James, Goose Creek, the Congarees, etc., while the left hand road went southwestwardly to the ferry across Ashley River, and up along the river to Dorchester. In a ditch at the side of the left hand road, by the railway tracks, is a granite post marking the parish line. This road leads to what is now known as Bee's Ferry, but it was established by Edmund Bellinger, second Landgrave of that name, who married Elizabeth Butler, daughter of Shem Butler and sister of

"YEAMANS' HALL," GOOSE CREEK

Joseph, and lived at Stoney Point (sometimes called Altaraxes and Rocky Point) although he owned much property in other parts of the low country. "Shem Town" was at one time something of a settlement, and Bellinger's Ferry was well known, as several Public Acts of the Assembly deal with vesting the right of the ferry in Mrs. Bellinger and her children.

Judge Smith states that just south of this fork in the Broad Path, and near the point where the road divides on the north, on the east side of the public road was an "Ordinary" or inn that existed from an early date and was called the Quarter House.

The Quarter House is frequently mentioned in early records. An Act in 1721 directs that "The road from Charleston to the Quarter House be made 40 feet in breadth," and an advertisement in 1731 names the owner. . . . "On Saturday the 4th of March next at the dwelling house of Mr. Hill Croft, deceased, commonly called Quarter House." Again, Thomas Cooper offers a reward for a horse that had strayed or been stolen if returned to him in Charles Town or to Mrs. Croft of the Quarter House.

Another advertisement dealing with this locality tells of the loss of a snuff-mill; "Lost on Saturday last between Charlestown and the Quarter House a Snuff-mill, with a silver Hinge and plaits on Top and Bottom. Engraven on the Top— Quod tibi hoc alteri—, on the Bottom—Non tibi ne alteri— John Hay. Whoever brings the said Snuff-mill to James Pain, Merchant in Charlestown, shall have 20s Reward."

The muster ground for the militia was here, and Gibbes' Documentary History says that in 1761 "Mr. Henry Middleton, coming from his plantation on Goose Creek met about forty Catawba Indians at the Quarter House." This place survived for many years, and was long called by the original name, even as late as 1832, when Wm. Dry offers to sell pine lumber at his "plantation by the Quarter House."

YEAMANS' HALL

Yeamans' Hall is said to have been bought from the heirs of Governor Yeamans by Governor Thomas Smith, and presented

21

to his son. Certainly a Governor Smith occupied it about 1693. Until shattered by the earthquake in 1886 this large two-story building set on a high basement was fairly well preserved. The surroundings are particularly beautiful, and in the family burying ground are found Poyas, Lockwood and Smith tombstones.

GOOSE CREEK SETTLEMENT

Goose Creek, sometimes spelled "Goose Crick," is one of the oldest settlements in the state outside of Charleston. The church still standing there was begun in 1714 and completed in 1719. Tradition has it that it was spared during the Revolution because of the fact that above its chancel there are the Royal Arms of England. In an historical sketch of this spot Judge Henry A. M. Smith says, "There was a very large settlement in Goose Creek at an early period. The early grants date as early as 1672 and 1673, and by 1680 all the lands on both sides of Goose Creek as far as Back River and Foster's Creek, and even to the headwaters of Goose Creek within five miles of the present town of Summerville, were taken up, and taken up almost entirely by Church of England people."

In 1732, according to Mr. Salley, an advertisement appeared in the *Gazette* designed "To encourage Tradesmen to settle contiguously in the Parish of St. James's on Goose Creek, John Lloyd, Esq., will grant building leases of 64 acres of land, viz., 8 Lotts consisting of 8 acres each Lott, all fronting the Broad Path, from the Brow of the Hill Mr. Rich Walker now lives on, to the Fence joining Mr. Hume's Land, on the North West side of the Broad Path. The Land is all cleared, and very proper for either Pasture, Corn or Rice, within 20 miles of Charlestown, and four of Goose Creek Bridge; and the Trades thought most proper to settle on it are, a Smith, Carpenter, Wheel-wright, Bricklayer, Butcher, Taylor, Shoemaker and a Tanner."

Judge Smith states that at Goose Creek "The only exception to the English settlements was a settlement of Huguenots. . . . One of the first, or rather, the two first to settle there were the brothers, Abraham Fleury de la Plein and

22

ST. JAMES' CHURCH, GOOSE CREEK

ST. JAMES' CHURCH, INTERIOR

Isaac Fleury de la Plein, who both received grants which became the center of a little French settlement. Isaac Porcher, the ancestor of the Porcher family in South Carolina, first settled in this country at St. James, Goose Creek, where he 'lived his life' and died."

THE OAKS

The beautiful manor house of the Middleton family was called The Oaks, and stood where Mr. Edwin Parsons has erected his magnificent home in colonial period architecture, a fitting and dignified successor to the old mansion which stood at the head of an avenue of venerable oaks which for nearly a quarter of a mile form a continuous arch over the broad approach to the house. These live oaks were planted, so it is said, in 1680, and the first mansion was built soon afterwards, survived the Revolutionary War and was burned in the latter part of the nineteenth century.

With an instinct for what was appropriate, the moving picture director who filmed "Little Miss Rebellion" selected, for some of the scenes of this story starring Dorothy Gish, this house, and used the avenue of giant oak trees as part of a scene depicting Juvenile Royalty accompanied by her mounted suite. The ensemble of this company in gorgeous uniforms and courtly trappings for their mounts revived for a few brief moments upon the screen all that colorful and stirring life of colonial days and flashed into existence the atmosphere of "Courtly knights and Ladies Faire" native to this fine old place; and that this type of life was by no means foreign to the Middleton family the following extract from the scrap book of Mr. Frank Holmes shows:

"Died at sea on the passage from London to Charleston, South Carolina, in October 1789, Lady Mary Middleton, the daughter of the unfortunate Earl of Cromartie and relict of the late Henry Middleton of S. C.

"The Earl had been banished from England for holding a correspondence with the 'Old Pretender,' who died at Rome in 1765 aged 78 years, his son Charles Edward at Florence in 1788 at an advanced age. His brother the Cardinal of York died at Rome aged 82 years."

23

CROWFIELD

Crowfield Hall, four miles from the Parish Church, was called after family property of the same name in England, said by Wm. Middleton as late as 1876 to belong to the family, and found in possession of Admiral Sr. G. Brook Middleton.

When Wm. Middleton, the son of Arthur Middleton who first built on Crowfield, returned to England (1758–1784) to take charge of the English Crowfield, he neglected very much the Goose Creek namesake. Mr. Rawlins Lowndes bought it in 1776 and resold it to Thomas Middleton, 1778, who then advertised it again for sale in 1786 as "containing 1400 acres of land on which stood a very commodious dwelling house of excellent brick, having twelve good rooms with fireplaces in each, besides four rooms in the cellar also with fireplaces." Crowfield, like Bloomfield, another Middleton place, boasted of unusually fine surroundings, comprising lawns, woodlands and formal gardens.

Goose Creek and its vicinity was famous for its scientific horticulturists, and the gardens prospered accordingly. "Not many miles from this locality," says Mr. J. I. Waring, "was situated the botanical garden of Andrew Michaux, the horticulturist. Its site has been located by the broken parts of many flower pots."

Eliza Lucas, in a letter to her friend "Miss Bartlett," gives a long account of an "agreeable tour" to Goose Creek, and describes Crowfield as "a seat of the Middleton Family" . . . The tour was designed to show her those parts of the country in which are "Several very handsome gentleman's seats, at all of wch we were entertained with the most friendly politeness. The first we arrived at was Crowfield, Mr. Wm. Middleton's seat, where we spent a most agreeable week. The house stands a mile from but in sight of the road, and makes a very handsome appearance; as you draw nearer new beauties discover themselves; first the beautiful vine mantling the wall, laden with delicious clusters, next a large pond in the midst of a spacious green presents itself as you enter the gate. The house is well furnished, the rooms well contrived and elegantly

24

furnished. From the back door is a wide walk a thousand feet long, each side of wch nearest the house is a grass plat ornamented in a serpentine manner with flowers; next to that on the right hand is what immediately struck my rural taste, a thicket of young, tall live oaks, where a variety of airy choristers poured forth their melody—and my darling the mocking-bird, joyned in the concert, enchanted me with his harmony. Opposite on the left hand is a large square bowling green, sunk a little below the level of the rest of the garden, with a walk quite round bordered by a double row of fine large flowering Laurel and Catalpas—wch afford both shade and beauty. My letter will be of unreasonable length if I don't pass over the mounts, wilderness, etc., and come to the boundary of this charming spot, where is a large fish pond with a mount rising out of the middle the top of wch is level with the dwelling house, and upon it is a Roman temple. On each side are other large fish ponds, properly disposed wch form a fine prospect of water from the house—beyond this are the smiling fields dressed in vivid green.''

The property was in the possession of Henry A. Middleton at the time of his death, and in March, 1876, *The Washington Chronicle* says, Henry Middleton of Asheville, N. C., formerly of Charleston S.C. died yesterday at the residence of his brother, Commodore Middleton U.S. Navy, at the age of 79; he graduated at West Point 1816 but shortly after resigned his commission to engage in literary pursuits, married a niece of Sir Henry Pollock, resided for a long time in England and France, and was the author of several works of political character; his father, the late Hon. Henry Middleton, was Governor of South Carolina and member of Congress in 1816 where he served until appointed to represent our government at St. Petersburg, his residence for 10 years. His grandfather was Arthur Middleton, one of the signers of the Declaration of Independence, and his great grandfather Henry Middleton was one of the presidents of the first Congress in 1774, the father of the latter, Arthur Middleton, was one of the first Royal Governors of the colony.

25

OTRANTO

Otranto was another Middleton residence. While Edward lived at The Oaks Arthur dwelt at the Otranto plantation, his residence being at the spot where the Otranto Club House now stands; but Mr. Waring states that "The place now known as 'Crovatts' was the original Otranto, and was owned by the Hamiltons, who constructed a private race track, which started in front of the house and ran in a circle for one mile, in order that guests could sit on the piazza and have a full view of the course and races."

"From 1796 to 1806 the Reverend Mr. Porgson," says Dr. Burgess in his chronicles of St. Mark's Parish, "occupied the house known now as the Otranto Club House as a rectory." But this is not the first parsonage for Goose Creek church. The first one, according to Dr. Burgess, was the old brick parsonage at Goose Creek built about or just after 1714 when the present church was built. An old plat represents the form and shape of 100 acres of land given by Capt. Benjamin Schenkingh to the parish; "One acre thereof for to build a church on, and the rest for ye use of the Rector or Minister of said Parish, for ye time being," the conveyance from him, "ye said Schenkingh, to the Church Commissioners" being dated 1706. At the same time there was donated by Arthur C. Middleton four acres upon which the first parsonage was erected. Evidently something happened to the original parsonage, as Mr. Porgson occupied the present club house in 1796, the avenue of which tradition says was planted by Captain John Cantey.

The good parson Porgson was a devoted disciple of Isaak Walton, and could not refrain from his favorite sport even on Sunday. One Sunday morning while walking to church carrying his sermon under one arm and his fishing rod on his shoulder he stopped on the bridge to see how the fish were biting. He suddenly hooked a large trout, and in his anxiety to land his fish he forgot his sermon, which slipped from beneath his arm and fell into the water; there being a strong ebb tide it floated away, and the congregation probably had no sermon that day even if the minister had his trout.

26

"MEDWAY," ON BACK RIVER, ABOVE GOOSE CREEK
The home of Landgrave Smith and now owned by Mr. S. G. Stoney
The oldest brick house in South Carolina outside of Charleston

OTRANTO CLUB HOUSE, GOOSE CREEK

According to Dr. Johnson, tradition has it that the romantic marriage of "Mad Archie" Campbell, famous in the Revolution, to a young lady of Charleston took place at the rectory of St. James, Goose Creek, and that they were married by the then rector, the Rev. Mr. Ellington. "Mad Archie" Campbell was a member of the family of the Duke of Argyle, to which family the last Royal Governor, who lived on Meeting Street in what is now the Huger house, also belonged.

According to the chronicles of the Brisbane family, compiled by E. Haviland Hillman, F.S.G., from 1801 to 1804 Otranto was owned by John Stanyarne Brisbane (Born 1773—died 1850), son of James, and grandson of William the Emigrant. "When John Brisbane's father, James Brisbane, was banished from Charleston in 1782 he intended taking John with him, but at the last moment, as the vessel was about to sail, John got into one of the small boats on which passengers had come on board, hid under a seat and returned to shore, where he remained with an old aunt, probably Susannah Stanyarne. He married, 19th March, 1795, Maria Hall, the daughter of the Hon. George Abbott Hall and Lois Mathews. From 1801 to 1804 he owned the plantation on Goose Creek called Otranto, where the Otranto Hunting Club now is, and later had his country seat at Malona (Acabee Woods), Ashley River."

At one time Otranto Club was the residence of Dr. Garden, well-known botanist and correspondent of Linnaeus, the naturalist, who named our beautiful Gardenia after his correspondent. "Subsequently," says Mr. Waring, "it was owned by Mr. Philip Porcher, and was once known as 'Goslington,' meaning Little Goose, a name said to have been bestowed upon it by the Hon. James L. Petigru on the occasion of a brilliant dinner party given in the ancient building, now the Otranto Club House.

It is a low structure with attics and dormer windows; the porch is about one foot from the ground and extends around three sides of the building; its roof is supported by heavy brick columns. It is situated on a hill leading down to Goose Creek, and is altogether charming in conception and execution. Frank

E. Slyde, a man of artistic nature and appreciative of all that is fine in these old southern places, connected with the National Headquarters of the War Camp Community Service, recently visited this place, and speaks of the Club House at Goose Creek as a place where "One need but release his imagination to see the gay folks at the various parties in the beautiful, plain, quaint rooms with the furnishings so odd, and to hear the clink of glasses and the hale and hearty salutation of 'Heigh-ho, friend, we bid you enter.'"

THE ELMS

The intimate daily chronicles of Goose Creek between the years 1754 and 1781 may be found in the journal of Mrs. Ann Manigault, whose grandson, Gabriel Manigault, married Margaret Izard, and who is mentioned frequently as "Grandson G." This private record deals with the different prominent families of the settlement, and contains many intimate items of people prominent in colonial life, among others the family of Izards, who spread out at one time in several branches in the neighborhood, and whose home place, "The Elms," was on Goose Creek. Mr. Joseph Ioor Waring, a descendant of one of the Waring settlers of the Dorchester and Goose Creek neighborhood, says that all that remains of this fine old home of a prominent family is "A single tall column of the lofty porch, standing like a monument over its departed glory." In this house Mr. Izard entertained LaFayette very lavishly when he made his tour of the country, one of the octagonal shaped wings of the house being fitted up in great elegance for his entertainment; here he spent a night, and ever afterwards this wing was known as LaFayette's Lodge."

Says Mr. Waring, "It is difficult now to find even a path leading to the old house. Around the ruins, in the spring of the year, amongst wild grasses and weeds, bulbs and garden plants still grow, marking the site of the flower garden." The family, like the home, has vanished, but in the Museum of Fine Arts in Boston hangs a large double portrait of Mr. and Mrs. Ralph Izard, painted by the celebrated artist Copley. This picture was found in London for Mr. Charles I. Manigault, a grandson of the originals of the portrait.

The Izard family intermarried, among others, with the family of the last Royal Governor, Campbell, but before that time the will of Ralph Izard bequeaths (1722–1724) "All that my tract of land situate, lying and being on or near the south side of Goose Creek in the County of Berkley." A memorial tablet to his memory, and his hatchment, may be seen on the walls of Goose Creek Church, and his remains are interred in the cemetery just outside.

Part of the northern portion of the Elms, an Izard estate, after passing through several hands, came finally into the possession of Dr. Eli Geddings, a famous physician of Charleston. His property is described as "Bounding north on Crowfield."

The city residence of the Izard family is found still standing in Charleston; a square brick building on the north side of Broad street one door west of King.

MEDWAY AND ITS NEIGHBORS

Medway is sometimes called the Back River Place, and "Back River," says Oldmixon, the historian, "falls in Cooper River about two miles above Goose Creek." At the confluence of Cooper River with this its second western branch, lying between Goose Creek and Back River is a considerable extent of arable land separated into several plantations.

The first of these, lying on the eastern side of Goose Creek, is known as Red Bank, and on this place there was formerly an extensive pottery for the manufacture of tile, etc. A little beyond Red Bank on the western side of Back River is Parnassus, once owned by the Tennent family. Here is a beautiful avenue of oaks. Near this avenue is a lonely headstone inscribed:

<blockquote>"Rose; a faithful servant."</blockquote>

a mute reminder of the deep affection which existed between master and servant in the days gone by. Away out in the woods were two more grave stones inscribed respectively "Hector" and "Joe." These are said to mark the burial places of two noted "deer drivers," who were buried on two well-known "stands." More reminders of the old days when the deer driver was a valued possession, and generally a very lazy but privileged fellow, whose main responsibility was the care of the horses and hunting dogs.

Beyond Parnassus, situated on a bluff on Back River, is the ancient house called Medway. This house was built in 1682. It is by far the most interesting and best preserved, as well as oldest, house of early times. This was the home of the first Landgrave Smith, who was Governor of the Colony. It is said to be the first brick house built outside of Charleston. Its curious old Dutch gables are very quaint. The ceilings are low, the rooms spacious and the fireplaces huge. Near the house is the grave of Governor Smith, marked with a heavy slab, where sleeps the former master of Medway and "sometime" Governor of the Colony of South Carolina.

To this gentleman has been falsely ascribed the first cultivation of rice in the colony, "but," says Mr. Salley, "the first settlers of South Carolina who came over in 1670 came with instructions from the Lords Proprietors to attempt the cultivation of rice, and it had become a considerable industry in the province before Landgrave Smith came into the province in 1684."

Mr. William Dunlopp was in 1687 "Lycenced To joine together in the holy Estate of Matrimony . . . Thomas Smith Esq and Sabina de Vignon Dowager Van wernhaut provided there be noe lawfull Lett shewne to you to the contrary." Tradition has it that this wife was a beautiful Baroness, and the "Ancient Lady" has much to say on this subject. She also says, "We see that drink was served to guests in goblets of' pure silver in 1692. Yes, the Blakes, Boones, and many other gentlemen were asked into the Back river parlor to drink beer, smoke a pipe, and take a sly chew from the landgrave '*Tobacco Box.*'" . . . Her description of Back River mansion is from "heresay"; "I am told that it is a low building, with a dutch roof, of very inferior bricks, yet such is the strength and quantity of mortar, which holds them together, that it continues a strong and very comfortable dwelling. It remained

THOMAS SMITH
One of the Landgraves of South Carolina. From a painting

"MEDWAY" ON BACK RIVER
First brick house built outside of Charleston. Home of Landgrave Thomas Smith.
From an old print

many years in the family," but the place is now in possession of Mr. Samuel G. Stoney, who is preserving all its quaint and rural charm.

Many ghosts are said to walk inside of these low-ceilinged rooms, with their large fireplaces and narrow windows. At a certain window, with its small panes of glass, is seen sometimes a shadowy lady, who sits and watches for the coming of the young husband who never returned, having met his death while deer hunting. In another room he who is so bold as to sleep therein sometimes wakes in the night to see an old gentleman seated comfortably in front of the fireplace smoking his pipe.

"It was just the place for ghosts to walk, for strange voices to be heard, for unusual things to happen," says John Bennett, who has immortalized the atmosphere of romantic mystery with which Medway is enveloped in his book, "The Treasure of Pierre Gailliard," in which he revives the eerie sense of desolation and haunting allurement found only in the discovery of a well-built brick house in such an isolated spot.

In an old walled cemetery at Medway on a part of the original tract, is a moss-covered slab of marble over the remains of Rev. Elias Prioleau, a native of Poms and Saintonge, one of the Huguenot emigrants who, on the Revocation of the Edict of Nantes, came with others to South Carolina. According to a mural tablet erected to his memory in the Huguenot Church, Charleston, he became a minister of that faith, and the stone at Medway also recites this fact, and states that this family sprang from one of the Doges of Venice. Miss M. Elise Langley, of Charleston, S. C., has in her possession some interesting documents or mementos of Antoine Prioli, who died in Venice 1623, and from whom the family sprang. The Rev. Elias Prioleau died at his farm on Back River on Midway, now Medway, in St. James, Goose Creek, and there his remains repose.

DEAN HALL

At what is known as the T, Cooper River divides into two branches, to the east and to the west. Many large plantations lie along both banks of both branches. Fronting the Cooper River proper, directly opposite to where it branches, stands what is known as Coming's Tee plantation on which is found a beautiful house. If the reader will picture the capital letter T, and place Coming Tee at the place where the shank of the letter joins the arms, he will have a working conception of this river and the plantations in the vicinity. The left arm of the T will correspond to the western branch, and the right arm of the T will correspond to the eastern branch. Strangely enough each branch divides in turn, or rather is formed by two branches joining to form the head-waters of the rivers, those of the western or left hand branch of Cooper River being Wadboo and Biggon Creeks, and those of the eastern branch being Quinby Creek and the river itself. There is another peculiar fact to be noted in connection with the two branches of this river, and one that will serve to assist the reader in visualizing the lay of the land, and that is that the Colleton family (from whom the county derives its name) owned a Barony at the head of each main branch of the river. On the western bank of the left hand branch lay Fairlawn Barony, and a little further, on the right of the left hand branch, was Wadboo Barony, while the grant of a Barony of 1200 acres, called the "Cypress Barony," is situated on the head-waters of the eastern branch of Cooper River around Huger's Bridge. Many of the houses on Cooper River still standing are found upon portions of land formerly belonging to the Colleton family, but now in possession of various other old families of that section.

A great curve occurs in Cooper River to the west just before it divides at the T, and upon a peninsular, nearly an island, formed by this great curve and the turn of the western branch is located Dean Hall plantation, an enchantingly situated country place. With the handsome house and the outbuildings Dean Hall is said to look more like a village than a plantation, and is rightly considered one of the show places of the river, having been set in fine order by its latest owner, Benjamin Kittredge.

"DEAN HALL," COOPER RIVER, BELOW THE TEE

MAUM PATIENCE AND HER PET GOBBLER

The exact age of Dean Hall and the buildings thereon is not known, but a clue is afforded by an advertisement appearing in the *South Carolina Gazette* September 2nd, 1757, when the place was for sale. It was then the property of Sir Alexander Nesbit, a Scotch Baronet, and was bought in by his sons, Sir John and Alexander. Sir John married a Miss Allston, but was, before his marriage, a man of sporting instincts and affable manners. He caused many a flutter in the dove-cote if an incident taken from Irving's "History of the Turf in South Carolina" is to be believed. Many of the gentlemen of the neighboring plantations were ardent followers of the Sport of Kings. Strangely enough this apparently idle hobby was destined to have a deep significance at the time of the Revolutionary war, because the "Swamp Fox," Marion, and his men, commanded the use of extraordinarily well-bred horses in their guerilla warfare against the British, and other cavalry leaders knew where to apply for a good mount.

Chief among these men who raised good horses were Daniel Ravenel of Wantoot, and the Harlestons. The love of the sport, as well as some of the original stock, survived the Revolution. In February, 1796, a race was run between John Randolph, of Virginia, and Sir John Nesbit of Dean Hall. Each rode his own horse; Randolph won. Many of the married fair ones were heard to confess after the race was over, that although Mr. Randolph had won the race Sir John had won their hearts, and that they much preferred him in a match to his more successful competitor.

The sporting instinct has manifested itself in a succession of owners, and although rice planting was the chief industry, hunting has flourished there. This is very natural on account of the fact that the plantation rice fields, alternately flowed (flooded) and drained, afforded splendid reserves for wild duck and deer, in conjunction with the pond-like place where the water was compounded for irrigating the rice fields in time of drought.

The house itself is of brick, set six feet from the ground upon an arched foundation. A veranda surrounds three sides of the lower story, its low, over-hanging eaves imparting a tropical appearance to the entire building. This veranda, reached by a double flight of stone steps, is also the entrance, giving access to the hallway which runs the entire length of the square establishment, dividing the house, and affording ventilation as well as light. Upstairs, there being no piazza, all the rooms look out over the river into the park-like woods of the estate. Thus, because of its favorable situation for water sports, hunting and inland excursions into adjacent fields and woods, Dean Hall has been the scene of much cultured hospitality, and during the lifetime of the Nesbits it was visited by an English scientist, Sir Charles Lyell. During the occupancy of the Carsons Dean Hall not only housed many distinguished visitors, but also had much to show them when they arrived in the way of paintings and sculpture, and many rare and valuable books.

Concerning his family, Mr. James P. Carson has this to say: "The name Carson is quite common throughout the country and frequent advertisements concerning property owned by them were seen in the *Gazette* before and after the Revolution. There was a Dr. James Carson who owned plantations around here, and there are Carsons buried in the church yard on Edisto Island, but none of these are my kindred. As a small boy at the circus which I attended with my father we met Elisha Carson, who was my father's cousin. There was a William Carson, who was also a cousin, and to avoid the miscarriage of their letters my father inserted the A in his name.

"James Carson, my grandfather, was born in 1774, and in 1816 died at the age of 42, and is buried at Ballston Spa, New York. At an early age he came to Charleston and was a factor, the firm name was Carson and Snowden, which was dissolved in 1797. He then continued the business, and on his retirement was succeeded by his clerks, Kershaw and Cunningham, who, in their turn, were succeeded by Robertson and Blacklock.

"James Carson (1774–1816) married Elizabeth Neyle (1764–1848) on May 6, 1796. She was the daughter of Samson Neyle, a prominent merchant; she probably had money, was ten years older than James, who evidently had the commercial

34

instinct. They had two children, Laura, who married Henry Brevoort in 1816, and my father, William A., who married Caroline Petigru in 1840. In 1805 James bought the Stuart house at the corner of Tradd and Orange Streets, which remained in the family until about 1850.''

In 1820 William A. Carson, who married Caroline Petrigru, a daughter of Hon. James L. Petigru, the brilliant lawyer, bought Dean Hall. This was found to be the most valuable piece of his property at the time of his death, which occurred during the year 1854, at which time he was a wealthy man and left much property to his executors and trustees for the benefit of his wife and children.

The "Ball Book" says that at one time Dean Hall was bought by "Elias Nonus," who had inherited a fortune from his uncle, Hugh Swinton Ball. He married Miss Odenheimer, daughter of Bishop Odenheimer, of New Jersey, moved to Pennsylvania in 1865, and died there in 1872.

In writing of the Carson tenure of the property, Mr. James Carson says, "My father, William A. Carson, was a rice planter who wore out his life watching a salty river, and died at the age of 56, when I was 10 years old." The property was sold by Mr. James Carson to the present owner, Mr. Benjamin Kittredge, of California, who married Miss Elizabeth Marshall, of Charleston.

CHAPTER III

WESTERN BRANCH OF COOPER RIVER
ABOVE THE "TEE"

COMINGTEE AND BEYOND ON THE EASTERN SIDE

HIRTY miles from its mouth at Charleston, Cooper River divides into two branches, eastern and western, like the letter T. On the little peninsula thus formed Captain Coming settled, and named the place " Coming's Tee." The original grant did not cover the whole of the present Comingtee plantation, for the next owner, Elias Ball, purchased and added two adjoining tracts in 1703 and 1704, and in 1735 bought a third tract, described by his son in 1752 as "lying between the T of the river, lands of his own, a creek between Nicholas Harleston (then owner of Rice Hope) and the northwestern branch of Cooper River."

The plantation has always been considered as two tracts, "Comingtee" and "Stoke." "Coming's Tee" was settled by Capt. John Coming and his wife, Affra Harleston (a sister of John Harleston, of Mollins, Essex County, England). John Coming was a half-brother of William Ball, farmer of the Devonshire section in England, who never came to America, but sent his brother, Elias Ball, in his place at the time of Capt. Coming's death. These are the same Charleston Comings mentioned in Charleston history as owning land at "Oyster Point," and as giving "Glebe lands" to St. Philip's Church.

After Capt. Coming's death his half-brother, Elias Ball, came over to America to look after the estates of the widow Coming. He married Mrs. Coming's sister, Elizabeth Harleston. Capt. Coming and his wife were childless, and after the death of the latter some time in 1698 or 1699 Coming Tee

36

passed to Elias Ball, who was hardly more than a youth when he took possession of his inheritance; but he was a great sportsman and frequently commanded scouting parties after Indians. His first wife died about 1720, and 11 months later he married Mary Delamere, a girl the age of his eldest daughter.

Of Mary little is known, and nothing remains of her personal belongings but two books, a prayer book of the Church of England and a collection of quaint old pamphlets bound together in one volume. A human touch concerning the life of these dead and gone people is found in accounts of the eleven months following the death of the first Mrs. Elias Ball, and the trouble the bereaved and perplexed widower had with his children. It is said that in his memorandum book the name of "Mary Delamere" is scrawled across page after page right through the daily accounts. The way out of all perplexities was beginning to present itself, with the result that Elias married Mary.

There were soon two sets of children, as Mary had by this marriage seven, two of whom died young, and two girls died at about fifteen years of age, but another daughter, Eleanor Ball, lived and married Colonel Henry Laurens, the celebrated patriot. The exact date of Elias' death can only be surmised, but Eleanor Laurens' name appears in his will in 1750, and in a codicil in 1751. His burial place also is a matter of conjecture, supposedly in West St. Philip's Churchyard in Charleston.

The Balls were English people from Devonshire, and in the Ball Book's description of the house that Elias Ball built in Carolina, a map of Devonshire, England, from Speed's Atlas, is shown. This map contains Ball places in England, "Stoke," and "Combe-in-tene" settlements near the mouth of the River Tyne, and reveals the similar relative positions of the "Stoke" and "Coming Tee" tracts on Cooper River in America, to their English counterparts.

The Carolina Stoke had a barn, and negro houses, and was where the Brick Mill builded by Elias Ball now stands. The name Stoke appears in the will of Elias Ball when he leaves the plantation under discussion to his nephew, John Ball, Jr., but the dwelling house was always on Comingtee, which also had its own barn, corn house, negro quarters and gang of negroes.

The first owner of Comingtee, Capt. Coming, probably built on or near the site of the present dwelling. It is not known whether he or Elias Ball built the brick house now there, and there is no clue to the exact date of this building, but it is said to be one of the two oldest houses in the Parish (the other being Exeter, high up on the Western Branch).

Tradition has it that the bricks for this structure were brought from England, and it is thought that the brick house was built by Elias Ball, while the Comings dwelt in a wooden cottage which stood on the neighboring slope, opposite the large sycamores in the avenue, and which was standing as late as the year 1865, at which time it gave evidence of being quite an old place. In front of this wooden house were two beautiful live oaks which still mark the spot. For many years it was used as the overseer's residence, but after the overseers lived at Stoke it became the sick-house, or plantation hospital for the negroes. Rumor held that, as is the case with most old plantations, the family burying ground was near the house, and as the graveyard at Comingtee was thought to be near the wooden house, it would seem that this was the original dwelling.

A family memorandum book says that there were two houses at Comingtee in the day of the first and second Elias; in proof of this an entry in 1736 is made, "To half a days work on the old house." Some house, old or new, underwent repairs and alterations after 1731, and in 1738 "something was done" to the garret windows of the brick house that took several days' work. In 1743 and 1763 the house was shingled, and was repaired at a cost of 400 pounds.

The Ball Book says: "The old brick house was built, as was then customary, without piazzas. This was evidenced by the horizontal bands in relief on each side and gable of the building (known in architecture as ' lines of relief ') placed there for artistic effect. . . . The old house contained origin-

"COMING TEE" HOUSE, ON COOPER RIVER
Where the river divides into two branches

STRAWBERRY CHAPEL, COOPER RIVER

ally only two rooms on each floor, with no passage-way between the two lower rooms. Into the larger of these the front door opened. The staircase also came down into this larger room. At a later day the panelled partition was erected, forming a passage-way, and cutting off the South room from the stairway. The rooms on both floors had the old-time wide fireplaces with high mantels, and heavy cornices around the room. Wooden panelling cut off deep closets on each side of the chimneys on both lower and upper stories, with narrow gable windows in them for light. When the piazzas were added, the lower rooms were so much darkened that it became necessary to remove the lower closets and enlarge the gable windows to double their original size. . . . The house when built was not rough-cast, as it has been for over a hundred years, but was of plain brick-work, finished with pointing mortar." A wooden addition as large as the original house was added in 1833 or 1834 by John Ball, the owner at that time.

Both the house and the wooden addition have deep cellars with fireplaces large enough to roast an ox, and no doubt many a turnspit has sat here in this corner (himself half roasted) when helping to prepare a roast pig or Christmas turkey for the guests above.

Comingtee had a beautiful old-fashioned garden with a straight walk down the middle, between flower beds bordered with jonquils, snowdrops and sweet old-fashioned roses, while crepe-myrtle trees faced each other across this walk. An old brass dial in a sunny spot marked the passage of the hours.

This place is beautifully situated and easy of access. In addition to the water front there are two land approaches to Comingtee; one the avenue which comes to the house from the north and leads from the public road that goes up the western branch to upper St. John's and its settlements; the other (called quaintly the "So' Boy Avenue") leads to the house from the public road that winds up along the eastern branch, leading over Bonneau's Ferry to French Santee.

On this plantation there is a chain of reservoirs for flooding the adjacent rice fields at need, and the one between Comingtee and Fishpond (the Harleston place) has been much discussed and disputed about. It was supposed to belong jointly, and the full history of this reserve would embrace the history of the entire countryside until 1874 when agreement was made concerning the break in the dam which caused the first quarrel.

The first Elias, called "Red Cap," lived at the plantation until 1740, then he moved to Charleston, and his son Elias took possession. About this time John Coming Ball, second son of the first Elias, married; he built and settled at "Hyde Park," a plantation on the eastern branch. Elias, the second, was a bachelor, and becoming lonely he built and settled at "Kensington," the next plantation to Hyde Park, in order to be near his brother. He subsequently married Mrs. Lydia Chicken, a widow, and their son, the third Elias, inherited and dwelt at Comingtee. Elias the second was buried, by his own request, from his old home there.

The plantation remained continuously in the Ball family, and was famous for its hospitality, even when its owner or occupant was a bachelor (which happened sometimes during the long period that Comingtee was in this family); yet so perfect were the arrangements made for guests that in every sleeping room was to be found the old four-poster, double bed and a trundle bed or crib.

The property rested finally with Alwyn Ball, Jr., of Rutherford, N. J., who removed the wooden annex and restored the brick building in the old style; he recollected and replaced in their old places all the family treasures of furniture, plate and paintings. A history of the Balls would touch in some vital way the lives of most men and women of prominence in the early history of the state, and would include a record of many interesting events, but space permits of only brief mention of the lives of some of them in connection with the homes they builded and occupied. Through the courtesy of Mrs. I. G. Ball, Jr., (neé Jane Johnson, daughter of Dr. John Johnson, D.D., soldier, scholar and priest of God) an unusual opportunity was granted for scanning family records and extracting and quoting from precious passages of the Ball Book, compiled by Mr. A. Alwyn Ball, of Rutherford, N. J., the last Ball owner of Comingtee.

CHILDSBURY AND STRAWBERRY CHAPEL

Dr. Irving, in his "Day on Cooper River," states that it was at Childsbury that the British forces in the Keowe expedition were landed from their transports and marched under Governor Littleton: and that at the same place Col. Wade Hampton took fifty prisoners and burned four vessels laden with valuable stores for the British Army quartered near Biggin Church.

At Strawberry Ferry—*i.e.*, the plantation of that name—says the same writer, the "Strawberry Jockey Club" used to hold its annual meetings. The club having been dissolved in 1882, the race course was ploughed up and converted into a corn-field.

The earliest mention of the name Strawberry appears to be in the act of 17th February, 1705, which declares that "ye Inhabitants of the Eastern & Western branches of ye T of Cooper River are willing at their own proper Cost & Charge to make a fferry at y^{ee} Plantation of Mr. James Childs Known comonly by ye name of ye Strawberry Plantation."

The old cypress on which the rates of ferrage was painted has become mortised into a tree on the Strawberry side—the tree had overgrown it at least 100 years ago. From this it is safe to conclude that the signboard has been there for several generations. The primitive ferry is still in use by those who wish to pass across the river.

The town must have assumed some position during the life of James Child, after whom it was called, and in February, 1723, an Act was passed which recited that James Child had by his will given 500 acres for a common, and money for the support of a free school, and also a place for a market in the town, and that "the inhabitants of Childsbury are very much incommoded as well for want of certain market days in each week to be appointed for Childsbury town" as for want of public fairs to be held there at least twice a year. A beautiful little chapel is still in use at Strawberry.

41

MEPKIN

Mepkin, on Cooper River's western branch (eastern side) above the "T," consisted of 3000 acres and was the country home of the Laurens family, Henry Laurens having bought it in 1672 from the John Colleton estate. The entrance gates and avenue to Mepkin are still intact, but the fine old house has fallen to decay, although it was built of bricks on a high basement. The edifice was two stories in height, and was constructed after the same general square plan of the Laurens town house.

The diary of Timothy Ford says, "Within sight of Washington is the seat & Plantation of his excellency Henry Laurens, agreeable prospect of which induces us to visit it to-day (Tuesday). Contrary to our expectations he had gone to town, we were not however disappointed of viewing the place which displays the beauties and advantages of nature no less than the ingenious improvements of its owner. He is a rare instance of method, whereby his plantation raises itself above those of this country in which everything is done immethodically by the round about means of force & Labour."

Henry Laurens (born in Charleston 1734, died there 1792) was a swarthy, well-knit man, somewhat below middle size; a man very much the master of himself and his moods and passions. His lips, as shown in the portrait of him by Copley, recently discovered in London, were naturally so firm as not to need to be compressed. The nose was not long, drooping just a little at the end to hide the nostrils, and his eyes were very watchful. The whole man looked aggressive and just a bit cocksure. The face was roundish and firm about the jaws.

Henry Laurens was the first son of John Samuel Laurens. He was raised as a merchant and the wide general education he possessed was obtained after arriving at manhood through his habit of extensive reading. In 1744 he was sent to London to obtain training as a merchant, and in 1736 he was prominent in the organization of the first fire insurance company in the United States. In 1739 he closed out his Charleston business and returned to London, where for many years he carried on an extensive trade, largely with America. In 1749 he was made agent for the colony in England, a position which he held until 1750. In 1771 and 1774 Laurens was again in London, but as a retired Carolina merchant and rich planter.

Young Laurens is said to have met "the beautiful Eleanor Ball," daughter of Elias Ball, at a plantation on Cooper River, and they were married on July 6, 1750, when he was at the age of 26. Of Laurens' 12 or more children who reached maturity only three survived their father.

While Laurens was a great merchant, he was something more. Though keenly engaged in business, he looked upon public affairs as vitally a part of his life. In the Indian War of 1761, in the full tide of his wealth getting, he accepted a commission, collected recruits and marched into the Appalachian Mountains.

Henry Laurens was first elected to the House of Assembly in South Carolina in 1757 and continued to be elected except on one occasion until the Revolution. Toward the end of October, 1777, Hancock resigned the presidency of the Continental Congress, and on November 1, 1777, the position was conferred upon Henry Laurens by a unanimous vote. It was during his presidency that a strong friendship between LaFayette and Laurens developed. When LaFayette was wounded Laurens took him in his own carriage to the officers' hospital near Yorktown.

In October, 1779, Henry Laurens was commissioned to go to Europe to purchase leather for the use of the colonial army. He sailed on the Mercury, which was convoyed by a 16-gun vessel, but his vessel was captured by a British ship while off the coast of Newfoundland. He carried valuable papers, which he endeavored to destroy by casting overboard, but they were recovered from the sea and used against him. He was first taken before the admiral at St. Johns, N. F. Thence he was taken to London and was committed to the Tower of London on the charge of high treason. In the beginning of December, 1781, his release, owing to the interest of Edmund Burke and Franklin, was assured. The release was made with the view of exchanging him for General Cornwallis. On

43

the last day of the year 1781, unable to stand except on crutches, Laurens was released, and in 1782 was appointed Peace Commissioner to Paris. His services, terminating only with his departure for America, were of great importance and entitled him to be considered the first minister of the United States to England.

This distinguished father had a scarcely less distinguished son. John Laurens (born in South Carolina in 1755, educated in England and France) served on the staff of General Washington during the Revolution; also served with Major General Lincoln in South Carolina in 1779, and was wounded at Coosawhatchie Bridge. He was a special envoy to France in 1781, returned to America at the end of the year and took part in the campaign in South Carolina in 1782, and was killed in a fight with the British at Chehaw Neck, on Combahee River, August 27, 1782.

A portrait of John Laurens is to be found in the State House at Columbia, S. C., and through the efforts of Colonel John Dargan was only recently publicly "unveiled" with suitable ceremonies, as a tardy recognition of the services this son of Carolina rendered to his native land. The act of unveiling the picture was done by Laurens descendants of a collateral branch of the family, John Laurens having left no "hostages to the future."

In writing to this son during the Revolution Henry Laurens once closed his letter with the following lines:

"My Dear Son
    I pray God protect you
    & add to your knowledge
    & learning, if it be necessary,
    discretion—
                    HENRY LAURENS."

Like all rice planters, Henry Laurens possessed a town house, situated at the southeast corner of Laurens Street and East Bay; it has only recently been destroyed. As originally built the house was of nine-inch-long brick, and so substantial from the cellar to the heavily hewn timbers of the spacious attic that even after the many years it stood firm and true until torn down to make room for the Seaboard Air Line R. R.

With it perished colonial carvings, marble mantels, set-in book cases, thick walls, secret doors, and, on the upper floor, a wonderful ballroom. It was in this room that Henry Laurens' sister, a young girl, was laid out when she died. She lay facing a window, and her love for the garden, which used to extend to the river's edge, worked a miracle; a storm came up, and through the open window rain dashed into her face. A watcher, noticing that the little maid's eyelids quivered, called help. The maiden revived and lived to be an old lady.

The incident left such an impression upon her brother that his will directed that his body should be burned at death. He concluded his will with these words:

"I come to the disposal of my own person. . . . I solemnly enjoin it on my son as an indispensable duty that as soon as he conveniently can, after my decease, he cause my body to be wrapped in 12 yards of Tow Cloth and burnt until it be entirely and totally consumed and then collect my bones, deposit them wherever he shall think proper."

This request was duly complied with, and his body wrapped in tow cloth and burned on his plantation in an iron coffin at night. The slaves gathered round the flaming funeral pyre, while just below the dark waters of the Cooper River swirled and eddied at the foot of Mepkin Bluff.

ELWOOD

According to the Ball Book, Alwyn Ball, son of the first John, married, early in life, Esther McClellan, and lived at Elwood plantation, a place situated a little above Comingtee, on the same side of the western branch. Alwyn combined a passion for hunting with a gift for music. His house was in Cordesville, "the summer pineland village." It was afterwards purchased by his nephew, Keating Simons Ball. The building was quaint in appearance, with an enormous shed that made it look like an East Indian bungalow.

Alwyn Ball died in Charleston in 1835 at the early age of 28 years, in a house on a part of the lot now occupied by the

St. Francis Xavier Infirmary, and was buried at Strawberry Chapel, on Cooper River, near his old home.

His funeral procession was very dramatic, as his remains were to be taken up the river on a boat. The cortege wound its way through the city streets to the wharf where the boat awaited. First went the hearse, behind which was "Josh," a faithful servant and huntsman, leading his master's hunting horse saddled and bridled; with them were Mr. Ball's favorite dogs, a couple of deer hounds. The family followed in proper conveyances. When the wharf was reached the coffin was placed on its trestle in the bow of the boat, the dogs guarded it all the way up the river. When the coffin was being lowered into the grave Josh carried out his master's last directions by sounding a loud blast on his hunting horn, which was then thrown into the grave and buried with the young master who so often in life had answered its summons to the chase.

RICE HOPE

Rice Hope, adjoining Comingtee, was the property of "venerable Read," one of the last surviving heroes of the Revolution, who became possessed of this property by marriage with Sarah Harleston, eldest daughter of Col. John Harleston. This plantation was banked and cleared in part from its native wilderness in 1795 by Dr. Read. The titles are as follows:

John Harleston's "Will, dated 2 Octo. 1790, devised Rice Hope Plantation on the East Bank of the Western Branch of Cooper River to his daughter, Sarah Read, with right of survivorship to her husband, Dr. Wm. Read, and after their death to the issue of the marriage. Dr. Wm. Read survived Sarah, his wife, and died in April 1845 leaving I. Harleston Read and Elizabeth A. Parker the only surviving children of the said marriage, who thus became entitled to one moiety each."

It would seem that Harleston Read bought his sister's share from a "Conveyance dated 2 feby. 1846, from Peter Parker and Elizabeth A., his wife, to I. Harleston Read of an undivided moiety of 'All that certain plantation or tract of land called Rice Hope situate lying and being etc. . . . measuring and containing in the whole 1709 acres more or less, comprising 271 acres of Rice land and Marsh, and the residue provision, wood, reservoir, pine and other lands.' The bounds are given as 'to the north partly on Cooper river, the Childsbury Township, and the Strawberry Ferry tract of land belonging to the Estate of Ball, to the east on lands of the Estate of Ball and lands of Calhoun, to the south on lands of Calhoun, and Ball, and on Cooper river, and to the west by Cooper river.' "

Beyond Rice Hope are found the following plantations, which do not, however, contain houses: Washington, North and South Chacan and Sportsman's Retreat.

ABOVE THE TEE—THE BLUFF AND BEYOND ON THE WESTERN SIDE OF THE WESTERN BRANCH

The Bluff is opposite Strawberry Ferry, and consequently one of the ferry slips is on this plantation once owned by Major Isaac Harleston.

In the Ball Book: "From a letter of Wambaw Elias we learn that Elias of Limerick was not on speaking terms with his cousin the gallant Major Isaac Harleston. There is no clue to the cause of this quarrel, unless on the principle that— 'Lands intersected by a narrow frith abhor each other.' "

The house at the Bluff is a long, low, rambling old building, quaint enough, yet having no particular quality except permanency, but being of deep interest on account of the Moultrie family, whose country place it was for many years. It passed finally, by marriage, to the Ball family, and is now used as a hunting club.

Timothy Ford, while visiting at Washington, a neighboring place, said in his Diary (1785–1786):

"We employ much of our time in sporting with our guns, which also give me an opportunity of seeing the different plantations in the vicinity of Washington. They are chiefly rice plantations & of course there prevails a sameness thro the whole—but still there is a variety in regard of buildings, avenues, walks & gardens. There is a common taste for improvements of this kind among the planters here about. On Wednesday M^rs. Edwards being informed that Col^o. Moultrie brother of the Governor & Att. Gen. of the State has arrived at his seat about 2 miles hence with some company from town proposes that we all take tea there in the afternoon by which means I have an introduction to him, his Lady, Miss Smith and M^r· Moultrie his nephew from England. Miss Smith knows well that she is thought handsome; she possesses accomplishments, some sense, & a great deal of vanity. . . .

"M^rs· Edwards invites the company to dine with her on friday. Thursday we spend in romping about the plantation Barns &c. & in viewing the negroes at work at the rice— On Friday the company dine with us & in the evening we attempt to dance but find the music so bad that we are obliged to desist. I am more confirmed in my opinion of the rattling disposition of Miss Smyth; of the innumerable merits of Miss Beckworth & the hospitality, generosity, affability, & goodness of M^rs· Edwards. M^r· and M^rs· Holmes are no less entitled to my highest esteem & gratitude. On Saturday we all received an invitation to dine on Sunday at Col^o· Moultries, where we meet an accession of company from Charleston. Dinner is served up at 4½ oClock & the desert by candle light—On Monday we form a maroon party to visit some saw mills about 8 miles hence which in this country are considered objects of curiosity."

From a sketch by the late Dr. James Moultrie, with annotations by A. S. Salley, Jr., we learn that Dr. John Moultrie, the Emigrant, and the progenitor of the Moultrie family of South Carolina, was born in Culross, Shire of Fife, Scotland. He was a physician of eminence and a graduate of the University of Edinburgh. He came to Charles Town, S. C., anterior to 1729 in which year his name appears among the signatures of the original founders of the St. Andrew's Club, now Society. Born 1702. Died in 1771. He married first Lucretia Cooper, and, after her death, Elizabeth Mathewes. By his first wife he had the following children: John, Royal Lieut.-Gov. E. Florida; William, Major-General in American Revolution; James, Chief Justice E. Florida; and Thomas, Capt. in American Revolution. By his second wife he had one child, Alexander, Attorney-General of South Carolina, who married Catherine Judith Lennox, and whose daughter Catherine married her cousin, Dr. James Moultrie, fifth son of Hon. John Moultrie, M.D., of Charleston, S. C., by his sec-

48

ond wife, Eleanor Austin, daughter of Capt. George Austin of the Royal Navy and Ann Ball. Hon. John Moultrie received the degree of M.D. at the University of Edinburgh in 1749. He returned to Carolina, where he practiced his profession until 1767, when he removed to East Florida and was appointed Royal Lieutenant-Governor of that Province, which office he continued to hold until Florida was ceded to Spain, at which time he removed with his family to England. He is buried in Sheffnal Church, Shropshire. He had several children, but we are concerned with only two of them, John and James.

In an old book of memoranda by Lydia Child is the following entry: "January 5th, 1762, Mrs. Eleanor Austin ran away with Mr. John Moultrie and was married." Tradition hath it that Capt. Austin, her father, was opposed to this match. Capt. Austin, who had been a merchant in Charles Town, returned to England, where he lived upon his estate, Aston Hall, in Shropshire. After a lapse of some years the Hon. Henry Laurens undertook and effected a reconciliation between father and daughter after this manner: "When he went to England he took with him a picture of Mrs. Eleanor Moultrie and her two sons, John and James, which, in the absence of Capt. Austin from home, he hung in the dining room at Aston Hall," and upon Capt. Austin's return he was much incensed with his servants for allowing a stranger to take such a liberty, but finally the reconciliation was effected through Mr. Laurens' action.

Mrs. Jane Moultrie, wife of Maj. George Austin Moultrie, writing to Mrs. E. A. Poyas in May, 1849, says: "The picture you allude to of Mrs. Eleanor Moultrie and her two sons, James on her lap and John, my husband's father, standing by her knee offering her a rose, still hangs where Mr. Henry Laurens, perhaps, first placed it, in our dining room at Aston Hall." Capt. George Austin lies buried at Sheffnal Church. He bequeathed Aston Hall to his grandson, John Moultrie, who married in England Catherine Ball, daughter of a Tory, Elias Ball, called "Elias of Wambaw," formerly of Wambaw Plantation, South Carolina, afterwards of Bristol, England,

4   49

and his wife, Catherine Gailliard, a South Carolina woman from one of the plantations adjoining Wambaw.

So John remained in England, but James returned to South Carolina, and was evidently the "nephew from England" referred to by Timothy Ford as visiting Mr. Moultrie. He was a doctor, having received his degree at the University of Edinburgh, and returned to Charleston, the place of his nativity, and married in 1790 his cousin Catherine, daughter of Alexander, fifth son of the Emigrant, as spoken of before.

The fourth son and fifth child of this marriage was named William Lennox, and like his father followed the profession of medicine. He was twice married, his first wife being Hannah Child Harleston, by whom he had seven children, and after her death he took for his second wife Juliet Hall Ingraham (daughter of Capt. Nathaniel Ingraham) by whom he had two children, Mary Louisa and Eleanor Catherine. The latter died in infancy, and the former married in her twenty-third year Isaac Ball, Esq., Planter. Thus the Bluff passed into the hands of the Ball family where for many years Mr. and Mrs. Ball and their large and interesting family resided until their removal to Charleston, where they are now to be found as members of the "Kingly" Balls, their sons having married among the Weissenger, Grimke, Jervey, and Porter families, while their daughters have married among the Ficken and Rhett families.

The most distinguished member of the Moultrie family is Major General William Moultrie, some of whose descendants are found in the Brailsford family of South Carolina. The life and achievements of General Moultrie are too well known to be listed, and are briefly told by a memorial tablet to be found in the vestibule of St. Philip's Church, Charleston.

PIMLICO

Pimlico, next to the Bluff, has an interesting history, concerning which the Ball Book has this to say (page 140):

One of Alwyn Ball's brothers, Hugh Swinton Ball (1808) married "Miss Anna Channing, daughter of Walter Channing, of Boston. They had several children, all of whom died very young. His wife and himself both perished in the wreck of the steamer Pulaski, on their way from New York to Charleston. The boiler exploded on the night of the 14th of June, 1838; the vessel was blown to pieces, and many of the passengers were lost. Soon after their death, a lawsuit, which lasted several years, arose about the property. As the survivor was to inherit the bulk of it, the question was, which one *was* the survivor—a question not easily decided after a scene of such confusion and terror. The court finally decided in favor of the plaintiffs—Mrs. Ball's family—the evidence (as I have heard) showing that Mrs. Ball's voice had been heard calling in the darkness for Mr. Ball; and the presumption was, that, had he been living at the time, he would have answered her. By this decision, not only his wife's property, which was considerable, but more than half of his own, went to the plaintiffs. His intention had been to leave his plantation Pimlico to his nephew, Elias Nonus Ball, son of his brother, Elias Octavus; but the plantation and the negroes had to be sold for division. His nephew, however, found himself in possession of a very comfortable property on coming of age." After the sinking of the Titanic in 1914 this case was cited in court.

A wonderfully built and well-finished, hipped-roof wooden house is found at Pimlico. Its side faces south on the river, but Pimlico is approached on the landward side by a famous oak avenue that curves in from the public road a mile distant. It is now a sportsman's estate, once the home of people who not only gloried in the out-of-doors, but who skillfully used the beauties of nature as a worthy setting for a southern plantation residence. According to the present front elevation the original plan of the house provided for tall columns within the exterior walls, indicating the presence of a portico, but the recent addition of a small modern piazza has changed considerably the perfect simplicity of the old design.

Inside the house a cultured atmosphere of fine colonial days is immediately restored by the presence of exquisitely finished, hand-carved woodwork on the windows, wainscoting and mantels. The stairway, a perfect example of its kind, rises from the rear of a long entrance hall, adjoining which

51

are two large, perfectly proportioned rooms. The exact date of this house is hard to place, but it is of a similar type of house found all up and down the river. However little we know of the date of the construction of this building, the plantation itself was among the grants made to the three sons of Sir John Colleton, described as being opposite to Mepkin, near Strawberry Ferry and on the other side of the river, on a plantation called Mepshew, and now known as Pimlico.

POINT COMFORT

Adjoining the plantation of Mepshew (said in Dr. Irving's day to belong to the Ball estate, and only interesting on account of the land titles and Indian name) is found Point comfort, said by Dr. Irving to belong to R. W. Roper, now in possession of a Charleston family, connections of the Roper family, which is to be remembered particularly by the hospital bearing their name and which was founded by money left through the estate of this particular branch of the family. The house at Point Comfort was built by Mr. Roper, and resembles the Roper house on John's Island. Both are going to ruin.

On the plantation can be seen the remains of this beautiful house built of brick and conforming to the strictest architectural code. It is said by Mrs. R. P. Tucker (Cornelia Ramsauer) to be the most satisfying situation for and design of a home of elegance and beauty, but now gone to ruin, although Mrs. Tucker states that even yet a student of architecture would find a perfect example of early American architecture at its best in the front and side elevation of this large brick house.

The house is situated upon a knoll, and is surrounded by oak trees draped in moss which give a sombre aspect to this once busy plantation home, once well planted, well planned and well developed, now the lonely abode of vagrant winds.

Underneath the house is a series of large arches acting as supports, the enclosed part of which affords space for the household offices and constitutes a basement. Over the central front arch is built the "grand stairway," after the fashion of French Colonial houses, viz., with a central landing at the piazza level descending on either side. This stairway is of marble with iron balustrades.

The house itself, irrespective of the basement, has two stories and an attic. The lower floor has two very large double windows, in the French fashion, which are found on either side of the house, and lead from the piazza directly into two large front rooms, which may be at will thrown together. Inside there are (so far as the casual inspection possible from the outside reveals) splendid examples of paneling and woodwork. The house at Point Comfort will soon be a thing of the past unless steps are taken to restore to its pristine beauty this fine old place worthy of a better fate.

WAPPAHOOLA

There stands at Wappahoola, on a creek bearing the name, a delightful old house built of black cypress, said to have been constructed under the personal supervision of the owner (a Mr. Porgson) by slave labor. This property has, of course, a set of outbuildings, and is a fine and complete example of an artistically planned home of a farm house type.

It is raised a few feet from the ground, and the front elevation shows the usual veranda with its low-hanging eves, the second story being without piazzas of any kind. As this type of house is met with in a modified form in so many instances along the Cooper River it must have been adopted because found to be absolutely the best for the daily regime of plantation life, while entirely suitable for the residence of a gentleman and his family of antebellum days; thus the houses at Wappahoola, Pimlico, Quinby and Limerick are all modeled on this general plan, with slight variations.

The house was said to have been built by Mr. Porgson, but in Dr. Irving's book it is ascribed to E. Lucas; it is better known as the home of Frank Heyward, whose father's town house was that wonderful old brick house on Legare Street now owned by Lamb Perry, just south of the Smythe house on the eastern side.

Frank Heyward married Fannie Ferguson, a daughter of James Ferguson and Abbie Ann Barker, and Wappahoola is still called the Home of the Heyward family, being the residence of a son, and a daughter, Marie, and another daughter, Mrs. G. Cannon, while another daughter, Panchita, Mrs. William Grimball, resides in Charleston.

DOCKON

The plantation next to Wappahoola is Dockon. Dr. Irving says Dockon plantation near Wappahoola was originally the property of Jacques duBose, and owned in 1742 by Samuel and Joseph Wragg, passing to Ropers, Lucas, and Fergusons, in whom it was vested a century later. Mrs. Samuel G. Stoney gives the information that the Dockon house was burnt, but that a beautiful avenue is left, and an unpretentious wooden house. According to Mrs. Stoney there was at Dockon a very valuable library at one time. Certainly a literary flavor of a spicy quality emanates from a famous novel called "Verve Cliquot," written by Mrs. General Ferguson, who was a lady from New Orleans and visited at Dockon. Mrs. Stoney is also the authority for the statement that at one time there were three Ferguson brothers well known in Charleston soceity, Dugué, Tom, and Sam, all being dead now except Major Thomas B., who was at one time Minister to Sweden and Norway.

The progenitor of this flourishing family was Thomas Ferguson, who became a man of property and standing in South Carolina. "He was," said Dr. Johnson, "born on a piece of land seven or eight miles north of Charleston, between the Dorchester and Goose Creek roads; and when an infant was removed by his parents, on a pillow, to a ferry of which they had become managers, sometimes called Ferguson's but more commonly called Parker's Ferry. Young Ferguson grew up proficient in all outdoor sports, and Mr. John Parker, then a boy and heir to the ferry (afterwards a member of Congress) became much attached to young Ferguson."

Mr. Ferguson's first outfit was very limited. It consisted of two negroes and a buck saw. He continued, however, to work hard, secured the good opinion of his friends and neighbors, and finally became overseer to several plantations, gen-

"WAPPAHOOLA," WESTERN BRANCH COOPER RIVER

erally rising from that position to that of manager. He soon became independent, wealthy, popular and influential. He married happily and advantageously. In fact, if all that Dr. Johnson's Traditions tell of him is true, he may be said to have married early and often, having had no less than five successive wives.

It is narrated in Charleston of a certain dignified gentleman who was frequently married, that upon the occasion of his last marriage his eldest son, by his first wife, failed to attend the wedding. When asked why he thus absented himself from this ceremony he is said to have replied: "Pshaw! I haven't got time to go to all of Pa's weddings."

"Pa" seemed to have had a short memory also, for a lawyer is said to have been handling some property that the gentleman had acquired by one of his first marriages and to have remarked: "Now this property came to you when you were married to Miss So and So."

The old gentleman protested that he had never married that lady, "Only thought of doing so." Finally convinced, however, that he actually had married the lady in question, he is said to have given in by saying casually, "Oh, yes, so I did by the way, and a very good woman she was, too."

Be that as it may, Mr. Thomas Ferguson was certainly five times married, and, according to Dr. Johnson, his wives were: (1st) a Miss Elliott; (2nd) the widow North, of the Perry family, by whom he had two children, James and Anne, the latter of whom became Mrs. Charles Elliott and subsequently Mrs. Richard Berresford; (3rd) Miss Martha O'Reilly, a handsome woman, by whom he had four sons who grew up and married; (4th) the widow of Andrew Rutledge, and daughter of General Gadsden; and (5th) Miss Wragg, who survived him, with two sons.

Col. Ferguson was one of the most influential men in the State and gave his best services to the upbuilding of South Carolina. His home in Charleston adjoined the Barker property on Tradd Street. To reach this latter charming place, now in the possession of the Manigault family, one has to go down a delightful old-fashioned lane which opens into a beautiful old garden. To the north and to the west of the Barker house were two lots bought in 1762 by James Postelle and Charles Pinckney and conveyed within a few months to Thomas Ferguson, who erected thereon his dwelling.

Mr. Ferguson was a large planter of the parish of St. Paul, and it is interesting to note in addition to the previous data of this family given in the history of Dockon, that Major Thomas Barker Ferguson, at present visiting in Charleston, says that the first map of Charleston shows a Ferguson house built outside of the town limits. Tradition, he says, has it that the Fergusons came over with Oglethorpe. There were three branches of this family, one settling at Philadelphia, one in the West Indies (from which branch the family in South Carolina came) and the third in Holland, and when Major Ferguson was at a diplomatic dinner in Holland he noticed that he was being closely observed by his host, the reason for this observation appearing later when Major Ferguson was told that he very strongly resembled members of the Ferguson family in that country.

It will be remembered that Mr. Thomas Ferguson, the founder of the family, and the grandfather of Major Thomas B. Ferguson, made his start in life near Parker's Ferry, and Major Ferguson says that his grandfather was related to the Parkers. It is interesting to note in this connection also that Mr. Paul Sanders at Ritter says that his brother now owns and lives in a quaint old wooden house on a high brick basement placed upon land exactly opposite to one of Thomas Ferguson's first plantations.

As Mr. Ferguson was married five times and had children by each marriage he seems to have disposed of the difficulty of dividing his property by leaving to each set of children the property acquired through their mother. There were, it appears, twenty-six or twenty-seven children by these various marriages.

Major Ferguson states that, should he live five years longer, until 1926, three generations of his family, that is from his grandfather's birth in 1726, his father's birth, 1784, and his own in 1841 and his life prolonged until 1926, these three generations which should be six generations (as commonly computed) will cover two hundred years; a fact unique in American history.

The Ferguson connection with Cooper River property comes in when Mr. Thomas Ferguson married Miss Anne Wragg, Dockon being part of the Wragg property. The children of this marriage were Samuel, DuGué, Thomas Barker, Joseph Sanford, and Fanny, who married Frank Heyward and lived at Wappahoola. (Major Ferguson has this to say in regard to Wappahoola, that the house there was built by Parson Porgson.)

The last mention made of the progenitor of this large and flourishing family, Mr. Thomas Ferguson, is when he was appointed aide to General LaFayette, who visited this country in 1821. Thus it will be seen that the dwellings, names and histories of the Barkers, Broughtons, Fergusons and Fitzsimmons are closely interwoven.

Dr. Sanford Barker was the brother of Major Theo. G. Barker, and their mother was a Miss Millican, whose father was the builder, for the Broughtons, of the house next under discussion.

Thomas Ferguson not only merited, but received the friendship of the distinguished men of his day, his friendship with Christopher Gadsden being a matter of history, where it is recorded that "an extrordinary intimacy and attachment existed between General Gadsden and Mr. Ferguson, and continued to the end of their lives."

SOUTH MULBERRY

A discussion of the geographical arrangement of the plantations on the western side of the western branch of the Cooper River shows that the first house situated near the water after leaving Pimlico is South Mulberry, formerly included in the Mulberry tract upon which North Mulberry was built. The two Mulberry tracts, north and south, were originally included, by error, in Fairlawn Barony, but their history will be discussed in connection with the history of Mulberry house.

On South Mulberry stands an old wooden house sometimes called "Home Place," the chief charm of the place being the garden filled with rare shrubs cultivated by Dr. Sanford Barker, who married Christina Broughton, of North Mulberry. Dr. Barker was a botanist who failed to record his scientific achievements, but one who loved to botanize, and with whom many noted scientists also botanized on long "visits" to South Mulberry extending over many months at a time

The Barkers, Broughtons, Fergusons and Fitzsimmons were all connected by marriage. The first mention of Barker in connection with Cooper River is found in Mills' "Statistics," which tells of the massacre by the Indians of the garrison at Schinskins. "A similar act of perfidy on the part of the Indians was committed about the same time, a little above the Eutaws, at a place called Barker's Savannah. The commanding officer, Col. Barker, from whose defeat the scene of action acquired its name, was drawn into an ambuscade by the treachery of an Indian named Wateree Jack, who pretended friendship, and lured the white people into a snare."

The Barker family residence in Charleston was found on the southern part of a lot on Tradd Street nearly opposite to Logan Street.

THE MULBERRY

Mulberry, also called " The Mulberry," or " Mulberry Castle," was built in 1714. The land on which the house stands was purchased from Sir John Colleton by Thomas Broughton, afterwards the first Lieutenant-Governor under the Royal Government, and one of the Council who signed the celebrated " Church Act." Mr. Salley says that " at a very early date there was a landing at ' The Mulberry ' on Cooper River. Col. Thomas Broughton bought the place and built there, in 1714, a handsome house which is still standing—one of the handsomest examples of the provincial architecture of that date to be found in America to-day."

According to Mills' " Statistics," " In the Indian War of 1715, St. John's and St. Stephen's parishes were the frontiers of the province. In or near them were three forts: the first on

"MULBERRY CASTLE," WESTERN BRANCH COOPER RIVER, BUILT 1714

The old Broughton place; now owned by Mr. C. Chapman

Cooper River, about 3 or 4 miles below Monk's Corner, on the plantation of Mr. Thomas Broughton, called Mulberry; the second on Mr. Daniel Ravenel's plantation, called Wantoot; the third on the plantation of Mr. Izard, called Schinskins, on the Santee River. The garrisons at Schinskins were all massacred in consequence of their own imprudence in permitting a number of Indians to enter the fort under the cloak of peace and friendship.''

Dr. Irving declared that as late as 1842 an old cannon, the relic of bygone days, was still to be seen in the yard upon an ancient mound, which mound was doubtless the remains of the old fortifications at Mulberry.

In the "History of Fairlawn Barony," Judge Smith says: "On 6th September, 1679, an additional grant was issued to Sir Peter Colleton for 4423 acres on Cooper River, lying adjoining to and south of the Fairlawn Signiory.

"The tract included in this last grant was afterwards known as 'Mulberry,' although it would appear, from what subsequently occurred in connection with the sale to Thomas Broughton, that the 'first bluff bank,' commonly called the 'Mulberry tree,' was within the lines of the Fairlawn Signiory.''

In January, 1708, Sir John Colleton, son of Peter, executed a conveyance to Thomas Broughton of the tract of 4423 acres granted to his father in 1679, describing it as on the "Westerne Branche" of the T in Cooper River, which said plantation is now called or known as the Mulberry plantation, a part of which continued in the Broughton family for two hundred years. The error of misunderstanding about the exact location of "bluff bank" commonly called "the Mulberry tree" caused Thomas Broughton to assume that it was on his tract purchased from Sir John Colleton, and accordingly he placed his settlements upon it only to find that this was a mistake and that he had builded upon a southeastern part of Fairlawn Barony. This was rectified in a neighborly fashion by Sir John transferring to Colonel Broughton 300 acres off that of Fairlawn, and receiving in exchange a similar number of acres off the northwestern part of Mulberry and a hundred and fifty pounds additional in money.

Long ago when rice was grown at Mulberry "The Meteor" says: "The hill at Mulberry was covered with fine oak, cedar, elm, catalpa, and other forest trees, which, with luxuriant vines of wild grape and supple-jack, made groupings of beautiful foliage over the Spanish bayonet and fan palmetto that grow at will on the graceful grass-covered slopes as they trend toward river and forest. From the windows of the house on this plantation miles of riceland lie in view, which are in soft shades of brown and black when ploughed in spring, bordered by the green banks curving with the course of the river, to be followed in June by the tender yellow-green of the growing rice and in September by a waving expanse of golden grain.

"The square red brick building stands on this hill, which ends abruptly in a bluff thirty-five feet high on Cooper River, and slopes towards the forest and ricelands. The exterior is like the picture on the Broughton family tree of the house at 'Seaton' in England, the home of the Broughtons. A Dutch roof (now Mansard) with dormer windows, covers the main building, at the four corners of which are built detached rooms called 'flankers,' which connects with the house by space for a door way. These 'flankers' have each a pointed roof, surmounted by an iron vane six feet high, of light arabesque design, upon which swings as weathercock an oblong plate of iron, out of which the date 1714 is cut. Above this date the vane ends in a royal crown. Seen as these 'flankers' are, from some distance across the low-lying rice fields, they give a quaint, unusual look to the house, and probably led to its being called Mulberry Castle."

The bricks at Mulberry are unusually good. They are varied in shade, the darker or overburned ones being used at the corners and openings as quoins. The entrance to the house is from a porch into the large dining "hall," as it was called, with high ceiling, large windows and the broad fireplace of the time, in front of which stood a heavily built, solid mahogany table, the top being near two inches thick. The walls of this and the adjoining "parlor" were covered with family portraits. The foundation of the house encloses a cellar, deep and wide enough to contain kitchen and store room, with ample space for the wood required to fill the wide hearths above. Being so much larger and stronger than the neighboring houses, it was a refuge for many families, during the troubles with Indians first, and afterwards with British scouts. Loop-holes for muskets made in heavy window shutters gave means of defence from the four sides of the house. Trap doors in the floors of each "flanker" lead to shallow cellars paved with "French flagstones," in which ammunition was kept. When the "Broughton" of the day was at home, during the war with England, he was liable to surprise from British scouts. He therefore provided a way of escape through a subterranean passage from one of the flankers.

A letter from Mrs. Nath. Broughton, addressed to "Nath. Broughton Esqr., In Charles Town, These June ye 15: 1732," gives fascinating glimpses of the domestic life at Mulberry and neighboring places:

"My Dear

"I sent on Sunday to wassamsaw about the fouls, my father having forgot to tell me what you desired till Saturday, there-fore could send no sooner M^r· Lawson sent me worde his wife had none fit for yeus as yet, he came down on Tusday and tould me had heard of Some at wampee but could not possably git them at wassamsaw till last night or this day, and as my father thought it was time the things should goe down I have done my best, could get but 3 dozen yong fouls in all the nabour-hood which I send with 14 young gees, they have bin well fed but it is so short a time that —— be but little the better, I design 2 of them for cosin Manigault if you think well of it should have sent her some fouls if they could have bin had but hope to make it up another time, pray give my affectionate servis to her, I was sorry to hear by M^r· Le Bas she was not well and wish her better health . . . nancy being in want of gounds desier M^{rs}· La Tour will get withall to make her a couple, I desire it may be something that looks well they not being for comon wair, my sister Broughton desiers her to get her a pair of mens gloves at M^{rs}· ceraus (Sereau?) that will fit cosin manigault she gives her servis to you and all with you, pray give my love to M^{rs}· La Tour I hope she will excuse

61

my not writing to her, I shall be glad to know whether my neess mazick is brought a bed desier to be remembered to her if you see her, I wish Capt warren a happy voiage, we are all as the doct left us, but have heard my——has had a bad night I hope to hear by the——unity you continue mending which will be a great Satisfaction to

Dear Life
your affectionate wife
H. CHARLOTTE BROUGHTON.

I send 4 chairs to be bottomed, since you are likely to receive some mony should be glad M$^{rs.}$ La Tour would bye me a gound as I desired her.''

The town residence of the Broughtons is difficult to locate in those early days, but in 1771 the following advertisement would seem to place one of them at least on Tradd Street:

"So. Ca. Gazette, April 4, 1771. Mr. Fournier, Miniature Painter, &c. Is removed to Mrs. Rivers in Tradd St., almost opposite to Mr. Andrew Broughton's: and having now, in a great measure, recovered his health, is ready to wait upon any Gentlemen or Ladies who may be pleased to favor him with their Commands.''

The Broughtons married into neighboring families on the Cooper River, and Mulberry was for many years the residence of Major Theo. G. Barker, whose mother was a Miss Millican (whose father built the house for the Broughton family). After being in the hands of Major Barker, whose wife was Miss Louisa Fitzsimmons, the property passed on to other owners. The history of the Fitzsimmons family is wrapped up in the history of lands belonging to the Fitzsimmons and Hammond families near the Georgia line. Space does not permit of more than a brief mention of the Fitzsimmons family, some of whom are now living in Charleston and the vicinity. The old family place near Beech Island is in possession of Mrs. J. P. Richards at "Red Cliff," a former home of the Governor Hammond noted in history as using the famous expression "Cotton is King." The Hammond and Fitzsimmons families have intermarried, and Christopher Fitzsimmons Hammond had in his possession some portraits by Peale of ancestors of both branches of his distinguished family. The

Fitzsimmons burying ground is found at the Cottage tract on the Georgia side of the Savannah River. Beech Island, another Hammond house, still stands.

Samuel Barker Fitzsimmons resides at old Wiltown. He has in his possession a most exquisite set of Crown Derby china and many rare pieces of glassware, along with portraits and historic furniture which came to him when the Barker estate at Mulberry was broken up.

Mulberry finally passed into the hands of Mr. Clarence E. Chapman, who acquired the property when it was in disrepair, having been unoccupied for approximately ten years. He has been much interested in restoring this old place, and has kept intact all of the original interior furnishings of wood and ironwork possible. Mr. Chapman has even dismounted certain pieces of ironwork, sending them north. He consulted experts, and had the pieces duplicated in order to fully restore the original property correctly from an historical standpoint; he has also reduplicated the correct furniture for such an establishment, and has treated "The Mulberry" with the respect and reverence worthy of its lineage, for the Ancient Lady says that at Strawberry Chapel "the oldest inscription that is legible is 1757, on the stone that covers Mr. Nathaniel Broughton, of Mulberry Castle, in St. John," who built the house in 1714.

LEWISFIELD

Lewisfield, comprising 1000 acres on the river front, adjoining Exeter to the north and Mulberry to the south, was transferred by Sir John Colleton, 4th Baronet, on the 15th of September, 1767, to Sedgewick Lewis. At the time of sale this 1000 acres is stated to be known as the "Little Landing," but after passing into Lewis' hands it acquired the name of Lewisfield, which it has ever since retained. Through intermarriage, the place subsequently passed into the Simons family, in whose possession it continued for many years. Johnson's "Traditions" says that Keating Simons married Miss Sarah Lewis in 1774 and "thereby became possessed of a rice plantation and negroes, on the western branch of Coopere river, which he called Lewisfield," which still retains that name, and was in possession of his grandchildren in 1851. After serving his country, when Charleston fell into the hands of the British, Keating Simons became a prisoner on parole, and retired, as he had a right to do by capitulation, to reside on his plantation, Lewisfield.

Many of Simons' neighbors were unguarded in their expressions of hatred to the British victors. (Mr. Broughton, of Mulberry, was one of these, who for his discipline had a troop of horses quartered on his land.) Shortly after this Lord Cornwallis, passing down—says Dr. Johnson—from Camden to Charleston, sent a courier to announce that he and his "family" would dine with Mr. Simons the day after. "Accordingly Mr. Simons provided amply for his reception; killed a lamb for the occasion and poultry and other plantation fare in abundance, and arranged his sideboard in accordance. But his lordship had his cook and baggage wagon with him and was well served by those who knew his inclinations. Accordingly, they killed the old ewe, the mother of the lamb; and on Mr. Simons telling the Scotch woman, the cook, that this was unnecessary, and showing the provisions, she replied that his lordship knew how to provide for himself wherever he went."

The story goes on to show how Mr. and Mrs. Simons were invited to sit at their own table as guests, but Mr. Simons, while accepting for himself, said that "He could not think of his wife becoming a guest instead of presiding at her own table," and told his lordship that Mrs. Simons was "otherwise engaged." At this dinner a great game was played over the wines, Mr. Simons generously providing some of his best, but again his lordship "enquired of his aides if they did not bring with them some of his old Madeira, and called for a bottle or two." His lordship pretended to enquire the history of it, whether "London particular," or imported directly from Madeira, and the young gentleman had an answer ready for the occasion. It proved, afterwards, that the wine had been plundered from old Mr. Mazyck's plantation when it had been visited by Cornwallis.

"DOCKON," WESTERN BRANCH COOPER RIVER

"LITTLE LANDING" OR "LEWISFIELD." THE STEVENS HOUSE
WESTERN BRANCH COOPER RIVER

Mr. Simons remained on parole at Lewisfield waiting to be exchanged, until the middle of July, 1781, when General Greene sent his cavalry down into the lower part of the State, even within sight of Charleston, and Colonel Wade Hampton commanded part of this expedition. It seems that the gallant Hampton was at that time courting Mr. Simons' youngest sister, then living at Lewisfield. "Love rules the court, the camp, the cot," and "Love-directed-Hampton" came near to Lewisfield. He galloped up the avenue to see his "lady love," but found instead a party of British from two vessels at the landing, which vessels were fast aground. Nothing daunted, Hampton (being an elegant horseman, in the habit of galloping his steed and at this speed stooping from his saddle to pick up from the ground his cap, sword, whip or glove) galloped back to the main road, vaulted upright in his saddle, waved his sword over his head and shouted to his command to return.

This they did, and engaged the enemy. Some of the British escaped, although many were taken and the boats burned. Suspicion falling on Mr. Simons as being accessory to the surprise and capture, an expedition of Black Dragoons was immediately sent out from Charleston with orders to bring him in dead or alive, but being warned, he did not await their arrival, broke his parole, and joined General Marion in the Swamp. Meanwhile his house and plantation were being searched for him, but luckily he was away, and remained with the old Swamp Fox as an aide, to whom he continued firmly attached, not only to the end of the Revolutionary War, but also to the end of his life; at the death of General Marion, Simons' loyalty was transferred to his family, and at the death of Mrs. Marion (so says Dr. Johnson, from whom all the above narrative is extracted and quoted) she left her plantation and negroes to Mr. Simons' eldest son, Keating Lewis Simons.

Lewisfield is now in possession of Mr. Charles Stevens, whose wife was the fascinating Mary Wharton Sinkler, of Belvidere. An amusing story is told that at Lewisfield, during the Civil War, a clever ruse was employed by the owner's family to save their valuables. It was given out that a relative had died in Charleston, and that the body would be interred upon the plantation. Accordingly a coffin was brought, but in it was secretly placed the family silver, plate, etc. An elaborate funeral was held and the valuables buried. As the negroes never discovered the ruse employed, raiding parties could not extract from them information they did not possess, and the valuables remained hidden safely until after the strife was over and the former owner returned to his home. One day he decided to recover his buried possessions, taking with him an old negro man, who had been present at the "funeral" years before, to assist him. The owner waxed so hot in the search that the old darkey, who was helping to dig up the supposed relative, exclaimed: "Lord, Maussa! By dis time you sho mus be unjint 'um" (unjoint him).

The house at Lewisfield is the regulation square pine or cypress building, facing the river landing. The establishment is set up on a high brick foundation, as a precaution against the rising of the river in freshet times. From the ground a high flight of steps leads to the wide piazza which forms the front to the lower story of Lewisfield, and lying along this piazza are the two front rooms of the place. There is no "front door" proper, but entrance into the house is made (as is oftentimes the case in houses of this section) through long French windows opening directly into these rooms. The only other entry into the house is at the rear where another flight of steps is found leading to the back hall, which penetrates only half the depth of the house, and affords space for stairs leading to the upper story, while separating the two rooms in the rear.

In all these old plantation places, which are ringed around with rice fields and blue-gum and cypress swamps, the outbuildings are set a little way from the main building in order to dispense with the household offices going forward in the main house. The servants like this arrangement, as it gives them greater freedom, and a little domain all their own. Many a southern child has looked with delight upon a stolen visit to the servants' quarters and there learned folk-lore stories akin to those "Uncle Remus" told the "Little Boy." No one lives at Lewisfield now, and the name is being changed (against history) to "Chacan," an adjoining place across the river, also owned by the same Stevens family, the very handsome house upon which was unfortunately burned.

EXETER

Sir John Colleton, the fourth Baronet, made the following transfer of property—"On the 15th September, 1767, to Mary Broughton, 988 acres on the river front, adjoining the 511 acres transferred to Thomas and Nathaniel Broughton." In this deed the 988 acres is styled "Exeter" plantation, by which name it has ever since been known. Miss Marie Heyward, of Wappahoola plantation, is the authority for the statement that the house at Exeter was built by Governor Broughton for his daughter.

Exeter house is two miles north of Mulberry. It is a quaint dwelling of bricks of English measurement laid in Flemish bond. The two houses are in plain sight of each other; Exeter, with the date 1712 engraved in its brickwork on the chimney-side, and Mulberry with the date 1714 in its weathervanes, are companion houses in historic interest. The plantations of Mulberry and Exeter were Broughton residences, but Sir Nathaniel Johnson was supposed to have lived at Exeter at one time, before he lived at Silk Hope, on the eastern branch of the Cooper River.

A portrait of Sir Nathaniel was at one time in possession of Dr. Barker, of South Mulberry, and one of his wife, said to be Anne Overton, a descendant of the general of that name who served under Cromwell, hung for a time at Exeter along with other interesting portraits. Wherever he lived, it is certain that Sir Nathaniel Johnson was buried at Silk Hope, in St. Thomas' Parish, and from respect to his memory his grave was surrounded by a brick wall by Mr. Gabriel Manigault, who purchased the plantation, many years after the death of the old knight, from his descendants.

In "Cameos of Colonial Carolina," exquisitely written by that most "perfect, pure and gentil" knight of the pen, the Rev. P. D. Hay, which Cameo appeared in *Harper's*, Vol. LXVI, No. 391, 5, a full history of Sir Nathaniel Johnson is given, and Exeter is described as being his home.

"We have but to step over the threshold of one of the old houses to cross a chasm of two centuries. Let us, for instance, visit Exeter, the country home of Sir Nathaniel. As we enter, two cabinet pictures, representing respectively a blonde and brunette of the time of Charles II, welcome us, clothed, as to their shoulders, in wonderful folds of white and blue and crimson, Their stories and their names are alike forgotten.

"Skied up over a door of the hall is the portrait of a young Huguenot maiden dressed as a shepherdess, and taken in London, it is said, by Sir Peter Lely, as she passed on her way from France to Carolina. On the left of the chimney a robust English matron appears in heavy bronze satin, while over her shoulders is thrown a snowy kerchief of lawn. On the opposite side is her daughter as a younger matron, born about 1703, with a complexion as fair as the wide band of pearls encircling her neck, and a face eloquent of sweet womanly virtues. She is dressed in blue silk, cut away from the neck only enough to show its slope, the waist just under the arms, wide sleeves held open by a fall of lace, a heavy piece of corded silk several shades lighter than the dress passing down the entire front, looking as straight and stiff as a cuirass of steel. In another place we see a boy of five clad in a short-waisted light gray surtout reaching almost to the ankles, white stockings, and crimson shoes. Into a room with walls so peopled it would not seem very strange to see the good Sir Nathaniel himself walk, dressed in a shag gown, trimmed with gold buttons and twist, silk tops for his legs, and a camlet cloak thrown over his martial shoulders.

"But paintings are not the only art treasures which these colonial houses contain. Pieces of old jewelry are here—diamonds and brilliants set in silver; rare specimens of napery, which have escaped by successive miracles the accidents of great wars and fires, expressing in exquisite damask-work legends such as Elijah fed by the ravens; antique musical instruments, which have by turns shivered to the Cavalier tune of 'Green Sleeves,' or pulsated responsive to the rhythm of some soft air born among the vine-clad hills of France; time-stained inventories of the furniture once filling a stately English home in the days of Charles I; and deeds of the same period conveying now in their heiroglyphical characters to the heirs nothing but doubt and confusion. These, with fragments of old lace, moth-eaten letters, vellum-bound diaries of the time, and remnants of beautiful china and glass, may yet be seen.

"EXETER," NEAR MONCK'S CORNER, WESTERN BRANCH COOPER RIVER

"With such a treasury to choose from, it would not be difficult to furnish forth an old-fashioned tea table on the lawn at Exeter, realistic in its minutest details; nor would it be hard to fill the punch bowl again with genuine Barbadoes shrub, if Carolinians could be made to agree whether the sweet orange and lemon should be used in the brewing or the juice of the sour orange alone. . . .

"Judging from the size of the tea service, genuine Bohea must have been a rare commodity in those days, and in looking over an old bill I find Dr. William Rind to have been a debtor to Alexander Cramahe and Co. 'to I lb. Bohea tea, £4 10s.' Dr. Rind was a gay bachelor, and in case the reader should wish to know what was required by a man of fashion during the first half of the eighteenth century, I will quote another bill against him by the same firm:

"To 1 Wigg Comb ....
To 1 pr. Pumps..............................
To 1 Thread hose..............................
To 7 yds. blue silk ....
To 1 doz. gold breast buttons..................
To 2 bottles treacle water......................
To 1 pair glaz'd white gloves....................
To 1½ doz. silver breast buttons @ 25s..........
To 1 prayer book ....
To ¼ cask rum..............................

" . . . Sir Nathaniel . . . served the colony as Governor for two terms. He was the first one of these officials who set an example of civil service reform by alienating from himself the monopoly of the Indian trade—a perquisite which his predecessors had apparently enjoyed without embarrassment.

"Governor Johnson was at pains during his administration to conciliate the Indians, and they did him 'yoeman's service' when the province was invaded.

"In the parish register of St. Thomas and St. Denis, one of the parishes which he founded, under the date 1712, we may now read these words:
"The Right Honble Sir Nathaniel Johnson.
Buried ye 2^d of July.
His grave lies on Silk Hope plantation."

Since the days of Sir Nathaniel Johnson Exeter has passed through many interesting adventures, and was near the scene of action of some sharp encounters during the Revolutionary War. It is now in the hands of Mr. A. J. Jones.

The Colleton mansion house stood on Fairlawn Barony at a spot about a mile east of the present Monck's Corner station, on the Northeastern R. R. (the county seat of Berkeley County) between the main public road and Cooper River, and about a mile from the river. It presents the remains of the most extensive brick mansion house and offices, and adjacent buildings in South Carolina of the period. During the war of the Revolution, the British turned it into a fort and storehouse and when they were compelled to evacuate the post, set it on fire, and destroyed it in 1781.

When the British retreated, states Mrs. Graves, the daughter and heiress of Sir John Colleton, "they burned down the mansion . . . and destroyed every building, including a Town built on the Barony for the residence of several people belonging to the estate, with the granaries, mills, &c. On this occasion, in addition to the furniture, paintings, and books, plate, etc., a large sum of money which was in my father's strong box, and my jewels, were lost, either destroyed or plundered." Finding that desolation brooded where plenty formerly had revelled in her gayest mood, the mansion at Fairlawn was never repaired nor rebuilt; a crumbling mass of broken brick and tile, with fragments of glass and pottery in a jungle of weed and shrubs is all that marks its site.

The account of Mrs. Graves' life is taken from a little publication by her, entitled "Desultory Thoughts on Various Subjects, by Louisa Carolina, Wife of Rear Admiral Richard Graves, of Hembury Fort, Devonshire, and Daughter of Sir John Colleton, Baronet, Born Baroness of Fairlawn, Landgravine of Colleton, and Sovereign Proprietress of Bahama. Printed at the British Press 1821." The only known extant copy of this work in South Carolina was the property of Theo. G. Barker, Esq.

"Mrs. Graves in so entitling herself was under some misapprehension. She was not the descendant of Landgrave Colleton, but of the Proprietor, and was therefore not Landgravine; nor is the female heir of a baronet a baroness," says Judge Smith. Mrs. Graves comes in as a descendant of one of the John Colletons, who was twice married. She is the child by his first marriage, his wife being Anne Fulford, daughter of Frances Fulford, of Great Fulford. His marriage to Anne Fulford having been dissolved by Act of Parliament, he married in 1774 Jane Mutter, and died in September, 1777, at Fair Lawn and was interred at Biggon Church. By his will he left all his property to this daughter (by his first wife), Louisa Carolina, who married Capt. (afterwards Admiral) Richard Graves, of the British Navy, and during her lifetime the sale and breaking up of the rest of the Barony took place; although the final sales of the last of it were not had until after her death.

The following sales were made by Admiral Graves and his wife, *viz.:* 1st November, 1815, to A. C. Mazyck—Ellery; 26th March, 1816, to M. W. Smith—416 acres, no name.

Under a family arrangement the estate had been transferred to Samuel Colleton Graves, the son of Admiral and Mrs. Graves, and he made sales as follows: to John White—Moss Grove; to Keating Simons—no name to tract; to John White—the tract called Gippy Swamp; to Samuel G. Barker (Trustee)—the tract called the "Old House."

Fairlawn Barony has furnished the background for a historical romance of colonial days. The "Story of Margaret Tudor," by Miss Annie T. Colcock is drawn from some of the Shaftesbury papers. Miss Colcock has made romance fit into history better than any other recent writer of fiction dealing with colonial history of South Carolina excepting perhaps Miss Annie Sloan in her "Carolina Cavalier."

INLAND PLANTATIONS OF FAIRLAWN BARONY
GIPPY

In addition to the plantations lying along the western bank of the river were several inland tracts sold subsequent to the breaking up of the Barony. The history of these tracts is of no special significance, except that one of them, Gippy, originally bought by Alonzo White, possessed a river landing. A list of these plantations includes Fairfield, Castle Ruin, Bamboretta, Moss Grove and Gippy, upon which latter a house still stands, and is now found in the possession of Mr. White's descendants.

A picture of this shows the southern aspect of the house, and gives a fair idea of the plantation home of that period. For many years Gippy was the residence of the Stoney family, representatives of which are found throughout the State, and a direct branch of which is located in El Paso, Texas.

FAIRFIELD, CASTLE RUIN AND BAMBORETTA

Behind Mulberry, having no river landings, lie the three places known as Fairfield, Castle Ruin and Bamboretta, all originally part of one tract.

On July 26th, 1769, John Mitchell, of Salisbury, North Carolina, acquired 1004 acres of Fairlawn Barony, "not situate on the water front, but bounding to the East on the public road to Moncks Corner." He died, leaving two sons, John Mitchell and William Nesbit Mitchell, and by his will his plantation, which he styles "Fairfield," is left to his son John, who died in 1800 and left it to his son William, with remainder over to his brother, William Nisbet Mitchell, should his son die before twenty-one years of age, without children. The child must have so died, as we find William Nisbet Mitchell in possession of the whole, which at his death appears to have been divided into two plantations, one called by the original name of Fairfield, containing some 470 acres, and the other of some 521 acres, on which William Nisbet Mitchell lived, called Castle Ruin and Bamboretta.

"This William Nisbet Mitchell directs, in his will on record, that the burial ground at Fairfield, in which his brother and his children were buried, and in which his own body was to be deposited, should, by his executors, be enclosed with a substantial brick wall." The foregoing is quoted from an article in the *South Carolina Historical Magazine* dealing with Fairlawn Barony.

Showing how tradition in some instances differs greatly from actual facts, an extract from Dr. Irving's "Day on Cooper River" says: "Mitchell directed in his will that his body should be burned. He died in 1826; many years before his death he purchased an iron chest or coffin, he used it during his lifetime as a cupboard or bin. After his death his body

"GIPPY," WESTERN BRANCH COOPER RIVER

was burned and ashes put in this iron chest and locked and key thrown into Cooper River. In his will he directed that his remains were not to be buried, but placed above ground in the woods on two brick piles with brick enclosure around it. This wish was complied with, and body placed near his former residence about two miles West of the 28 mile stone on the Moncks Corner road, where it may be seen to this day. The burning of his body was conducted by Thomas Broughton, Esq.'' It is said that the old iron coffin is in use as a drinking trough for horses.

Beyond Fairlawn Barony lay Wadboo, Keithfield, Somerton and several other plantations of great historical significance and interest, but as no houses now stand upon these places we pass them over with this bare mention.

CHAPTER IV

EASTERN BRANCH OF COOPER RIVER ABOVE THE "TEE"

WESTERN SIDE OF EASTERN BRANCH OF COOPER RIVER

FISH POND AND THE HUT

CROSS the river from Dean Hall, and near Comingtee on the western side of the eastern branch, are Fish Pond and The Hut. At the time Irving wrote his "Day On Cooper River" they were owned by John Henry Ingraham. These plantations were originally the property of the Harlestons, who settled there to be near their sister, Mrs. Affra Comings, at Comingtee. The plantations on this part of the river front were not large, and were in comparatively close proximity so as to form a social neighborhood of society, the members of which were in easy circumstances and more or less connected by ties of blood or marriage or early association.

According to Theodore D. Jervey, the Harlestons were identified with the history of South Carolina from the settlement of the Province. They were descended from an old and illustrious family of the county of Essex, England, and bore a conspicuous part in the Wars of the Roses, being adherents of the house of York. One member of the family, Sir John Harleston, was governor of Havre du Grace in the reign of Edward IV, another was Vice-Admiral Richard Harleston. In the family records John Harleston is described as of South Ossenden, while his son is later described as of Malling. More than one hundred years prior to this—about 1532—we find the same name and place in the County of Essex, England.

The first of the name to come to Carolina was Affra, who married in 1672 Captain John Comings, the mate of two vessels, *The Carolina* and *The Blessing,* plying between this province and England, and whose Carolina home was the plantation at Comingtee, which she later left to Elias Ball, who had married her sister.

Affra Comings was a woman accustomed to wealth and refinement. "Her father's 'inventorie' shows the furniture of her early home Mollyns from 'the seller, the parlour, the Inner parlour, the hall, the kitchen, the larder, ye great Chamber, the hall chamber, the painted chamber, the nurserie, the buttrie chamb^r the back chamb^r the gallerie' to 'the garretts'."

Mrs. Comings died in 1699 and as she had no children she devised all her estate, at her husband's request, in "joint tenancy " to the aforementioned Elias Ball, and her nephew, "John Harleston in the Kingdom of Ireland, the son of John Harleston late of Malling in the county of Essex in the Kingdom of England." The family tradition places the arrival of John Harleston in America at 1699 or 1700. From letters to him and his replies to same soon after his marriage to Elizabeth Willis in 1707 it is apparent that he was a person of importance in the province and that he must have occupied close personal relations with its rulers at that time. A letter of John Harleston to John Page (subsequently Lord Mayor of Dublin) displays the position they held in the colony:

"The Chief Justice M^r· Nicholas Trott, who is my Perticuler Friend in Carolina . . . Invited him & his wife to my Weding & set him at table with the Governor & Capt of men a ware that lay in oure harbor that saime time, & with the best of the Country."

Perhaps the most distinguished public member of the family of Harlestons was Isaac Child Harleston, who had a notable record during the Revolution, winning the title of Major, and being elected a member of the first Provincial Congress. He was a great horseman, and upon the death of his cousin John, son of Edward, by a provision in John's will, he became sole owner of the celebrated imported stallion Flimnap. The will reads as if this cousin had a deep respect for the Almighty even though he was a thorough sportsman. It states:

"Also my moiety of the above mentioned stud horse Flimnap as also my wearing gold watch and the old-family watch I give unto my cousin Isaac Harleston, son of John Harleston, deceased."

Speaking of Flimnap, a celebrated visitor to South Carolina in 1773, Sir Joshua Quincy, witnessed a race between this horse and Little David, in which £1000 were won and lost. He writes:

"At the races I saw a fine collection of excellent, though very high-priced horses, and was let a little into the 'singular Art and Mystery of the Turf.'"

Isaac Harleston was a great favorite with his brother-officers of the Revolution, as the following letter will show:

"Dear Isaac

The Genl: & Col: if I remember were not determined to dine with you, when invited—I was there last Night—and they then, upon my taking leave—s^d they sh^d see me at your Quarters at dinner to-day—this hint I give that you may exert yourself for Eels & fresh butter of which the Genl: & Col: are very fond—Shubrick is to land at your wharf—Remind me when I see you of a small anecdote of Col: Wigfall

Mond^y morg—"   Y^{rs} R. Smith.

BONNEAU'S FERRY, PRIOLI AND THE VILLA

As there are few old houses left on this particular part of Cooper River it is best to briefly mention the places in their order, so that the continuity of the sketches will be preserved. Anyone interested in land titles will find all of this definite information thoroughly discussed by Judge Smith in the *South Carolina Historical and Genealogical Magazine,* and no effort is made in the present volume to re-cover that ground, the human-interest story being featured in these accounts of the old houses.

Early in 1712, when Charles Craven was governor, Bonneau's ferry was in existence. When a courtship was taking place in the neighborhood the ferryman prospered, and one of the Ball account-books has item after item put down to ferriage.

TOWN HOUSE OF THE BALL FAMILY, VERNON STREET, CHARLESTON.
Built about 1800

Prioli, next to the Hut, was sometimes called Bonneau's Ferry, while it was the property of Dr. T. G. Prioleau. This arose from the fact that Samuel Bonneau had lived there at one time. He left two daughters, one of whom married John Ewing Calhoun, and the other Zekiel Pickens. The latter sold to Mr. Prioleau and moved to Brick Yard, a plantation on the other side of the river.

The Villa, next to Prioli, was originally called Gerard's Plantation. It was once owned by John Harleston, Jr., son of Edward Harleston, who married the daughter of Thomas Lynch. After Harleston's death his widow married Major James Hamilton, and their son was the General Hamilton of "Nullification" days. They resided for a time at the Villa, then sold it to Frederick Rutledge, who married Miss Harriet Horry, and it was then called "Harriet's Villa."

RICHMOND, FARMFIELD AND BOSSIS

Richmond and Farmfield, the two plantations next above the Villa, were Harleston places, Richmond being for a long time the seat of Colonel John Harleston, who had purchased a large tract of land comprising both Richmond and Farmfield from Dr. Martine. In the subsequent division of property Richmond fell to Colonel Harleston's daughter Jane, who married Edward Rutledge, and Farmfield to his daughter Eliza, who married Thomas Corbett.

On the first of these plantations there formerly stood a noble mansion, placed on the brow of a hill about 200 yards from the river side. In 1842 it was owned by Dr. Benjamin Huger, who married a Miss Harleston, and their son, William Harleston Huger, was one of the best-known physicians of Charleston. He married Miss Sabina H. Lowndes, a daughter of Charles T. Lowndes.

William H. Huger attended, as a youth, a private school conducted by Mr. Christopher Coates, after leaving which he went to the South Carolina College, where he graduated in 1846, and after a short vacation entered the Medical College of South Carolina and studied in the office of Dr. Peter C. Gailliard. After completing a course in medicine he went to

Paris to continue his studies. He took a course of lectures and a hospital course in the French capital, his companions there being Dr. S. Weir Mitchell, Dr. Cornelius Kollock and his close friends, Dr. Christopher FitzSimons. When he had finished this course he returned to Charleston and began the practice of his profession, which he continued until his last illness in 1906.

Shortly after his return to Charleston from Paris, while a young man, Dr. Huger was elected physician to the Charleston Orphan House; this position he held to the day of his death. During the Confederate War he was stationed first on James Island, and later was put in charge of the army hospital in Charleston. After that city was evacuated, Dr. Huger was sent to the hospital at Cheraw, and afterwards transferred to Sumter. Like all of the Harleston people, he was passionately fond of horse-flesh, and greatly admired fine stock. He was for many years a steward of the Old South Carolina Jockey Club.

Richmond plantation has on it an old burying ground; the inscriptions found on the tombstones include Harleston, Corbett, Read, Withers, and Rutledge names.

Adjoining Farmfield is Bossis, a plantation once owned by Nicholas Harleston the first. It had at one time belonged to a Mr. Bosse, hence the name of the property. Mrs. D. S. Lesesne, of Charleston, has now in her possession some of the old plantation belongings from this place when it was owned by the Harleston family.

EASTERN SIDE OF EASTERN BRANCH
OF COOPER RIVER

THE HAGAN

Just at the point where the Cooper divides into its two branches there is situated, on the eastern bank, a plantation known as The Hagan. The first grant covering this was one made August 24, 1688, to Samuel Wilson of 1000 acres, described as bounding west on Ahagan Creek, which was the Indian name for a creek of considerable size flowing from the southward into the eastern branch of the river at the T. It is variously spelled Ahagan, Hagan and Ehegging Creek. The high bluff on the river near the mouth of the creek is called Ahagan Bluff.

In 1748 Daniel Huger bought the Hagan tract from William Moore, and two other tracts adjoining the same plantation from Mr. Hull and Bonneau. Wm. Moore had received this plantation from his grandmother, Sarah Rhett, wife of William Rhett, who acquired the land in 1720 from Henry Miller. He had gotten it in 1708 from nieces of Thomas Gun, who obtained the property in 1690 from Samuel Wilson, to whom it had been granted by the Lord Proprietors.

Mr. Huger acquired other lands on French Quarter Creek, and was also owner of "Limrick" plantation, within the Cypress Barony. He was one of the wealthiest landholders in the neighborhood, possessing a place as far south as Ashepoo. He had much property in the city of Charleston, and in his will bequeathes:

"To son Benjamin my corner House in Charles Town fronting the broad Street with my other four Houses adjoining it and fronting Church Street. To son Daniel Corner House in Charles Town, fronting on Elliott Street and to Son Isaac tenement adjoining in Elliott Street."

John Huger, son of Daniel, was left by his father "the plantation called the Hagan."

In 1782 a battle was fought at Videau's Bridge on Brabant plantation between Coffin's cavalry of the British Army and a detachment under Col. Richard Richardson, and although the Americans later suffered defeat, the British were the losers in the first attack, and "Mad Archie" Campbell was captured by two Venning brothers. The horse of one brother refusing to carry double, Nicholas Venning took the prisoner behind him on his horse. Finding that he was making an effort to escape, Nicholas, as ordered, shot him. Mortimer Venning, his grandson, recorded the incident, and kept in his possession the sword his grandfather had worn, which, however, was lost, together with other valuable possessions, after the War between the States. The sword was made of a saw-blade

79

bound with wire to a wooden handle, and was used by Nicholas Venning until the close of the Revolution.

The old house and residence at Brabant shared the fate of so many of the family residences in St. Thomas' Parish; destruction by fire, and abandonment, consequent upon the complete overturn of private and public fortunes by the war of 1861–1865.

BEYOND FRENCH QUARTER CREEK—PLANTATIONS CONTIGUOUS TO THE RIVER

CHERRY HILL, CEDAR HILL, THE BLESSING, CAMP VERE

According to Dr. Irving, Cherry Hill was owned by Capt. Duncan Ingraham, and Cedar Hill by James Poyas. Both of these places had previously been in the Laurens family. He also says that the The Blessing plantation, north of French Quarter Creek, extending along the river as far as Camp Vere, was owned by the late Henry Laurens.

The history of Blessing and Camp Vere is recited in a celebrated law suit in which are quoted several old wills. Extracts from that of Margaret H. Laurens, found in the *Bill for Instruction and Relief,* published in the records of the Court of Equity in the Charleston district in the case of the executors of M. H. Laurens vs. Annie Isabel Laurens and others, show that Margaret Laurens was the widow of Frederick Laurens, of Camp Vere, and that the said Margaret purchased a plantation on Cooper River called The Blessing.

In the suit in which these papers appear a most interesting story is told. It seems that Margaret Laurens had an adopted grandson, Alfred Raoul Walker, to whom she left a legacy of $20,000 upon certain conditions. He was the infant child of Benjamin Walker, then a resident of Canada. The boy, apparently, was a minor at law, living in Charleston with his godmother, Miss Susan Quash, when Mrs. Laurens' will was probated. The adopted grandmother being dead, the question arose as to how Raoul was to be supported and educated, and as to what would become of the legacy if he should die under 21 years of age, or should fail to comply with the conditions prescribed by the will of Mrs. Laurens, *viz.:* that he was to receive none of the capital until he had studied and acquired a profession. The will naïvely reads, "I earnestly recommend him not only to acquire a profession, but to practice it." She also recommended to him to assume the surname of his great-grandfather, Mr. Pinckney. The celebrated Dr. John D. Irving, who wrote "A Day on Cooper River," was a witness to this will.

MIDDLEBURG

On the plantation of Middleburg, situated in old St. Thomas and St. Denis' Parish, across the river from Richmond, stands a fine old wooden house, very difficult to describe except as belonging to the farm house type. Here also is still standing a rice mill, built in 1800 of black cypress; one of the first toll-mills for rice in operation in South Carolina. Rice was sent here from Georgetown and other distant places.

Middleburg is best identified as the residence of the Simons family. Judge Smith says that the plantation of Middleburg is in a personal aspect one of the most interesting in the State. It was the starting point of the Simons family, one of the most prolific and well known from its character and widespread connection in the low-country. The first owner and settler of the place was Benjamin Simons, the first immigrant of the name. The record does not show exactly when he arrived, but he is supposed to have been one of the French Huguenot immigrants. The name Middleburg, which is found attached to the plantation from a very early date, is supposed to be after Middleburg, the ancient capital of the province of Zeeland in Holland; however, any connection, if any, which Benjamin Simons might have had with the foreign Middleburg is not generally known.

The first Benjamin Simons took out grants for considerable acreage in this parish, and was well to do. Benjamin Simons the second had 13 children, and Benjamin Simons the third, who married Catherine Chicken, made large additions to the Middleburg tract. The immigrant Benjamin Simons married Mary Esther duPre, and the graves of both are found at Pompion Hill Chapel.

After the death of the third Benjamin, Middleburg was partitioned among his three daughters. The home place, Middleburg, was allotted to Lydia, who married Jonathan Lucas, and after her husband's death it was left to their son, Jonathan Lucas. The Lucas family retained it until long after 1865, so that the part of Middleburg granted to Benjamin Simons in 1704 remained in one family over a hundred and sixty years, and passed later, with Horts and Smoky Hill, to Mr. John Coming Ball, with whom it now rests.

A study of the Simons family has revealed the fact that Keating, James, Robert, Morris and Edward Simons took up arms in the cause of American Independence. Our own time shows the names in recent history of Colonel James Simons and Dr. Manning Simons as distinguished descendants of these no less distinguished ancestors.

LONGWOOD

Longwood plantation adjoins Pompion Hill Chapel, which stands on land between Middleburg and Longwood on the Cooper River front. On June 12, 1738, Longwood was conveyed by Benjamin Simons to Thomas Hasell, who, in 1747, conveyed it to John Hasell; the latter in 1750 disposed of it to Samuel Thomas, Rector of St. Thomas' Parish as early as 1738. It afterwards became the property of the vestry, who sold it in 1784 to Capt. Thomas Shubrick; from then it passed to Gabriel Manigault.

Alfred Huger, a former Postmaster of Charleston, once owned the property called Pompion Hill; during his ownership, and presumably by him, the name of the place was changed from Pompion Hill to Longwood. The reason for this is not known, but the old name fell into disuse as applied to the plantation, and was restricted to the bluff on which the Chapel stands. The plantation is still called Longwood, and after Mr. Huger's death after the war of 1861–1865 it was sold away.

QUINBY

Quimby, now corrupted to Quinby and sometimes Quenby, was originally the ancestral seat of the Ashby family, who

"QUIMBY," EASTERN BRANCH COOPER RIVER
The Ashby home, now a Ball House

"MIDDLEBURG," EASTERN BRANCH COOPER RIVER
The ancestral home of the Simons family

had so named their Carolina place, after their place at Quimby, England. This plantation is situated opposite Bossis, and adjoining Longwood to the northeast, on the east bank of the eastern branch.

Elizabeth Ball, once Mrs. John Ashby, was three times married. Upon her tombstone it is recorded that she was a woman of rare economy. She was the third daughter of Elias Ball the first, and when she was about the age of sixteen, married in 1727 John Ashby, a widower with one son, of St. Thomas' Parish. His home was Quimby, the Ashby place about eight miles up the river from Comingtee, and on the opposite side; but Love and Capt. Bonneau's ferry found the way to bridge the distance, and so Elizabeth and John consented together in the Holy Estate.

Their married life must have been of brief duration, for his will dates 1728. It was generous to his widow of barely eighteen, and his plantation is left to his son and heir, John Ashby, along with Webdoe on the Santee, but should this son die without heirs both plantations were to go to Elizabeth, who was to have the right of residence until John became of age.

Eleven months after Mr. Ashby's will was made, a marriage contract was signed between his widow and John Vicaridge, a merchant of Charleston. Elizabeth married still a third time, becoming Mrs. Richard Shubrick, of Belvidere. She died September, 1746, at the age of 35, and was buried alongside of her sister, Ann Ball-Daws-Austin, in St. Philip's Churchyard, where her tombstone may still be seen by the south door. In 1802 Mr. Roger Pinckney bought Quimby from Thomas Shubrick and sold it later to John Bass for his son Isaac.

It was on the plantation of Quinby that Lt. Col. Coates' command, of 500 infantrymen and 100 cavalrymen, was attacked by Lt. Col. Lee with the Legion, and Lt. Col. Hampton with the State Cavalry. Marion and Sumter, coming up with reinforcements, continued the engagement. The Americans killed 40 British and took 140 prisoners, quantities of baggage, and about 100 horses. Those who fell were buried by the roadside, lining the road that leads from Quinby Avenue to Quinby Bridge.

LANDS ADJACENT TO HEADWATERS OF EASTERN BRANCH OF COOPER RIVER—CYPRESS BARONY

Landgrave Thomas Colleton, second son of Sir John, received, in addition to the two grants to himself and his two brothers, a grant in 1681 of 12,000 acres, called the Cypress Barony, situated on the headwaters of the eastern branch of Cooper River.

LIMERICK

In 1707 the Lords Proprietors permitted the Cypress Barony to be alienated and divided into smaller tracts; thereupon it was parceled out, 5000 acres to Dominick Arthur, and 3500 acres to both John Gough and Michael Mahon, who took out new grants for their portions. Michael Mahon was a native of Limerick, Irleand, as was also Dominick Arthur, and the name of Limerick became attached to the part of their shares subsequently sold to Daniel Huger, son of the first Huger emigrant, who made Limerick his place of residence.

With the sale and partition of the Cypress Barony, and its plantation equipment, the family of Landgrave Thomas Colleton lost all touch with the province. In later years all the part of the Cypress Barony allotted to Michael Mahon and John Gough, with 734½ acres off the Arthur portion, had become the property of members of the Ball family.

It is impossible to relate all of the notable achievements of the family of Hugers. Daniel Huger the third, to whom Limerick had been devised by his father, conveyed it on March 12th, 1764, to Elias Ball of St. John's Parish, Berkley County, as containing 4564½ acres. It continued to be owned by the Ball family for over a century and a quarter, not passing from their hands until after 1890.

There stands to-day on Limerick, the old plantation dwelling which has attained the venerable age of two hundred and odd years. Though slightly run down at the heels, it is certainly a quaint and curious old-fashioned affair that has stood

84

"LIMERICK," A PRIMITIVE HOUSE NEARLY 200 YEARS OLD
A Huger house

AVENUE OF LIVE OAKS, "LIMERICK," EASTERN BRANCH COOPER RIVER

the acid test of years. A glimpse of the swamp around the headwaters of the Cooper are seen in the background of the illustration. This house is fairly typical of the dwellings of that day and time in those isolated regions, as is the magnificent avenue of oaks which marked the approach to most of these plantation residences.

Elias Ball, of Limerick, was held in high esteem by his brother parishioners, who erected a mural tablet to his memory in Strawberry Chapel, an honor bestowed on no other layman of that parish. He was strong-willed, kind-hearted, clearheaded, resolute, generous and affectionate. On his plantation his word was law, although he was kind to his slaves. As an illustration of his undisputed sway the following anecdote is told:

One of the overseers on the plantation was to be married, the feast was ready, the company had assembled, minister and groom were on hand; but the bride at the last minute refused to be married at all. She would listen to neither coaxing, threats nor arguments. Mas 'Lias fortunately happened to be on the plantation; to him a little negro boy was sent.

"Mas 'Lias, Mis' Katie say she wun't married."

"Tell Miss Katie I say she 'must married.' "

Back sped the messenger in hot haste with the tidings—and she *was*.

Isaac Ball, second son of John Ball, Sr., came into possession of Limerick at the death of his uncle a few months after (1810). He married his cousin, Eliza Catherine Poyas. They settled at Limerick and lived a happy useful life. Having no children they adopted a little nephew of Mrs. Ball's.

Limerick passed to William James Ball, whose wife, Julia Cart, had charm of manner equal to her beauty of face. After her death in 1858, near the close of the Civil War, he married his cousin, Mary Huger Gibbes, and lived at Limerick, where he died in 1891.

Ebenezer Roche owned and settled Windsor before the Revolutionary War. He died in 1783, and his executors sold the place to Edward Harleston. In 1786 Edward Harleston moved to Fish Pond, and sold Windsor to Joseph Brown, a son-in-law of Rawlins Lowndes, who sold it in 1788 to Evan Edwards. The widow of the latter continued to hold it until 1840, when it was purchased by Dr. Irving.

The place was in a high state of improvement, with a large park well stocked with deer. The fine family mansion on the hill was destroyed by fire in 1815, and a little cottage built, in which Dr. Irving lived.

HYDE PARK AND KENSINGTON

The present house at Hyde Park, the plantation across the river from Silk Hope, was built about 1800 by the second John Ball (born 1760, died 1817), who was living at Kensington when it was constructed. The original house, built in 1742, by John Coming Ball, younger son of Elias the first, was burned some time after 1772.

The second John Ball, of Kensington, was known in the family as John Ball, Sr. At the age of 16 he was managing his brother Elias' plantation interests. Before he entered the army in the Revolution he married his cousin, Jane Ball, daughter of John Coming Ball and his wife Judith Boisseau. He must have been a thrifty man, for at his death in 1817 he owned the plantations of Kensington, Hyde Park, White Hall, Midway, Belle Isle, on the Santee River, St. James, or the Saw Mill tract, Marshlands, near Charleston, and a large brick house in the city at the northeast corner of Vernon Street and East Bay.

On Kensington plantation, which adjoins Hyde Park on the western bank of the river, there is an old three-story house. It was constructed by slave labor, of cypress from the plantation. Instead of nails, round wooden pegs are used in the construction, while in the outbuildings all of the nails are hand-wrought. There are large piazzas downstairs, and old batten doors and shutters. Although it was built on the river opposite Silk Hope, the dwelling house fronted on the road which led from Bossis and Hyde Park, and was not far from Cordesville. Kensington passed into the hands of Dr. John Irving, and back again into the Ball family.

86

A plantation in olden times was a community in itself, which required thorough organization and complete system; and whatever the evils which were inseparable from the institution there were many and great compensations, such as the present conditions of affairs do not afford, nor have afforded since the sudden freeing of slaves worked such hardship upon these people by forcing them into an economic struggle for which they were absolutely unprepared.

McCrady writes:

Though unsuited to the climate, the models of the houses were after those of the houses in London and the English country seats. The furniture and carriage horses, chaises or coaches (of the planters) must all be imported, and tailors and milliners often brought out the fashions from London (for the use of the well-to-do). Households were organized on the English model, except in so far as it was modified by the institution of slavery.

In every well-organized planter's household there were three high positions, the objects of ambition of all the negroes on the plantation. These were the butler, the coachman, and the patroon. The butler was chief of all about the mansion; his head was often white with age. His manner was founded upon that of the best of the society in which his master moved. He became an authority upon matters of table etiquette, and was quick to detect the slightest breach of it. He considered it a part of his duty to advise and lecture the young people of the family upon the subject. . . .

The coachman . . . was scarcely less of a character than the butler. He had entire charge of the stable, and took the utmost pride in the horsemanship of his young masters, to whom he had given the first lessons in riding. The butler might be the greatest man at home; but he had never the glory of driving the family coach and four down the great "Path" . . . to town and through its streets.

The oldest plantations were upon the rivers; a water front, indeed, and a landing were essential to such an establishment, for it must have the periago (a colloquialism for a large canoe used in those days) for plantation purposes, and the trim sloop and large cypress canoes for the master's use. So besides the master of the horse—the coachman—there was a naval officer too, to each planter's household, and he was the patroon—a name no doubt brought from the West Indies. The patroon had charge of the boats and the winding of his horn upon the river told the family of his master's coming. He, too, trained the boat hands to the oar and taught them the plaintive, humorous, happy catches which they sang as they bent to the stroke, and for which the mother of the family often strained her ears to catch the first sound which told of the safe return of her dear ones. Each of these head servants had his underlings, over whom he lorded it. . . . The house was full, too, of maids and seamstresses of all kinds, who kept the mistress busy, if only to find employ for so many hands. . . . Outside the Overseer was responsible for the administration of the plantation.

The type of life which proceeded at Hyde Park may be considered typical of that which went on in all the attractive homes and estates up and down the river. These old places were extremely beautiful, although the houses were not imposing from an architectural standpoint; many of them were situated on high bluffs overlooking the Cooper River and its tributaries. Before the eye of the beholder stretched out mile after mile of rice fields, all under bank. The dwellings were surrounded by lawns, gardens and meadows, while extensive woodlands formed a background to the rear.

No one can imagine the life which went on in these establishments. A little glimpse of the country life in South Carolina in "Ye Olden Tymes" has been preserved in a poem written by Catherine Gendron Poyas, a niece of "The Ancient Lady," called "Limerick." In this she tells of the neighboring places:

"Through pleasant fields, on river-banks we stray,
    Where beauteous Cooper winds his placid way,
    Now classic grown, since Irving's spreading fame,
    Has given it, for aye, a place and name!

To Richmond hill, or Farmfield, we repair,
    Or Bossis, sylvan spot, where balmy air
    Revels on sunny day, 'mid fragrant flowers,
    Or gently whispers 'round its woody bowers.
    Perhaps, on Hyde-Park's breezy hill, we stand;
    Or Kensington, whose ancient oaks demand
    The admiration that we show before
    The pleasant mansion opes its friendly door."

88

The sports in which the guests indulged are glowingly described; then she speaks of childhood days:

> "Oh, carping care! O sorrow! little then
> Dreamt I you waited on the steps of men;"

and tells of playing whoop-and-hide

> "Beneath the moon's pure, placid silvery ray—
>
> But one will say, 'some nights there is no moon;'
> I'll show you where we passed those evenings, soon—
> In some old negro's cot, where blazing nigh,
> The ample pine log sent its flame on high.
> There would we sit around the chimney wide,
> List'ning the tales of ghosts—of one who died
> In the old war—and still is heard or seen
> At dead of night, upon the road between
> This gate and Kensington,—a neighboring place—
>
> Sometimes this horrid phantom comes, they say,
> As gallant steed, carparisoned and gay;
> Anon it changes to a savage dog,
> That fiercely one attacks; then, as a hog,
> Goes grunting on its way—but oh, most dread!
> It last appears—a man without a head!
>
> But lighter tales sometimes we would require,
> As close we crept around the cheerful fire:
> Of what 'old master' used to do and say;
> Of how 'mass Jack a courting went one day';
> And many a pleasant tale of lady fair,
> With rich brocade, and gems, and raven hair;—
>
> But turn we now from childhood's joys and cares,
> To the bright dreams of youth's extatic years;"

The day begins with a stag hunt, and the band of gallants hoping to catch a glimpse of the girls before they start:

> "They wait, they loiter o'er each cup of tea,
> In hopes, before they start, the girls to see;
> To win a smile—to have the old shoe tost—
> Without this charm, the field, the day were lost!
>
> The hunters off, the maidens find the day
> By far too long, and tedious on the way;
> But now at last the old clock strikes—'tis two!
> They fly upstairs to dress themselves anew;
>
> Hark! Hark! the huntsman's horn—they come, are near;
> The mistress orders—'bid the cook prepare
> To serve-up dinner in the shortest space;

89

And good old Joseph, quick, the side-board grace
With the refreshments, and with generous wine,
For, weary from the hunt, before they dine
They must some relish take . . ."

After dinner the ladies retire to the parlour:

"While still the gentlemen remain around
The social board, where wit and song abound.

'Tis Christmas—and the sable train rejoice:
Now in their humble cottages the voice
Of song and mirth is heard: . . .

Nor does the slave alone this season hail:
What though the Christmas lamp burns dim and pale
On our domestic altars, yet the day
Can never pass unheeded quite, away.

'Call in the rustic fiddler—clear the hall
Of chairs and carpets, for a mimic ball;
For merry Christmas must not pass us by,
Unless o'er polished floor our light foot fly.'

Crowding each door and window, now a throng
Of negroes press, and join their voice in song;
Their cheerful notes, unchecked, increase the rout,
And help the tune by fiddle old squeaked out;
Cotillions, country-dances, gallops, flings,
In quick succession each is tried—and brings
At last in turn, the graceful waltz—that dance
Conceived in Germany—brought up in France!

Old Limerick, to my heart forever dear,
Where are thy merry crowds dispers'd. Ah! where?"

POMPION HILL CHAPEL, EASTERN BRANCH COOPER RIVER

CHAPTER V

SANTEE, FRENCH SANTEE, SOUTH SANTEE, NORTH SANTEE

"SANTEE"

BY KATHERINE DRAYTON MAYRANT SIMONS

"Child of the coasts, by pale-eyed night,
Where the slim-stemmed lilies lie in white
    And cold;
Where the dank, green fennel hangs its wreath,
And summer's pulse-beats stir the breath
Of stagnant-pooled, dull-rainbowed death
    Deep gold;

Where the stars of the ghost-white dogwood bloom
Shine pale as pearl in the still night gloom
    Awake;
When the woodbine drips its honeyed blood,
And the spotted adder seeks her food
From the death scummed bowl of the still swamp flood
    And brake.

Nurse of the night's lone-woven spells,
Mother of tales that the Waxhaw tells
    Of thee:
In reach of thine moss sleeved arms' long quest,
Where the Waxhaw's campfire, burned to rest,
And the Waxhaw's grave-mound, scar thy breast;
    Santee! "

FRENCH SANTEE

IN ORDER to include local history belonging to territory adjacent to the headwaters of the eastern branch of Cooper River, to show the geographical connection obtaining, and to knit up the family connections, as well as to show why feeling against the Tories was so strong, extracts have been taken from a brief narrative of the life and services of Francis G. DeLiesline during the war of the Revolution, from the year 1777 to the year 1783 when peace was declared. He says of himself: "I was born

at my father's plantation at St. James Santee, about 40 miles from Charleston. My grand- and great-grandfathers were Huguenots who fled from the persecution of Louis XIV at the Revocation of the Edict of Nantes, and with many others settled there among the Indians about the year 1685, and this part of the country has ever since been called French Santee.

"My father died when I was very young, leaving my mother a widow with a handsome estate of slaves, lands and other property; when the war commenced I had just entered my fourteenth year and I volunteered my services in the company of Capt. John Barnett and with others to protect the coast, from the mouth of the Santee to Sewee Bay and Bull's Island, from the English privateers who were plundering and carrying off slaves and other property of the inhabitants. Our company remained on this service for some time, then marched off to Winyah Bay, near Georgetown, at Cat Island Fort, where we were enrolled under the glorious old banner of thirteen stripes, commanded by Capt. Davis, a Continental Officer. My company, after some time, was marched back to our former station at Santee, until Tarleton with his legion took possession of all the country from Charleston to Santee. Our company as well as all others broke up and everyone shifted for himself; my brother and three others and myself encamped in the river swamp opposite my mother's plantation, a little below Santee Ferry, to avoid Tarleton, as well as the Tories."

When Col. Washington came to aid Gen. Lincoln he found the country on the south of the Santee in possession of the enemy, and remained on the north side awaiting events, but it was not long before they suddenly crossed the river at Lenud's (Lanneau's) Ferry, made a foray about twenty miles down to Col. Ball's plantation, and surprised a British guard of fourteen men who were left with Ball to assist in collecting horses for Tarleton as well as to guard him. Tory Ball made his escape over the fence into Wamba Swamp near his house, where he had stables built for the horses he collected; he mounted one of the fleetest and pushed across the country for Strawberry Ferry, on Cooper River, the headquarters of Col. Tarleton and informed him of the capture of the guard, etc.

92

The Huguenot refugees on the Santee settled plantations or farms on or near the western bank of the river, northwardly from Wambaw Creek, and the community of French Santee, as it was known, built their church about fifteen miles north of the creek, giving it the name of the creek. The edifice built in 1767 is still standing, and is still known as Wambaw Church.

The point on the north side of the creek, near its mouth, was settled by Daniel Huger, and was called "Waterhorn." A monument to his memory was recently discovered by Alfred Huger, of Charleston, in a field not far from the chapel. In Mr. Lawson's description of his visit in January 1700–1 by canoe to this vicinity, he speaks of "Mons. Eugee's house, which stands about 15 miles up the river, being the first Christian dwelling in that settlement." In the Record of Daniel Huger is the following entry:

"Thursday, August 17th, 1704. My dear daughter Margaret Huger was married by License of the Hon. Sir Nathaniel Johnson, Governor, directed to Mr. Peter Roberts, Minister of the Holy Gospel at Santee, to Elias Horry, born at Paris in France."

His son, Daniel Huger, married Elizabeth Gendron; and the residence of Philip Gendron was on the Santee River, a short distance above the church, at or near Lenud's Ferry.

Another plantation in this vicinity was on the southern side of Wambaw Creek, nearly opposite Waterhorn, and was settled by Mr. Elias Horry. It was called Wambaw; and although Mr. Horry was not among the first set of immigrants, he became thoroughly identified with French Santee. He arrived in 1690, and married the daughter of Daniel Huger. The house, standing until a few years ago, and said to have belonged to Elias Horry, is described as follows: "It was a high and quaint structure. The high basement was of brick with two stories above of wood, and a roof with three gables. Steps led to the second story, and rested there upon a small veranda. This story was 'finished with wooden and rather heavy paneling.'"

In 1700 Mr. John Lawson visited the French settlement on Santee River, on a tour which he made through the interior of this State and North Carolina. In 1709 he published an account of his travels, under the title of "a Journal of a Thousand Miles, Traveled Through Several Nations of the Indians, &c." Remnants of the Pedee and Cape Fear tribes lived in the parishes of St. Stephens and St. Johns. "King Johnny" was their chief, with one other called "Prince." There were several Indians in the neighborhood of Pineville.

Associated with French Santee is Jamestown, where there is an old church, the site of which is known, and near it are graves which are remembered but now obliterated. The estate of the late Samuel J. Palmer now owns the land upon which Jamestown was laid out. It has long been known as Mount Moriah.

On account of freshets the French settlers moved higher up the river, into what afterwards became St. Stephen's Parish. This section had been gradually acquiring settlers, and had obtained the name of English Santee; in 1754 it was incorporated as a parish under the title of St. Stephens. The Parish Church is about 19 miles above the site of Jamestown. It will be remembered that the three parishes of St. Johns, St. Thomas and St. James Santee corner on Windsor plantation.

SOUTH SANTEE

FAIRFIELD

"Fairfield," the Santee home of the Pinckney family, which is the oldest place on the river, now belongs to Cotesworth Pinckney, of Richmond, Virginia. The Pinckneys are of English descent, sprung from a family widely scattered over England. It is said that the name is of Norman origin, and is variously spelled Pincheni, Pinchinge, Pinqueny, Pinkeni, Pinkeny, Pinkeney, Pinckeny, showing the changes through which the Norman word passed, until it settled down into the present form, Pinkney or Pinckney. Though holding extensive estates in many parts of England, their names are not prominent in political history.

"FAIRFIELD," THE OLDEST HOUSE ON SANTEE
Drawn by Alfred Hutty

The only event in the family history which rises above the general level is the claim of one of the name to the crown of Scotland, in the time of Bruce and Baliol, through his grandmother, Alice de Lyndsay. "Alice had married Sir Henry de Pinkeney, a great baron of Northamptonshire. Her grandson, Sir Robert Pinkeney, claimed the crown of Scotland at the competition in 1292, as descended from the Princess Margery, through his grandmother, Alice de Lyndsay."

Three branches of the Pinckney family emigrated to America; one to West Chester, New York, in 1684, one to South Carolina in 1692, and one to Maryland about 1750. William Pinckney, the jurist and statesman, is the most conspicuous figure in this latter branch. The first of the name who came to Carolina was Thomas Pinckney, in 1692. His wife was Mary Cotesworth, of Durham. He was a man of independent fortune, and built a house at the corner of East Bay and Tradd Streets, Charleston, S. C., where he lived and died. The Bay was not then encumbered with houses on its water front, but commanded a full view of the harbor, as the East Battery now does.

One personal anecdote is recorded of him. In looking out of his windows upon the bay, he observed a vessel just arrived from the West Indies, landing her passengers. As they walked up the street, he was attracted by the appearance of a very handsome stranger, and turning to his wife remarked, "That handsome West Indian will marry some poor fellow's widow, break her heart and ruin her children. His words were in part prophetic, for he died of yellow fever shortly after, his widow married the gay West Indian, George Evans, and though he did not break her heart, as she lived to marry a third husband, he often made her heart ache with his extravagance, squandering the patrimony of her children. Enough, however, was saved to enable them to have a liberal education.

Thomas Pinckney's three sons were Thomas, an officer in the British Army, who died young; Charles, the Chief Justice, and William, the Commissioner in Equity. Charles was educated in England, and there married Elizabeth, daughter of

Captain Lamb, of Devonshire Square, London. Returning to Carolina he became a successful lawyer and accumulated a large fortune and served as Speaker of the House and one of the King's Councillors. Having been married some years without children Charles Pinckney adopted his brother William's eldest son, Charles, as his prospective heir, and sent him to England to be educated; but a romantic incident in the family annals interfered with this plan.

In 1739 Colonel George Lucas, Governor of Antigua, arrived in Charleston with his family. The climate of the West Indies did not suit Mrs. Lucas; and her husband brought his family to Carolina, to an estate which he owned on the Stono River, ten miles by water and six miles by land from town.

His young daughter, just twenty years of age, was quite in advance of her generation, and that she anticipated, at the junction of the Stono and Wappoo Rivers, the cultivation of those tropical fruits which are pouring such streams of wealth into the once barren lands of Florida.

A letter written to a friend not long after her father's departure gives a vivid glimpse of the way in which she appreciated the responsibility thrust upon her.

"I have a little library in which I spend part of my time. My music and the garden, which I am very fond of, take up the rest that is not employed in business, of which my father has left me a pretty good share; and indeed was unavoidable, as my mama's bad state of health prevents her going thro' any fatigue. I have the business of three plantations to transact, which requires much writing and more business and fatigue of other sorts than you can imagine. But lest you should imagine it to be burdensome to a girl at my early time of life, give me leave to assure you that I think myself happy that I can be useful to so good a father."

Mrs. Lucas and her daughter were cordially received in Charleston society, but were especially welcomed in Colonel Pinckney's home. So open was Mrs. Pinckney's admiration for the young lady that, rather than permit her to return to Antigua, she declared her readiness to "step out of the way and permit her to take her place." This kind intention she actually fulfilled by dying the following year; and her husband was considerate enough to marry the lady his wife had chosen for him.

The marriage certificate issued May 25th, 1744, and signed by Governor Glen, authorized Charles Pinckney and Elizabeth Lucas to intermarry, and the said Charles Pinckney binds himself by a bond of £2000 to the faithful performance of the contract. Mr. Pinckney was also considerate enough to construct for her another dwelling which stood near the present Seaman's Mission.

Justice Pinckney bought a whole square on East Bay, and built a handsome mansion in the center of it, facing the harbor. The house was of brick, two stories high, with roof of slate. There was a wide hall running from front to rear. One of the rooms on the second floor was thirty feet long and had a high ceiling. The whole house was wainscoted. The mantelpieces were high and narrow, with fronts beautifully carved. In this house were born the two sons of Charles Pinckney and Elizabeth Lucas, his wife; namely, Charles Cotesworth Pinckney and Thomas Pinckney, who rendered great service to their country during the Revolution and afterwards.

"America is indebted," says Bruce Addington, in *Smith's Magazine*, "to women like Eliza Lucas Pinckney—possessed of the advantages of wealth and position, ardent, light-hearted, high-spirited, but right-minded and earnest and brave. They were women of fine ideals and fine achievement. Even when their dreams did not come true, when fate was adverse to them, they left traditions that have powerfully, however unconsciously, influenced the thought and point of view of posterity. In the South, as on the forgotten plantations of Rhode Island, this type of woman was the mistress of noble mansions, and of a small army of dependents, they keenly appreciated the duties as well as the privileges which this entailed. They cheerfully looked after the manifold affairs of household management, taught their servants and slaves the domestic sciences, and were untiring in work of charity. To their children they were the best of mothers."

From her marriage with Mr. Pinckney came the two generals, Charles Cotesworth, born 1746, and Thomas Pinckney, born 1750, and one daughter, Harriott, wife of Daniel Horry.

Charles Pinckney, one of the illustrious sons of Eliza Lucas, in his "Draft of Federal Government," which he laid before the Convention, included this clause: "The Legislature of the United States shall pass no law on the subject of religion." The clause was omitted in the form of the Constitution actually adopted; but the fact remains that the first step towards the removal of religious disabilities, and the establishment of equal rights, was made by this able son of South Carolina.

The honor of urging the subject in the Convention is due to Charles Pinckney, of South Carolina. His State followed his leading, and in 1790, upon a review of the Constitution of South Carolina, the clauses excluding Catholics from place and honor were stricken out.

The other son held, among other high offices, that of General in the Revolutionary War, first American minister appointed by Washington to the Court of St. James, and Minister to Spain in 1795. "Fairfield" was the Thomas Pinckney plantation home and a letter comes from him there in 1791 to Mr. Edward Rutledge (brother of Dictator John) concerning a communication from Mr. Jefferson asking whether it would be agreeable if he (Mr. Jefferson) should nominate Mr. Pinckney to the Senate as Minister to London. Mr. Pinckney said that almost every private consideration appeared against his accepting this position, but he writes to Mr. Rutledge: "Pray let me have your thoughts on these and any other subjects of immediate consideration, by a letter left for me in town, unless you should send an express. I am almost ashamed of requiring this of you but as you made me a governor, and now insist upon my being a minister, you must advise me in this situation, as you supported me in the former."

Mr. Rutledge advised acceptance, and as soon as he could arrange his domestic affairs Mr. Pinckney left home with his wife, who had been very ill, stopping over in Philadelphia to confer with the President. It has been alleged that Mr. Pinckney sought this appointment, but the Pinckney point of view

WAMBAW CHURCH (ST. JAMES'), SANTEE, BUILT 1768

is fully explained in portions of two letters. "My wife, I thank God, mends, though slowly. I have not ventured to open the subject to her. It would be too much for the weak state of her nerves. Poor Gadsden, too, is gone. My heart is filled with anguish, while my head is disturbed with this unfortunate appointment. Once more adieu. Your truly affectionate, Thomas Pinckney."

The mission to England does not appear more gratifying to Mrs. Pinckney than to her husband, as will appear in this letter from Judge Iredell written to his wife in Philadelphia under date, Charleston, April 19th, 1792. "Major Pinckney (the minister to Britain) and his family sail to-morrow. I have received such uncommon courtesies from him and his connections that I must earnestly entreat you to wait on Mrs. Pinckney soon after her arrival. . . . She is a most amiable woman, and none can be more free from any kind of pride or affectation. I am told that she has been in tears almost ever since her husband's appointment." The Pinckney address for the next four years was No. 1 Great Cumberland Place in London.

A letter written by Mr. Pinckney to the Secretary of State in America shows that the taint of rebellion still cleaved to our country and her representatives. "In my first communication I mentioned the civility with which I was received at St. James, and at the Office of Foreign Affairs. The only circumstance worth mentioning in my conference with the king was that Lord North's rope of sand appeared not to have been entirely effaced from His Majesty's memory; so I infer, from his mentioning the different circumstances between the Northern and Southern parts of our country tending to produce disunion. . . . I have been constant in every attendance at the king's levees since the return of the court to St. James, and, placing myself in the circle of foreign ministers, his Majesty never fails to have a few moments' conversation with me on the weather, or other topic equally important; but notwithstanding the great variety of incident that has lately occurred in European politics, he never touches upon that subject with me. The Queen also was very gracious but quite as non-committal in her attitude.''

America appreciated the service her distinguished son had rendered his country. When General Pinckney returned to South Carolina in 1799 the City of Charleston gave him a public dinner at the City Hall on Friday, February 8, 1799. The *City Gazette and Daily Advertiser* for the next day contains the following in its account of the ceremonies:

"The Hall, in the evening, was handsomely lighted up, and at the upper end was ornamented with the portrait of General Pinckney, under which the following transparent labels appeared, 'il faut de l'argent; il faut beaucoup d'argent?'— 'No, No! not a six-pence.' In front of the City-Hall was exhibited a transparent painting; a female figure appeared seated on a rock; at her side is the American eagle; at a distance she sees a dove returning, with the olive branch she had sent; she immediately seizes hold of several arrows, which lie at the foot of the American standard, and seems prepared for war. Over her head appears, 'millions for defence, not a cent for tribute.' ''

This traditional utterance is found upon the tablet to his memory in St. Michael's Church, and is still thrust upon him, though historians contend to the contrary. But if Mr. Pinckney was not beloved in England, he was properly appreciated at home. An intimacy existed between Mrs. Pinckney and Mrs. Washington, and a letter from her to Mrs. Pinckney (copied from "A Catalogue of Rare Letters") written in 1799, in return for Mrs. Pinckney's "oblig'in favors," thanks her for some "mellon seeds" and refers to Mrs. Pinckney's recent stay at Mount Vernon: "A place at which we shall always be gratified in seeing General Pinckney, yourself or any of the family. In which let me add a hope, if his military duties should call him to the State of Virginia, that you will always consider us as your headquarters during your abidance in it. . . . I will with pleasure send you the profiles of the General and myself, and feel the compliment of them being asked." She then mentions marriage of "Nelly Curtis to Mr. Lewis (who you saw here) who is at her mothers or she would write in reciprocating wishes of yourself and Miss Eliza and

100

"HAMPTON," THE HOME OF THE RUTLEDGES ON SOUTH SANTEE

would rejoice to hear of the happiness of her friend, Harriet Rutledge. Closed with sentiments of perfect esteem and regard, I am my dear Madame your most obedient H'ble Ser'vt. Martha Washington.''

Being on the highway between northern cities and Charleston, General Pinckney's house seldom lacked guests. Unless in old Virginia more genuine, habitual hospitality could no where be found than in the low country of Carolina. This feeling was embodied in the remark of a venerable citizen who lived in that vicinity, ''if I see no carriages under the visitor's shed when I return from my fields to dinner, I say to myself, my friends have not treated me well to-day.'' An English gentleman of fortune, Adam Hodgson, of Liverpool, who spent three years in exploring our country, having brought letters of introduction, visited General Pinckney at Santee and Eldorado. His impressions of this visit are recorded in a volume of ''Travels'' which he published in 1824. The first thing which struck him as he entered the house was the number and size of the windows, enough to make an Englishman shudder when he recalled the tax upon each pane of glass to which he was accustomed at home. The library was also a surprise. ''My host had an excellent library, comprising many recent and valuable British publications, and a more extensive collection of agricultural works than I had ever seen before in a private library. In works on botany and American ornithology the supply was large. The latter especially interested me, not having seen them before.''

He accompanied his host on his daily visits to the fields, the mills, and the hospital, and records his surprise when he heard this ''benevolent master order wine and oranges for some sick negroes.'' He inspected carefully the houses, the food, the clothing of the negroes and admitted that in these matters our laborers compared favorably with those of other lands.

HAMPTON

When the Horry tract at Wambaw was divided, although the portion upon which the original house stood was sold, yet the eastern moiety remained in the possession of descendants of the original settler on the distaff side; it having passed to the late Mrs. Frederick Rutledge, a daughter of Daniel Horry, and is now owned and occupied by Col. H. M. Rutledge, a grandson of Frederick Rutledge.

On this eastern tract there stands, a mile east of the original Horry house, a large and fine mansion. It was built in 1730, of yellow pine and cypress, over a brick foundation, by Mrs. Daniel Horry, widow of the French Huguenot who came over in 1686 and is buried just north of Hampton at Waterhorn. This house has long been the seat of refined hospitality, and is well known as "Hampton." It came into the Rutledge family through the daughter of Mrs. Horry, and has constantly remained a Rutledge home.

Of this place Archibald H. Rutledge, son of Col. H. M. Rutledge, says it is "one of the great rice plantations (containing 1285 acres) that lie along the coast country of South Carolina. It was the headquarters of the 'Swamp Fox,' the dauntless Francis Marion."

A mile or more of avenue leads to the massive old colonial house on Hampton, opening upon the wide lawn dotted by those sentinels of the centuries, which, with the white mansion, its lofty portico and its simple, but beautiful pediment supported by heavy columns, in its setting of giant oaks hung with Spanish moss, make a charming and impressive picture. Upon the occasion of a recent marriage in the family, although the guests were obliged to go by automobile, yet as one drove through the historic woods one's thoughts went back to olden times when the cavaliers and Huguenots, resplendent in cocked hats, ruffled shirts, knee breeches and brilliant coats, with dames and maidens in gay brocades of silk and satin, hastened along this way on similar errand bent.

Arrived at the house, instead of stately coaches with coachmen and outriders in livery, which one naturally would associate with this scene, the equipages of the guests were parked in front of the house, about the historic Washington oak, so called because the tree was spared from the axe by the request

THE DINING-ROOM AT "HAMPTON"

THE PORTICO AT "HAMPTON"

of George Washington when he visited Hampton late in the century.

Perhaps the most impressive feature of Hampton is the portico which must be traversed in order to gain entrance to the house. Once inside the hospitable portals of this colonial home the visitors find themselves in a great reception hall, amply supplied with antique furniture and decorated with family portraits. Some of the rooms possess landscape wall-paper like that found at Friendfield. One of the beauties of Hampton is its great ballroom occupying the entire east wing. This has an immense carved chimneyplace lined with Dutch tiles, in which it is said that five persons can stand.

Of course, this house has its ghost. The "Ghost-room," which is the guest room, is found over the dining-room. No one has ever seen there a "horrid spectre," for this ghost only makes a sound, and the noise is like someone moving a carpet stealthily over the floor.

At Hampton is kept a magnificent pulpit-bible, prayer-book, and "Book of the Institutions," presented to Wambaw Church by Mrs. Rebecca Motte, who removed to St. James Santee after the historic burning of her house at Orangeburg. At the time of the Revolution these were captured by the British and taken to England. Fortunately they were inscribed with her name, and tradition has it that a British officer who had received kindness from Mrs. Motte, seeing the books exposed in London on a book-stall, recognized the name of the owner, purchased the books, and turned them over to Mrs. Motte's son-in-law, General Thomas Pinckney, then Minister at the court of St. James, and were by him returned to the parish of St. James, Santee, where they are now kept at the Rutledge home at Hampton.

EL DORADO ON THE SANTEE

El Dorado, on the Santee, was built by, and was the home of, General Thomas Pinckney, our "first American Minister appointed to the Court of St. James, and Minister to Spain, 1795." It was the second home of General Pinckney, the first having been at Fairfield, not far distant.

The house at El Dorado, "situated on a sandy knoll, jutting out into the rice-fields, embowered by live-oaks with their outstretched arms and lofty magnolias with their glittering foliage," was a typical Southern home. It was surrounded by the native evergreen shrubbery through which ran winding walks. "The spacious mansion, which he planned and built with his own carpenters, is very suggestive of a French château, with its wide corridors, its lofty ceilings, and its peaked roof of glazed tiles. . . .

"After his return to America General Pinckney married another daughter of Rebecca Motte, Mrs. Middleton, the widow of a young Englishman who had crossed the Atlantic to bear arms in the cause of the colonies." He resigned Fairfield and purchased the present plantation, which he named Eldorado in remembrance of his Spanish mission, and from the golden buttercups which covered the land.

"The house here was built in conjunction with his mother-in-law. Mrs. Motte had sold her plantation on the Congarees, and removed to Santee to be near her daughters. . . . The large rooms, the lofty ceilings, the numerous windows, seem now unsuitable for a winter home, and suggest a lack of practical talent in the builder. . . . The planters in those days, however, occupied their homes all the year. . . .

"The air was redolent of nature's fresh perfumes. The yellow jessamine, the sweet-scented shrub, and other native plants, which fill our forests with their fragrance, met here in rich profusion. The sweet rose of France, the English and cape jessamine, mingled with the odors of the orange-blossom in perfect harmony. . . .

"From the windows of his stately home, General Pinckney could look out upon his own busy fields, and over many miles of rice-lands in the delta of the river. The banks and ditches which marked the separate fields, and the long canals which intersected the whole . . . all were spread out before the eye. The quiet of the landscape was often relieved by the white sails of a schooner on the river. . . ."

At the time of the Civil War, Eldorado, being so near the mouth of the river, was "exposed to the visits of vessels from the blockading squadron. . . . The house was shelled by gunboats from the fleet in 1863, and bears the scars of war upon its face. The mills were burnt by a hostile party, landed on the banks, and the house only saved from the torch by the timely arrival of a squadron of Confederate Cavalry under command of a grandson of its former owner. . . .

"Mr. Pinckney's love of agriculture was manifest all through the period of his English mission. . . . Through his second wife a large body of marshlands at the mouth of the Santee, adjoining the ocean, came into the possession of this noted agriculturist. It was covered alternately by fresh and by salt water, and so impregnated with the saline element as to be considered entirely unfit for cultivation. When the executor of the estate handed General Pinckney the titles to this portion of his wife's property, he apologized for offering a gentleman anything so worthless. But the new owner remembered that the rich lands of Holland had been redeemed from the sea; . . . and he imported from Holland a skillful engineer, who soon succeeded in protecting the land from the salt water, and introduced among the rice-planters of the State the Van Hassel system of embankment.

"By repeated experiments the saline nature of the soil was rendered fit for the culture of rice, and by enlarging the cultivated area, a large body of inexhaustible fertility was reclaimed, so that from this once contemptible estate a crop of twenty thousand bushels of rice was sent to market annually. Two of General Pinckney's children received the chief part of their inheritance from these lands."

In regard to the treatment of his numerous slaves, General Pinckney carried out the idea of the patriarchal relationship which the Southern planter felt towards them, making it possible for the slaves to glory in their masters, and to look up to them as the Scottish clansmen did to their ancestral chiefs.

"In the familiar picture of the Washington family by Savage, a stately black butler stands behind Washington's chair. That is General Pinckney's body-servant, John Riley, a freeman, for many years in his employ. His wife was Mrs. Pinckney's maid, who accompanied her mistress to England.

Not wishing to separate him from his wife during his residence abroad, General Pinckney carried Riley with him to England. As the painter who was then engaged on the Washington family picture had no black model at hand, he borrowed John Riley from the American ambassador to pose as one of Washington's servants. . . .

"Thomas Pinckney died on the 2d of November, 1828, in the seventy-ninth year of his age. The uniform companies of the 16th and 17th regiments of South Carolina troops, a squadron of cavalry, and a detachment from the United States garrison at Fort Moultrie, formed the military escort at his funeral. His horse, with its trappings and empty saddle, dressed in crape, followed immediately after the bier, attended by his three aides, Colonels James Ferguson, Lewis Morris and Frederick Kinloch, then the officers of the United States and State of South Carolina. . . . The procession moved from his house in Legare Street to St. Philip's Church, on the north side of which his remains repose. . . .

"The three swords which General Pinckney had used in the wars of the Revolution and of 1812 he bequeathed by will to his three sons, with the injunction that 'they never be drawn in any private quarrel, and never remain in their scabbards, when their country demanded their service.' In obedience to his example and his instructions, fourteen of his descendants served in the Confederate Army. . . .''

The story of the *Life of General Thomas Pinckney*, from which many extracts have been quoted, was written by his grandson, the Rev. Charles Cotesworth Pinckney, D.D., president of the South Carolina Historical Society.

NORTH SANTEE

The peninsula formed by Winyah Bay on the north, the Atlantic Ocean on the east, and the North Santee River on the south, with its various deltas, contains rich plantation lands adjoining the North Santee River. Many of the houses belonging to these plantations were not built upon the rice-lands, but upon the highlands on the other side of the river. Starting at the ferry, in order are Hopseewee, Fawnhill, White Oak,

"EL DORADO," ON THE SANTEE, ONE OF THE PINCKNEY HOMES

"HOPSEEWEE," (LUCAS HOUSE), NORTH SANTEE
Home of Thomas Lynch, the Signer

Rice Hope, Camp Main and Bearhill. Behind this latter plantation are three tracts, Mill Dam, Pleasant Meadow, and The Marsh, and on the river again are Green Meadow and Cat Island.

In 1855 the *Bishop's Journal* states that:

"Friday, 23rd (March)—At North Santee, preached on the plantation of Mr. Ladson."

The church at North Santee was then called the Church of the Messiah, and the Rev. Thomas J. Girardeau was rector.

HOPSEEWEE

Hopseewee on the North Santee River, now owned by the Lucas family, was built about 200 years ago by Mr. John Lynch, who received the land grant from the King of England. The house stands on a high bluff on the northern bank of the river, and is built of black cypress on a brick foundation. The original veranda fell into decay very many years ago, and was replaced about 1850 by double piazzas. The floor plan is that of the typical square old southern dwelling; four rooms on each of the two floors, all opening into the center halls, both upper and lower, which extend the entire length of the house. In the back of the lower hall is the stairway. The grounds are enclosed with ancient and majestic live-oaks, and beautiful japonica trees.

Thomas Lynch, Signer of the Declaration of Independence, was the son of the original owner, John Lynch, and was born at Hopseewee in August, 1749. He was educated in England, and in 1772 married Elizabeth Shubrick. He was a distinguished political figure in this country from the time of his membership in the Provincial Congresses of 1775–1776, until his death in 1779 when he was lost at sea. He is spoken of as the "Signer," having signed the Declaration of Independence during his term "as a sixth delegate" from South Carolina to the Continental Congress.

In 1762 Mr. Lynch sold the property to Mr. Robert Hume, a Goose Creek planter, and he in turn gave it to his son, Mr. John Hume, who died in 1845. It then came into the possession of Mr. Hume's grandson, Mr. John Hume Lucas, who used it as a winter home, and it has subsequently been always owned by descendants of the Lucas family.

A will of Jonathan Lucas, who was probably a famous member of the family in former days (dated 1874), speaks of " my mill and planting establishments," but there is nothing in the will to show where they are located; he may mean one on the plantation, or one that we know of in Charleston. As E. G. Memminger, Wm. Lucas, and W. J. Bennett were appointed executors of the will it would seem to indicate that this is the rice mill commonly called Bennett's Mill.

The following extracts are taken from the Year Book issued by Mayor Courtenay celebrating the Centennial of Incorporation:

"LUCAS' RICE MILLS

"The various contrivances for cleaning rice from the crude wooden mortar and lightwood pestle of the seventeenth century, as well as the later inventions of Guerard and others, all passed away when Jonathan Lucas introduced here his improved rice mill run by water-power.

"To this citizen we are indebted for the admirable machinery by which rice is cleaned and prepared for market— machinery which in its most improved state has been copied and introduced in the North and in Europe, serving materially to increase the consumption of the grain by supplying it in the most desirable condition to home and foreign markets. . . .

"He was a thoroughly educated millwright, was born in 1754 at Cumberland, England. Shortly after the war of the Revolution he sailed from England for a more Southern port, but through stress of weather the vessel was driven on this coast and stranded near the mouth of Santee River. It was there that he noticed the laborious process then in use, for cleaning rice from its hull, and preparing it for market. His was the thought and his the skill which accomplished the wonderful economic improvements upon the old 'laborious processes' by which the great forces of nature were soon to be harnessed to new machines, and the cultivation and preparation of this cereal to receive an impetus which subsequently resulted in greatly increased rice crops.

"In the year 1787 the first water mill was erected by Mr. Lucas, to whom the credit of the invention is understood to be due. This was built for Mr. Bowman on a reserve at his Peach Island plantation on Santee River. Jonathan Lucas,

Jr., inherited his father's mechanical talent and skill, and associated with him constructed on Cooper River in 1801 the first toll mill for cleaning rice. . . . He yielded at length to the invitations of the British Government, and passed the remainder of his days in England . . . (in 1822).

". . . The subsequent erection by Jonathan Lucas, Jr., and others of rice mills in Europe had the effect of drawing rough rice supplies not only from Eastern countries but from Charleston; under the influence of import duties on clean rice, that of Great Britain being equal to $4.00 per tierce of clean rice, mills were kept running in London, Liverpool, Copenhagen, Bremen, Amsterdam, Lisbon and Bordeaux, and Carolina rough rice was shipped hence in cargoes to those distant mills. . . ."

Other rice mills built on the Santee by Mr. Lucas, Sr., were on the reserve at Washo Plantation, for Mrs. Middleton, afterwards Mrs. General Thomas Pinckney; on a reserve of Winyah Bay for Gen. Peter Horry; on the reserve at the Fairfield plantation of Col. William Alston, on the Waccamaw River; and in 1791–92 Mr. Lucas built on the Santee, for Mr. Andrew Johnson on his plantation called Millbrook, the first tide mill. A year or two later he erected an improved tide mill at the plantation of Henry Laurens, called Mepkin, and in 1795, on Shem Creek, at Hardell's Point, in Charleston Harbor, he erected a combined rice and saw mill driven by water-power. This was the first mill erected in the immediate vicinity of the city.

". . . About 1840, Jonathan Lucas, the grandson, built a steam rice mill upon the Ashley, where now stands West Point Mill. This mill was burnt, and the present West Point Mill Company built on this site in 1860–1861."

This is located at the western end of Calhoun Street, within the city limits, and was operated up to the year 1919.

Hopseewee, at the present time, is the home of T. Cordes Lucas and his mother, Mrs. Wm. Lucas, and is in a remarkable state of preservation. The residents of the historic old place have a deep and thorough appreciation of it, and the writer has received much of the foregoing information through the kindness of Mrs. Lucas and her sister-in-law, Mrs. T. G. S. Lucas, of Charleston. At a recent exhibit of colonial relics at the Charleston Museum, there was displayed an exquisite wedding veil used by this family over one hundred and fifty years ago, loaned by Miss Sarah Lucas.

WINYAH BARONY

To the north of these, again, on the remainder of the peninsula occupying the territory between North Santee and Winyah Bay, is that portion known by the name of the Winyah Barony, deriving its name from its situation on the large bay. The barony was originally laid out to Landgrave Robert Daniel, whose ownership continued one day, Landgrave Smith being the second owner. It is frequently referred to as Smith's Barony.

Here Thomas Smith had dreams of founding a town, and the *South Carolina Gazette* for the week 16–23 July, 1737, carried an advertisement stating the situation of the proposed town, and setting forth its advantages. Evidently the lots did not sell, and some months later Thomas Smith offered inducements "to all poor Protestants of any Nature whatsoever, that are willing to come and settle" on the Winyah Barony. He died the next year, but before his death gave some of the barony to his eldest son, Thomas, who died before his father, but who devised 1000 acres of the 3000 given him by his father to his sister Justinah Moore. (It is to be noted that the 2nd Landgrave was twice married, and that he had by a second wife a younger son also named Thomas.)

The rest of the various tracts were disposed of by the will of Landgrave Thomas; it states that he had at the time 31 grandchildren and great-grandchildren. The land at Winyah Barony and other Smith lands in the neighborhood are fully traced in Judge Smith's able article on Winyah Barony.

One of the sons of Landgrave Thomas named his portion of the Smith lands The Retreat. It is interesting to note that the lines of Winyah Barony as originally laid out encroach upon several inland plantations later found in possession of other people.

"On 28th August, 1733, Mr. Thomas Lynch had obtained a grant for 4500 acres, lying mainly to the South of the

WINYAH INDIGO SOCIETY HALL, GEORGETOWN

From a print

Barony. It included, however, the valuable tidal rice swamps on Santee River which had been omitted from the barony grant. At the date the barony was run out the value of the tidal swamps for rice cultivation was not yet known. The lines of the new grant overlapped or interfered with the lines of the barony, and the result was litigation between Thomas Smith and Thomas Lynch. The exact result of this litigation the available remaining records do not disclose, but apparently by some settlement the title of the various purchasers from Thomas Lynch to so much of their land as was included in this 'overlap' was confirmed.''

Among the plantations affected by this overlap were Cat Island; Green Meadows; Tidyman's; Annandale; a Hazzard place upon which is found a fairly representative old house; The Marsh, and the Retreat. Cat Island extends completely across the peninsula, from North Santee River to Winyah Bay. Across the head of this island is found the Estherville Canal, for small boats. Cat Island is a Lowndes possession.

The location of the town called Smiths-Town, apparently fronted on Winyah Bay just west of Estherville plantation, and east of the east line of the Retreat plantation, where the highland comes to the beach or water's edge, without intervening marsh or mud flats.

Philip Tidyman, M.D., late of Charleston, owned a place in Winyah Barony. His will (1843) directs his executors to keep his whole estate together during the lifetime of his daughter, Susan Tidyman, and to have his plantations cultivated by his slaves as they were at the time of his death. After the death of his daughter, the executors are directed to sell his real estate, including the Cedar Hill plantation in St. James Parish. By the breaking out of the C.S.A. and the U.S.A. War, and the threatened invasion by the forces of the latter upon the plantations mentioned, the executors were compelled for the safe keeping of the slaves, to remove them from the said plantation and abandon the culture thereof. George A. Trenholm afterwards bought the Tidyman plantations in the Parish of Prince George Winyah (North Santee). After various legacies the will directs that the remainder of the proceeds of sales are to be equally divided between Mr. Tidyman's nieces.

CHAPTER VI

GEORGETOWN AND VICINITY

GEORGETOWN

HE ground on which Georgetown stands was originally granted to Mr. Perry, the ancestor of the present family of Kinloch, according to The Ancient Lady; through mistake it was granted a second time to the Rev. William Screven, the first Baptist minister in South Carolina and one of the first settlers in the Province, but was later reclaimed and recovered by virtue of the earlier grant. The town of Georgetown was projected approximately in 1732 or 1733, but the land was not granted for the purpose until 1734. The following year George Pawley, William Swinton, Daniel La Roche, and two others were appointed Harbor Commissioners to "lay out buoys, errect beacons, and regulate pilotage."

About the year 1740 the indigo planters of the Parish of Prince George Winyah formed a convival club and decided to meet on the first Friday of each month in the town of Georgetown. This was called the Winyah Indigo Society. The old Oak Tavern which stood in Bay Street was the scene of these monthly reunions. On the first Friday of May, each year, the anniversary meeting took place, when the important business of the Society was transacted, and then the annual dinner, with its songs and anecdotes, occupied the attention of the members for hours, and tradition reports it as a very merry function. Fees and contributions were paid in the staple crop of the section—indigo—and by the year 1753 the club was a rich association. A proposal was made that the surplus funds be devoted to the establishment of an independent charity school for the poor. The meeting rose to its feet. "Every glass was turned down without staining the table cloth," and the school of the Winyah Indigo Society was established and

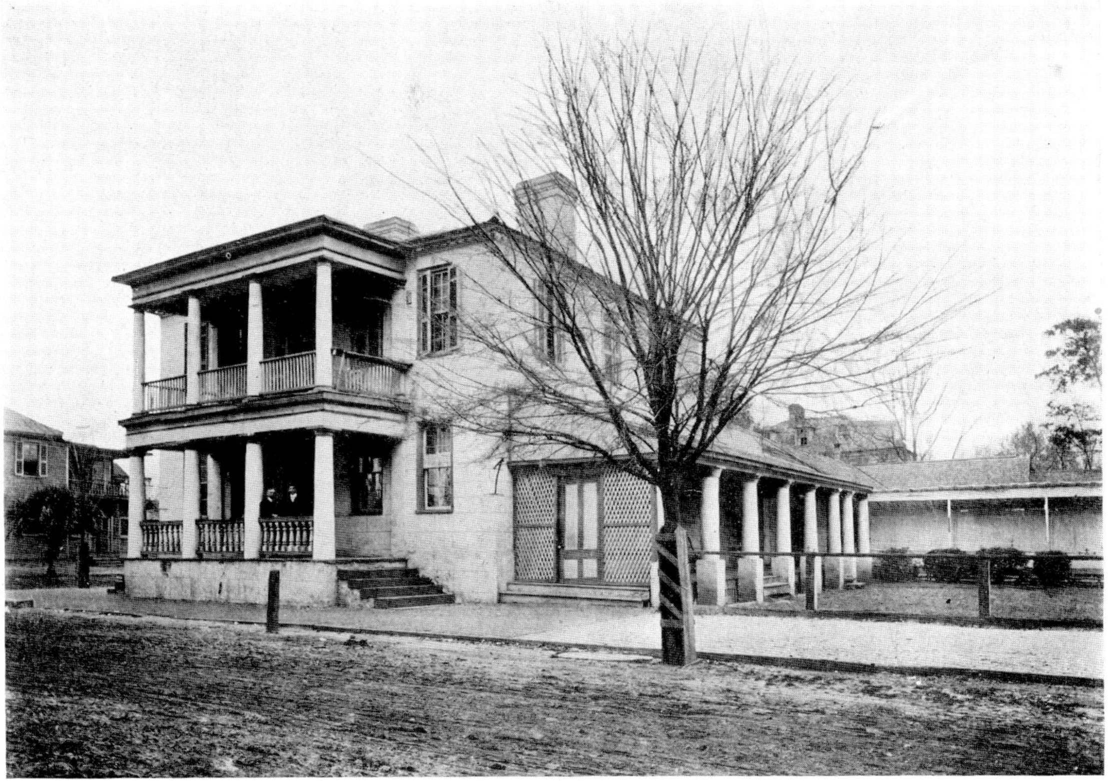

"WINYAH INN" GEORGETOWN

has continued its good work to this day. The holdings of the Society are among the most valuable real estate properties in the city, embracing the imposing and historic brick building which was used for years as an academy, and later for the graded school. It was probably to this building that the notice below refers:

"Charles Gee of the Parish of Prince George, Bachelor, and Catherine Bond of the Parish of Prince George, Widow, were married in the Public School-House of Prince George, by Banns, this Twenty Fourth Day of April in the Year of our Lord, 1770, by me S. F. Warren, Rector of St. James Santee.
This marriage was
Solemnized between us
In the Presence of   Charles Gee
                           Catherine Bond X her mark
                           Thomas Webb
                           Peter Maume (?)"

An autograph letter of George Washington referring to his reception in Georgetown, is greatly prized by the citizens of the town. It is in the possession of the Winyah Indigo Society, and is as follows:

"To the Inhabitants of Georgetown and Its Vicinity:
"Gentlemen—I receive your Congratulations on my arrival in South Carolina with real pleasure, and I confess my obligations to your affectionate regard with sincere gratitude. While the calamities to which you were exposed during the war excited all my sympathy, the gallantry and firmness with which they were encountered obtained my entire esteem. To your fortitude in these trying scenes our country is much indebted for the happy and honorable issue of the contest.

"From the milder virtues that characterize your conduct in peace, our equal government will derive those aids which may render its operations extensively beneficial.

"That your participation of every national advantage and your prosperity in private life may be amply proportional to your past services and sufferings is my sincere and fervent wish.

"G. WASHINGTON."

(Signed)
April 29th, 1791.

The building which was some years since known as the "Winyah Inn" (now used as a Masonic Temple) was the old "Colonial Bank of Georgetown," erected before the Revolution. It also served as headquarters for the British during the war. It is a substantial structure with spacious verandas supported by massive white columns. The old rice and indigo planters here deposited their wealth, and one of the iron vaults is still to be seen in the building.

THE PYATT OR ALSTON HOUSE

Mrs. John Rose Parker, now living in one of the few old structures remaining in the town of Georgetown, describes the place as being the Pyatt or Allston House, situated on the bluff in Georgetown directly on the Sampit River. It bears the honor of having had George Washington under its roof as a guest during his visit to the old colonial town in 1791 while on his tour of the South. It is now the home of the Pyatt family, direct descendants of Mr. Benj. Allston, who as a lad was with Marion's Command during the Revolution, and who made the old house his home about the year 1820. The records were lost during the war between the States, so that the exact date of its erection, and the name of the builder are unknown. It is a large brick building and must have been erected before the Revolution, as there was very little building done between the years 1783 and 1812. On a window pane in the long dining-room wing is the inscription, "J. W. Pawley September 2nd 1815," written twice in parallel lines. The exterior of the house has scarce been changed since that period. The land slopes directly down to the river in front, and it is quite probable that General Washington and his distinguished party landed there. Tradition has it that Marquis LaFayette was also entertained in this house, and it is of interest to know that the original character of a heroine of one of Simm's novels was mistress of this venerable house. Dorothy Singleton, widow of Colonel Singleton and second wife of Mr. Benj. Allston, was the prototype of the famous "Katherine Walton."

A handsome silver teapot bearing the monogram of Mr. Allston in large letters, is still used in the old dining-room by

114

THE PYATT-ALSTON HOUSE, GEORGETOWN
Rear view showing circular wings and quaint chimneys

the family, and needless to say is highly prized. The old mahogany sideboard, a Hepplewhite, and relic of Revolutionary times, still occupies its accustomed place in the room.

The picture accompanying this account of the Pyatt house is taken from the rear to show the unusual aspect of the place, the front view being more conventional. If one should attempt to describe the building they would have to employ the usual stereotyped phrases; a hipped-roof with dormer windows, the usual two story and a half plan, and chimneys on either end. The wide piazza downstairs is supported by six circular columns, an interesting feature being the double flight of brick steps, to the right and left, with an arched entrance underneath. The basement, in all probability, was built of "tabby," a favorite primitive cement much used by colonial builders on the coast. The round wing so prominent in the picture is at the rear. Perhaps the most striking feature is the atmosphere of dignity and age which this brick structure produces.

ALL-SAINTS WACCAMAW AND ITS PLANTATIONS

By Act of Assembly, May 23, 1767, the parish of All-Saints Waccamaw was taken off from the parish of Prince George Winyah. It was to consist of "all the lands which lie between the Sea and Waccamaw River, as far as the boundary line of North Carolina." William Allston, Joseph Allston, Charles Lewis, William Pawley, Josiah Allston, William Allston, Jr., and John Clarke, were appointed Commissioners for building a Church, Chapel of Ease, and Parsonage House at such places as they should approve within the parish.

The register now in existence begins in 1819, during the rectorship of Rev. Henry Gibbes, which lasted from 1819 to 1829. When Dalcho wrote in about 1820 he states that neither Journals nor Register were extant, but some earlier records were lost in the storm of 1893, when the house of Dr. Flagg, a warden, was swept away, for a badly defaced copy of the minutes of the vestry was rescued from the sea.

To show how the plantations are situated in relation to each other, extracts from a Missionary Tour, published in *The*

Southern Episcopalian of May, 1855, giving an idea of the itinerary of the Bishop, are here presented:

"Thursday 29th.—All-Saints' Parish, Waccamaw, afternoon . . . at Mr. P. Alston's plantation. At night same place. . . .

"Friday 30th.—At plantation of Mr. Weston. At night, same place. . . .

"Sunday, April 1st.—At All-Saints' Church. . . . Night . . . at the plantation of the late Mr. Francis Weston.

"Monday 2d.— . . . same place. At 12 o'clock laid the cornerstone of the Church of 'St. John the Evangelist,' in the upper part of All-Saints' Parish. Afternoon, at Mr. Motte Alston's, in Horry district . . . and at night . . .

"Wednesday 4th.— . . . at the lower Church of All-Saints' Parish.

"Thursday 5th.—Georgetown, at Prince George's Church. . . .

"Good Friday 6th.—Forenoon . . . Prince George's Church. . . . Night, at Prince Frederick's, Peedee, preached on Dr. Sparkman's plantation.

"Saturday 7th.—Night, at the plantation of Mr. J. Harleston Read. . . .

"Easter Sunday 8th.— . . . at the Parish Church. Afternoon . . . at the plantation of Col. Alston."

A different account of the same visit of the Bishop gives this information as to the movements of the clerical party:

"March 28th.—(Wednesday afternoon) Bishop arrived accompanied by Rev. Thomas J. Girardeau, of the Church of the Messiah, North Santee.

"29th.—This afternoon we visited True Blue, the residence of Col. T. Pinckney Alston. . . . Soon after 7 o'clock we proceeded to the Chapel. . . .

"30th.—Morning service in the Parish Church: . . . In the afternoon we visited Hagley, the residence of Mr. Plowden C. J. Weston. . . .

"31st.— . . . this evening Midway, the residence of Chancellor Dunkin .·. . (now, in 1921, in the possession of the Nesbit family).

"April 1st (Sunday).—Morning service in the Parish Church. . . . In the afternoon we visited the plantation of the late Mr. F. M. Weston, Laurel Hill. . . .

"2d.—Having spent the night at Laurel Hill . . . between 11 and 12 o'clock we proceeded nearly two miles beyond Laurel

Hill to Wachesaw, one of the few bluffs upon the river. . . . From Wachesaw . . . proceeded about five miles up the Parish to Longwood, a plantation belonging to the estate of the late Col. Ward. Here . . . a boat conveyed us three miles up the river to Woodbourne, the residence of Mr. J. Motte Alston. This plantation is on the West side of the Waccamaw, and lies between it and Bull Creek . . ., the principal channel of the Great Peedee. We were now in Horry District. . . .

"3d.— . . . returned by boat to Longwood, and thence in a carriage to the All-Saints' Parsonage.

"4th.—Wednesday in Passion Week: rode down the Parish six miles for morning services at the Southern Church . . . rode on nearly two miles to Fairfield, the residence of Mr. Charles Alston, sen. . . . From this plantation crossed Winyah Bay to Georgetown. . . ."

Oak Hill was the place of the LaBruce family, and was opposite the Oaks, an Alston home. Esther LaBruce married William Alston, and Elizabeth Alston married Joseph La-Bruce (April 6, 1821). In the Register of St. Thomas and St. Denis the name is given as Joseph Marbeut; the correct name seems to have been La Bruce de Marbeuf, the first part being the family name and the latter the place name, which was soon dropped. Waccamaw neck, according to Mrs. Flora La Bruce, was granted to Joseph La Bruce in the reign of George the second. He married into the Ward family and into the Alston family. The grant was at the head of Waccamaw River on Broutons Creek.

Joshua John Ward, of Waccamaw, was said by Dr. Johnson to have been probably the most successful rice planter in South Carolina. In 1845 he erected a monument to the memory of his relative, Colonel Hezekiah Maham, bearing the inscription, "Within this Cemetery/and in the bosom of the Homestead,/which he cultivated and embellished,/while on Earth,/lie the mortal remains of/Colonel Hezekiah Maham./ He was born in the parish of St. Stephens,/and died, A.D., 1789,/aged 50 years." Maham was a captain in the first rifle regiment, a commander of horse in Marion's Brigade, and Lieutenant-Colonel of an independent corps of cavalry raised by the authority of General Greene. The Ward place was at Brook Green, and is so mentioned on inscriptions.

THE OAKS

Mr. William Allston owned several plantations; Clifton, where it is claimed George Washington was entertained by Mr. Allston at breakfast, was selected as the heritage of his son, Washington Allston.

About fifteen miles from Georgetown, on the Waccamaw, and, like Brook Green, in All-Saints Parish, was The Oaks, one of the many plantations on this river owned by the Allston family. Here, in the year 1801, Joseph Alston, later Governor of South Carolina, brought his lovely bride, Theodosia Burr, daughter of Aaron Burr. Joseph Alston is buried in the old family burying ground at The Oaks, where there is a stone placed also to the memory of Theodosia Burr Alston, who was lost at sea. (There was another Allston burying ground at Turkey Hill plantation, near Waccamaw.) She is thought to have been captured by "Bankers" or pirates at the time of the war with England in 1812. The life of this poor woman was one of many sorrows, and through it all her love and adoration of her father was beautiful and unceasing. The monument to her memory tells briefly her pathetic story; it is also inscribed with the history of her distinguished husband:

"Sacred to the Memory/of/Joseph & Theodosia Burr Alston/and of their Son/Aaron Burr Alston/The last died in June 1812, at the age of 10 years/and his remains are interred here./The disconsolate Mother perished a few/Months after at Sea./And on the 10th Sept. 1816 died the Father/when but little over 37 years of age whose remains rest here with the Son's./The life of this Citizen was no common one to/the States, To its service he devoted himself from/his early years./On the floors of its Legislature, he was distinguished for his extensive information &/his transcendent eloquence in the chair of the/House of Representatives, for his impartial/correct decisions & every where he was/distinguished for his zealous attachments to his/republican principles./In the capacity of Chief Magistrate of the/State when bothe the honour and the responsibility/of the Office were heightened by the/difficulties and dangers of the War of 1812/he by his

PRINCE GEORGE, WINYAH, GEORGETOWN

indomitable activity & his Salutary/measures earned new titles to the respect &/gratitude of his fellow citizens./This great man was also a good one./He met Death with that fortitude with which/his Ancestor did from whom he received/his name & this estate & which is to be found only/in the good hoping to rejoin those whose loss had left in his heart an 'aching void,' that/Nothing on earth could fill.''

An interesting contemporary account of the Burr episode is had in a letter from Henry M. Rutledge to Henry Izard, which gives a closer view of the alleged conspiracy of Aaron Burr. It was obtained from the collection of letters and other manuscripts left by the late Dr. Gabriel E. Manigault and his brother, Louis Manigault, of Charleston, and was published in the *South Carolina Historical and Genealogical Magazine*. In part it reads:

Addressed: ''Henry Izard Esqu.
    Charleston
     South Carolina.
       Nashville March 25th—1807

Dear Izard,
 I arrived at this place, four days ago—after the most disagreeable journey, that I ever performed—The moment I passed the blue ridge, I perceived that I had plunged again into the depth of winter, & indeed I have scarcely experienced a fair day since. . . . I pushed my way however thro' the wind & water to Anderson's house, which is 25 miles from this—We set out the next day for this place, & called on our way at Genl: Jackson's where we spent an agreeable evening, in the course of which he made many enquiries respecting you. I found as you may presume, that Colonel Burr, furnished the most common topic in this quarter. I have not seen a single person, who believes that Burr ever intended to attempt a separation of the Western from the Atlantic States, or to possess himself of N: Orleans. They are all however persuaded that Wilkinson & himself, were connected in a scheme to attack the Floridas & other Spanish possessions, & that with the knowledge of the Executive, who expected every moment, a declaration of war on the part of Spain. And indeed, except Eaton's affidavit, who is supposed to have blended, what was said in jest & earnest I do not recollect any other evidence which might not be reconciled with this statement. Very little, not to say, *no* credit is here attached to Wilkinson's assertions

—Indeed there does not appear the slightest sentiment of hostility of the Atlantic States or to the Government of the Union in this quarter. . . ."

To return to The Oaks, the dwelling on this, one of the first places settled on the Waccamaw, has long since been destroyed, and the property has passed from the hands of the Alston family; but the site of the house is well defined and marked by a single brick chimney, all that remains of its former elegance.

OATLAND

A daughter of Mr. Benjamin Allston, grandmother of Mr. John S. Pyatt, of Georgetown, S. C., owned a plantation house on the Waccamaw called Oatland. She did not, however, make her home there, but once or twice a year remained for a short time at the plantation to look after her affairs, take stock of her business, and give out clothing to the negroes.

Her town house was on the southeast corner of Meeting and Charlotte Streets in Charleston. It was a handsome structure, a tall brick building placed at right angles to the street, with a Greek portico to the side, looking out upon formal gardens enclosed with high walls. There was about it an atmosphere reminiscent of an Italian villa. Up to a year or so ago it remained as originally designed, having passed from the Pyatt family to the Ancrum's, and then to the Edwards', who recently sold it to the Salvation Army.

LITCHFIELD

The Tuckers were a well-known family who owned many estates near Georgetown; a Miss Tucker married into the Weston family, thus forming a close connection between the two. The house most prominently associated with the Tucker family is the handsome old residence at Litchfield, which is still standing, although it has passed into other hands and been altered slightly during the intervening years.

A Miss Allston married Mr. John Tucker, and one of their two daughters married Mr. Frances Weston. After his wife's death Mr. Tucker remarried, and had six sons, all of whom were physicians and completed their studies in Paris. There

120

"PROSPECT HILL," WACCAMAW RIVER, NEAR GEORGETOWN
From a Drawing by Alfred Hutty

were three Dr. Tuckers on the Pee Dee, and two on the Waccamaw, and they practiced only on the plantations.

A Tribute of Respect adopted by the vestry of St. Paul's Church, Radcliffeborough, says of John H. Tucker:

"Although the larger portion of each year was passed in attending to his planting interests on the Waccamaw and Pee Dee rivers, yet when he was with us, he ever manifested a deep and heartfelt interest in everything connected with the spiritual and temporal welfare of our Church, contributing always liberally, in every way, to its advancement."

The will of this gentleman, who died about 1859, mentions as his property the plantations of Will Brook and Litchfield on the Waccamaw; Glenmore, Holly Grove and Moreland, or Bates Hill, all three situated on both sides of the Pee Dee River; and land on Sandy Island.

PROSPECT HILL

The plantation home at Prospect Hill on the Waccamaw has been said to be the most interesting house on the river. It was formerly owned by three distinguished families of this section, the Wards, Hugers and Allstons, and is now the property of the well-known "Bromo-Seltzer King," Mr. Emerson. The old house is still standing at Prospect Hill, and has had within its venerable walls many makers of history and celebrated personages.

The building itself is a wooden structure, with a double flight of stone steps leading from the large veranda. The arrangement of the iron balustrade is most unique; there is an inner railing which, from an opening in the center, runs right and left along the front of the piazza, then branches downward at either end, forming the outer railing of each flight of steps; the inner railing of the steps extends unbroken from the curve at the foot of one set of steps, across the front of the veranda parallel with the other railing, enclosing a small passageway a little below the level of the veranda, and down again as the inner railing of the other flight, all of which is made clearer by the illustration. The brick chimneys of the house are unusually tall.

121

Colonel and Mrs. Benjamin Huger (the latter was previously Mrs. Thomas Allston) entertained LaFayette at this elegant mansion during his celebrated visit to America. An account of his reception has been given by a Miss Allston, a relative of Mrs. Huger's, who was present at the occasion. The terrace was illuminated down to the river where he landed, and a great ball given in his honor at which the gloves worn were stamped with the head of LaFayette. The Hugers are also said to have entertained Washington at this historic home.

Colonel Benjamin Huger was a senator from South Carolina during Madison's administration, and was the brother of the Colonel or Major Huger, who attempted to rescue the Marquis de LaFayette from the dungeon of St. Olmutz. A tablet to the memory of Colonel Huger was destroyed by fire a few years ago when the Waccamaw Church, All-Saints, was burned.

Again Prospect Hill was the scene of much brilliancy when it was visited by President Monroe in 1825. He was conveyed from there to Georgetown in "one of the plantation barges, profusely decorated and adorned for the occasion with the United States colors proudly floating at its head. Eight negro oarsmen dressed in livery propelled the barge. The party was met at Georgetown by her most distinguished citizens; carpet was laid from the landing up to the place of reception."

The surroundings at Prospect Hill were in accordance with the magnificence of the dwelling. There are evidences of a richly cultivated garden, and the walls are hung with ivy, as are the railings of the old stone stairs. As the property of Mr. Emerson the place retains its original charm and distinction, and is considered of inestimable value as a true type of the colonial southern home.

The illustrations accompanying are made from descriptive drawings, it having been found impossible to secure permission from Mr. Emerson to proceed to his property, no reply having been received from several letters. This circumstance is unfortunate as it is understood Mr. Emerson has taken great delight in his historic home.

"PROSPECT HILL," REAR VIEW
From a Drawing by Alfred Hutty

FRIENDFIELD AND SOME ALLSTON PLACES

Friendfield, a plantation about six or eight miles from Georgetown, was the old Withers' homestead, once the residence of Daniel G. Wayne, grandfather on the maternal side of George F. von Kolnitz, of Charleston. It is on the Sampit River, and the house, apparently having had many additions built on, is most interesting, particularly the interior, a portion of which is shown in the illustration. At Friendfield is found the landscape wall-papering similar to that in the house at Hampton.

In old deeds we find this place frequently mentioned, and it seems to have been the scene of many marriages, as the following notice, one of several similar announcements, would indicate:

"James Landels of this parish, Bachelor, and Damaris Murrall of this parish, Spinster, were married in the Dwelling house of Capt. Richard Withers of this parish by License this 23rd day of February, in the Year of our Lord 1780 by me S. F. Warren of this parish, Clerk."

One of the Withers family, Frank, owned land up and down the coast. He seemed to have a passion for trading, and made a million dollars when cotton was three cents a pound. An interesting anecdote is related of how he rode to town on an Indian pony worth twenty dollars, and upon being offered eighty dollars for it by some merchant, took off the saddle and bridle, sold the pony, and walked home.

Friendfield was formerly a portion of 1515 acres, sold to Benj. Trapier, transferred to William Burnet, and divided in 1784 into two sections, Friendfield, the upper portion of 746½ acres was transferred by Burnet to Edward Martin, and the remainder subsequently known as Strawberry Hill, to Peter Foisseu.

Benj. Trapier acquired this 1515 acres by various law processes from the division of Hobcaw Barony, which took its name from the Indian name applied to the point of land opposite the town of Georgetown on Winyah Bay, and is not to be confused with the Hobcaw on the south bank of the Wando

123

River opposite Charleston neck, now called Remley's Point. Hobcaw Barony was one of the ten baronies aggregating 119,000 acres; laid out as early as 1711 and divided among the Proprietors by lot on November 21, 1718. From John, Lord Cateret, afterwards Earl Granville, "one of the first orators, purest patriots, brightest classic scholars and most ardent convivialists of his time," Hobcaw Barony passed to John Roberts, who purchased it for 500 pounds sterling, thence to Sir Wm. Baker, Nicholas Linwood, and Brice Baker, who appointed Paul Trapier as their attorney.

Paul Trapier was son or grandson of the ancestor of the family of that name, and at the time was apparently a merchant in Georgetown. It would be interesting to trace the different hands into which the Barony passed when divided. The Alstons acquired many portions of it, outside of that sold to Benj. Trapier. John Alston (also spelled Allston) was the founder of this distinguished family of South Carolina, and was the son of William Alston, gentleman, of Hammersmith (a part of London), Middlesex. He came to South Carolina in 1682 with James Jones, a merchant of Charles Town, as may be seen on page 123 of a book of miscellaneous records of the governor of South Carolina, covering the years between 1672 and 1692.

Mr. H. A. M. Smith says that the lower plantations, Marietta, Friendfield, Strawberry Hill, Fraser's Point, or Calais, and Michaux, were in 1860 all owned by the late William Algernon Alston; and that at one date or another the entire barony, with the single exception of Alderly, was owned by an Alston.

"Fairnfield" (Friendfield) in 1872, belonging to the late Joseph Alston, Esq., was advertised as consisting of the following tracts of land, containing rice, pine, marsh and swamp lands; Marietta, Strawberry Hill, Fairnfield, Marsh Island, Michaux's Point, Calais, and Clegg's Point; all lying contiguous to each other, forming a peninsula with the Waccamaw River on the west, and the Atlantic Ocean or its water on the east. "A single fence from 2 to 3 miles across the peninsula will enclose the entire tract."

FRIENDFIELD HOUSE. FRIENDFIELD NEAR GEORGETOWN. THE WITHERS HOME
From a print

Cherokee, another Allston place, was the plantation of Governor R. F. W. Allston, and was inherited from his grandfather, Benj. Allston. The former was Governor of South Carolina in 1857 and 1858. The plantation contains nearly 900 acres, and there stands on it a house in perfect order after all the intervening years from the time of its construction, on a very beautiful point overlooking the Pee Dee River, the front piazza commanding a view of ''a beautiful bend, the glimmering waters framed by dark oak branches.'' Cherokee is two miles from a white neighbor, and eight from Casa Bianca, the Poinsette-Pringle place. It was afterwards bought by the daughter of Governor Allston, who says, ''with my horses, my dogs, my book and piano my life has been a very full one.'' She speaks of going to church in ''our little pineland village,'' dining in the summer house, and then ''driving in'' to Hasty Point, which is named from Marion's hasty escape during the Revolution from the British officers.

Mention must be made, in writing, of the Allston family, of that distinguished artist, Washington Allston, one of the greatest of the pupils of Benjamin West, whose painting, ''A Spanish Girl,'' is one of the intaglio-gravure pictures illustrating ''Makers of American Art.'' Several years of his active life were spent in England, but he was a native American, having been born in the Waccamaw region of South Carolina in 1779. His father died when the artist was two years old, and when he was seven his mother married Dr. Henry C. Flagg, of Newport, chief of the medical staff of General Greene's army during the Revolution.

After graduating at Harvard in 1800 he studied art for a time in Charles Town with Malbone, the particular friend of Allston during his entire life, who in after years became known as Edward G. Malbone, a noted miniature painter. They went to London together, and Allston entered the Royal Academy, where he became a pupil of West's. He developed greatly in poetic and religious fields as well as in art, and the most celebrated of his paintings are of a religious nature. After spending many years abroad he returned to America about 1818 and spent the remainder of his life, until 1843, in Boston and

Cambridge. In prominent galleries of both England and America his paintings are hung.

CASA BIANCA OR WHITE HOUSE

Casa Bianca, the home of the famous Joel Poinsett, stood on the point of land between the Pee Dee and Black Rivers, eight miles south of Chicora. This was acquired by Mr. Poinsett through marriage with the widow of John Julius Pringle, formerly a Miss Izard, who spent her summers in Newport and her winters in Washington. She was a woman of charm and originality, and is said to have introduced in New York the fashion of wearing small, live snakes as bracelets at the opera. That the Izard women were always remarkable is shown by the celebrated witticism passed in Washington on one of them by a lady who declared, in speaking of the Bee and Izard families that they were "a proud lot from B to Z."

In connection with these aristocratic people, it is of interest that Mary Pringle, daughter of Mr. and Mrs. Julius Izard Pringle, whose mother was a Miss Lynch, and whose home was Greenfield, on Black River, several miles southwest of Chicora Wood, married into nobility, her husband being Count Yvan des Francs. Another family place was Weymouth, on Pee Dee River, six miles south of Chicora, the residence of Mr. and Mrs. Ralph Izard, the latter having been a Miss Pinckney.

A complete history of Casa Bianca is found in "A Woman Rice Planter," by "Patience Pennington." The life of the South Santee region is given in detail, and she describes in her own inimitable way the life on the rice plantations; telling of the negroes, their loves, hates, works and plays; of teaching the little children, and of the birds, beasts and flowers of Casa Bianca, where she spent her short married life. The tract consisted of 200 acres, which she afterwards bought.

Joel Poinsett was a Charlestonian of national, or even international reputation. His home had always been in the city of Charleston until his retirement from public life. A local notice in a Charleston paper in 1732 mentions his father in an account of the celebration of St. George's Day by the "Fort

THE DRAWING-ROOM, FRIENDFIELD HOUSE SHOWING PICTURE WALL PAPER

From a print

Jolly Volunteers'' at the "House of Trooper Pointsett, their usual House of Rendezvous.'' The son's residence was situated upon what is now Rutledge Avenue, a few squares above Calhoun Street on the east side. The house was a plain wooden one with columns in front, having somewhat the exterior appearance of a small church. It was recessed some distance from the street, and stood in the midst of a grove of live oaks; it was generally known as "Poinsett's Grove,'' and had probably been a farm before the city limits extended so far.

Mr. Poinsett had traveled much, and had observed in the cities of Europe the great usefulness of galleries of paintings and statues, their improvement and elevation of the tastes of the people, and with the hope of starting such an institution in Charleston he obtained land on Broad Street west of Logan, from the Methodist Church as the site of his proposed "Academy of Fine Arts.'' This was done in 1833, and he also got pictures and statues. If Mr. Poinsett's plan was not permanently successful it was at least a great step forward, and is now realized in the Gibbes Memorial Art Gallery on Meeting Street.

He married, as has been said, Mrs. John Julius Pringle, who owned a valuable rice plantation near Georgetown, and there, for the rest of his days, he passed the winters, some of his summers being spent in Greenville, S. C., where they also owned a farm, and for the fall months they sometimes went North.

Mr. Poinsett was rewarded for his great interest in science by having a beautiful flower named for him. It was described by two botanists, Wildenow and Graham, without its being known exactly which one had priority. The first called *Euphorbia pulcherrima,* and the second *Poinsettea pulcherrima.* It belongs to the family of Euphorbiacæ; is a native of Mexico, and was discovered there about the year 1828. It is commonly known, however, as the poinsettia.

The house at Casa Bianca stood on the bank of Black River; a picture of the front porch shows a two and a half story house with a piazza downstairs broken by a wing, and on the right a set-in gable roof over the steps leading out-of-doors. The pitch of the roof on the attic is also broken by a gable end fronting directly in the middle of the house. Sturdy chimneys give an air of English rusticity to the whole, which impression is carried out by the secluded look given the house by the surrounding trees. Patience Pennington speaks of it herself as a rambling old house; "even the garret with its ghostly old oil portrait of a whole family in a row and a broken bust of another member." In another place she says: "My predecessor at Casa Bianca was a woman of immense ability and cleverness. She spent much time abroad and was a good friend of the Grand Duke of Weimar to whom she sent an African as a present, he having expressed a desire to have one in his suite; in spite of war and turmoil, Tom, son of the gardener, was sent. The Grand Duke was delighted with him and treated him with great favor. Tom married the daughter of an 'honorable Councillor' lived happily and died from over exertion made in his efforts to render help when a fire broke out in the palace."

The garden at Casa Bianca was planted by Mr. Poinsett somewhere between 1830 and 1835. He brought many rare plants from Mexico, among others the gorgeous "Flor-de la Noche Buena" which in this country bears the name Poinsettia in his honor. There is very little left of the original garden, only the camelia bushes, the olia fragrans, Magnolia purpuria and Pyrus Japonica. The cloth of gold, Lamarque, and other roses grew rampantly, but visitors here have almost destroyed them, as they have the hedge of azaleas.

NORTH ISLAND AND THE HUGERS

An account of the Huger family has been given in connection with Limerick plantation on the Cooper River; a quaint old entry in the records of the State says:

"P M
August th 12th   This Day Came Daniell Huger of Sante
1697   Planter & record his mark of Cattell & hoggs &c:
             followeth, the left yeare Cropt the other wth an
             under & upper Keele, his brand mark as (here
             the device is drawn) margent."

Johnson's "Traditions and Reminiscences of the American Revolution" relate a most interesting event which transpired in 1777 while Major Huger was residing on his plantation near Georgetown. He was visited by two strangers, neither of whom could speak English, and having spoken French from his childhood, Major Huger invited them into his family circle. They appeared to be men of distinction, and told him that they had left France to visit America and had been put ashore near Georgetown, on North Island, wishing to proceed northwardly. One of them announced himself as the Marquis de LaFayette, the other as Baron von Steuben. They were hospitably entertained by Major Huger, introduced to his neighbors and friends, and then conveyed, in his own equipage, to Charleston, where they were well taken care of by the Governor and Council, and provision made for their journey to Philadelphia.

At the time of Provost's invasion, Major Huger and his family "lived in the enjoyment of ease, health and honor, in an elegant establishment, with all the enjoyments of domestic and social happiness. When he accepted the commission in the newly raised regiment, he had no earthly motive for thus devoting himself to the public service, but love of country, and his sense of duty to defend her dearest rights." He fell in executing his duty, having been Major of the second regiment of riflemen, in the Provincial service, his commission dated the 17th day of June, 1775.

This Major Benjamin Huger was the fifth son of Daniel Huger, a direct descendant of the Huguenot, Daniel Huger. In the cultivation of rice his father had prospered, and gave his numerous family all the advantages of education that America afforded, sending his sons in succession to Europe for the tour which was then considered indispensable to a complete education. They all profited by their opportunities, returning courteous and polished gentlemen, who at the commencement of the Revolution united with great cordiality in support of the American rights. John Huger was elected, by the Provincial Congress, a member of the council of safety, associated with Miles Brewton, Thomas Heyward, Arthur Middleton, and others, Henry Laurens being the President.

John Huger was afterwards Secretary of State. Isaac Huger was elected Lieutenant-Colonel of the first regiment; Daniel Huger was for several years a member of the Continental Congress; Francis Huger was elected quartermaster-general, and Benjamin Huger Major of the second regiment.

Major Huger's widow, a sister of Francis and Cleland Kinloch, lived to see her children well educated, married and honored. Her daughter married the Hon. Hugh Rutledge, chancellor of South Carolina; her oldest son, Benjamin, married the widow of Thomas Allston, and was many years a delegate to Congress from his own district, Georgetown; and her youngest son, after his daring enterprise to rescue LaFayette from the prison of Olmutz, was commissioned colonel of artillery, married a daughter of General Thomas Pinckney, and held the commission of adjutant general in his division of the Southern army in the War of 1812, against Great Britain.

At North Island, in Georgetown County, is erected a stone to mark the spot where LaFayette landed when he first came to this country to offer his service to the Continental Army. This enthusiastic young Frenchman who gave his services to the United States in their arduous struggle for independence, is now named in the history of South Carolina.

Farther up Winyah Bay from North Island is a plantation now owned by Mr. Bernard Baruch, a distinguished financier, whose father is a noted physician of New York, who originally came from Camden, S. C. Mr. Baruch's property is believed to have been one of the old Huger or Alston places, and indeed thought to be the place where LaFayette made his first landing at North Island.

CHAPTER VII

UPPER, LOWER AND MIDDLE ST. JOHN'S AND ST. STEPHEN'S

ST. JOHN'S BERKELEY

HIS parish was incorporated by the Church Act of 1706, but previously had many residents. The French settlers removed hither from French Santee and Orange Quarter, and it appears that as early as 1707 these people banded themselves together into a small congregation and in 1710 built themselves a church and called a minister.

"It is known from tradition," says *Huguenot Transactions No. 7,* "that this church was a small wooden building that stood a little east of the place now known as Simpson's Basin on the Santee Canal, about Midway between the present Biggin and Black Oak churches." The use of the church by the French was not continued. From Mr. Chastaigner's will we learn that after discontinuing the use of the church they held worship at Pooshee, a plantation owned by the Emigrant René Ravenel.

Concerning the plate owned by this church, Dr. Dalcho says:

"The Sacramental Plate, with the exception of the *French* Chalice, was, probably, purchased by the Parish. It has the following inscription on each piece: *St. John's Parish, South-Carolina in America.*

"A Chalice of Silver, gilt, was presented to the Parish. It had been used by the Protestants in France before the revocation of the Edict of Nantz, and was brought to Carolina by the Rev. Mr. Lessou, formerly Minister of a French congregation in this Province."

When the Parish of St. Stephen's became the resort of the descendants of the French, chiefly from French Santee, because of the freshets on that river, Upper, and Middle St. John's Berkeley became settled by some of the same people for the same reason. It is a strange thing to note that there are three very arbitrary divisions of St. John's, not easy for an outsider to understand. These divisions are known as Upper, Middle and Lower St. John's.

No more puzzling occupation can be devised than to correctly place the different families of the same name in their correct places. Suffice it to say, that the settlement in Upper St. John's was called Eutawville, where several houses are still found, and which will be discussed later; Middle St. John's settlement is called Pinopolis, here is found a Cain house, Somerset, a fair type of a St. John's plantation home in the nineteenth century. The roof of the house is slate. In Lower St. John's were the summer settlements of The Barrows and Cordesville.

The Cordes were another well-known family connected with this inland section of South Carolina. About the year 1665 Anthony Cordes, *un medécin,* arrived in the colony and resided on the French Santee, afterwards St. John's Berkeley, where he died in 1712. He came with the French emigrants, and is supposed to have accompanied them as their physician. His home was Cordesville. There was another Cordes place called Upton, but the homestead of this family was Yaughan, the residence of an ardent patriot who contrived during the Revolution to vastly annoy the British. Curriboo was the home of Thomas C. Cordes, who married Rebecca Jamieson. One of their daughters married Jonathan Lucas, Jr., and went to live in England. Milford, north of Blufort, was formerly the residence of Isaac DuBose, who sold it to Samuel Cordes; the latter also owned The Lane plantation.

What is said concerning the type of house in St. Stephen's Parish applies also to the houses in the three St. John's. Perhaps, however, the furnishings of the houses in St. John's were a little more elaborate than those in St. Stephen's, and in order to give a general idea of what was found in the old-time houses a few distinctive items will be mentioned.

"SOMERSET," THE CAIN HOUSE, PINOPOLIS

For illumination candles and lamps were used, the former being made on the plantations from the wax of the bay or myrtleberry plants. The lamps had bases of pressed glass, and bowls of cut glass. The wick attached to a double jet shows that a very volatile oil was used, probably spirit oil or alcohol. They were originally used with whale oil, and in many places the people burnt hog-lard. The crystal candlesticks of the period were made with marble bases, the sticks being of bronze, and glistening crystal pendants surrounded each individual candle-holder. On the hall table of every old establishment were kept the brightly polished brass candlesticks for the guests to take upstairs upon retiring.

The rooms in olden days, in these historic dwellings, were bright and cheerful and colorful. The artistically woven "carpets" were coverings for tables and bureaus, as well as for the floors. In summer the floor coverings were painted rugs, somewhat resembling our modern linoleum, and some were highly decorative. The owners took great pride in these. The corner cupboards which came into fashion about 1710 were considered as much a part of the house as the windows or the mantels. Many of the old houses with commonplace exteriors contained handsome marble mantelpieces, and rare old pieces of English and French furniture.

Persons familiar with the history of furniture in America would find in these old houses a perfect wealth of such belongings. There were sofas and settees, sometimes with cane seats; chairs decorated in French imitation of Chinese flower sprays; figures on fans from France; "what-nots" holding interesting bits collected by travelers; and many convex mirrors, with candlesticks attached. Among the most interesting things about these old houses are the enormous locks and large keys which were part of the defence.

Such furnishings were made possible by the wealth of the inhabitants, one of whom was Peter, an ancestor of the present Sinkler family. He died in Charleston, a prisoner of the British. Before he was carried from his plantation near Eutawville he witnessed the destruction of the following property; "twenty thousand pounds of indigo, one hundred and thirty head of cattle, one hundred and fifty-four head of sheep, two hundred head of hogs, three thousand bushels of grain, twenty thousand rails, and household furniture valued at £2500''; in addition to which the British carried off 55 negroes, 16 blood horses and 28 mares and colts.

Referring to personal belongings, the writer's mother, Susan DeSaussure, remembers when the ladies of this neighborhood wore the old-fashioned Caleche, or ''ugly,'' silk shirred, and worn around the front of poke bonnets to protect the face from the sun. They were fashioned in the Fifties, and somewhat resembled little buggy tops. Each different costume had a corresponding caleche. The ladies of that day carefully cherished their complexions.

Besides the Sinklers, the Mazycks, Porchers, Palmers, Ravenels, Cordes, Marions, Dwights, Gailliards and Gourdins were found as original Huguenot settlers of St. John's. It is almost impossible to untangle these families, and anyone who is interested may read ''Olden Times of Carolina,'' ''Ramsey's Sketch of St. Stephen's Parish,'' Mr. Isaac Porcher's article on this section, or Samuel DuBose's ''Reminiscences of St. Stephen's Parish.'' For instance, Mr. Mazyck Porcher, Carolina's Bourbon, lived at Mexico plantation, his grandfather, Peter Porcher, owned plantations called Peru, Ophir and Mexico. He lived at Peru and would often leave his home in the morning, ride to Ophir, a distance of 15 miles, thence to Mexico 12 miles, and back to Peru 10 miles, all in the same day. All of these men were fond of manly sports and in the Revolution Marion and Moultrie depended on them. In the struggle for American independence these men made fine cavalrymen. A few of the plantations upon which houses are still standing will be briefly discussed.

Old Field plantation was owned by Philip Porcher, who died in 1800. He paid taxes on over one-half million dollars worth of property, and had 464 slaves; among other real estate was a house in Archdale Street in Charleston, then a fashionable thoroughfare. Another Porcher residence was Indianfield, at which the semi-annual meeting of the St. John's Hunting Club is sometimes held even now. Massive moss-draped trees and beautiful lawns mark this romantic spot.

Dr. Isaac Porcher, the Huguenot emigrant, came to this country from the Province of Sainte Sévére, France. He is described (Burke's Peerage) as being Isaac Porcher de Richelbourg, doctor of medicine of the University of Paris, who married a Cherigny, of the Province of Touraine. Burke's account is incorrect, as has been proved by Mrs. Julia Porcher Wickham, a lineal descendant of Isaac Porcher. Mrs. Wickham made a pilgrimage to France to establish certain facts in connection with the Porcher family. Dr. Robert Wilson, President of the Huguenot Society in 1910, has also written much concerning Isaac Porcher. He states his ability to give with positiveness the origin of Dr. Porcher, from an old manuscript found years ago at Ophir plantation in St. John's Berkeley, which runs as follows:

"Isaac Porcher, né a St'e-Sévére en Beny, fils de Isaac Porcher et de Susanne Ferré. Isaac, Pierre, Elizabeth, Madeleine, et Claude, leurs enfants."

The emigrant's bible, which is still owned by his descendants of the pure Huguenot blood in St. John's, at Indianfield, contains on the flyleaf the notice of his wife's death written and signed by the emigrant himself; the date of this bible being 1707.

The refugee and his wife lived for some time in London, as records of the baptism of two of his children there prove, but he soon emigrated, and we find from an old document that he was in Charleston in the year 1687. He settled on land not far from Goose Creek where, in the old Huguenot cemetery there, his body is supposed to have been laid.

Further enumeration of the history of the family in France would reveal much of the internal history of that country, as the French branch of the Porchers was concerned with all the great affairs of that time. The history of Abbe Porcher de Lissaunay is closely connected with the Château of Cote Perdrix, near Sainte-Sévére, the only Porcher home in the old world of which we have any description. Mrs. Wickham wrote

135

an account of this place which has been published in the "Transactions of the Huguenot Society."

The last historic owner of "Peru" was Peter Porcher, whose fourth child, Major Samuel Porcher, had his plantation at Mexico, and married Harriot, daughter of Philip Porcher. At the time of the Civil War Mexico was owned by Mazyck Porcher, whom Mr. Yates Snowden has immortalized as "The Carolina Bourbon" in his poem of that name. A Missionary Tour to Upper St. John's and St. Stephen's says:

"We drove towards Mexico, an old family place now the residence of Mr. M. P. The ground about the house is much more broken than usual, its slopes being studded with fine trees, oaks and cedars; while the Santee Canal with its hedges and locks gives variety to the scene."

During the days of the stage-coach Hugh Legare often visited at the home of Philip Porcher, who had been his great chum at college. The house, which still stands, was built in 1812 by slave labor, and is of black cypress, the timber having been cut on the place. Its roof is of air-dried cypress or long-leaf pine shingles. It is called a double-story house, and stands on a nine-foot brick foundation the pillars of which are about six by three feet. The bricks were had from a brick kiln on the plantation; the hole where the clay was dug can still be seen on the edge of the woods. The interior decorations were done by a slave called Black Washington.

A most amusing story is told concerning an occurrence taking place at one of these houses during the courtship of Catherine Porcher (sister of Charles and daughter of Philip) by a Mr. Huger. He came a courting the lady, but evidently his manner of addressing her did not indicate that he would go mateless to the grave if she refused him, intimating that he would seek elsewhere. Thereupon she furled her fan and bid him begone to seek the other maid—a very proper display of spirit upon her part.

While in Charleston the Porchers occupied the house on Pitt Street now owned by Mr. Wm. Cogswell, which is nearly opposite to Bethel Methodist Church.

On the road between Mexico and Pineville, a distance of five or six miles, lies Belle Isle plantation, where are deposited the remains of General Marion. The tomb is in a neat enclosure which formed a family burying ground; it is a plain marble slab, slightly elevated upon a brick foundation, and bears a simple and most appropriate inscription. The house at Belle Isle is still standing, but is not in very good repair, nor is it inhabited. To Shirley Carter Hughson, now Superior of the Order of the Holy Cross, belongs the credit of properly marking Marion's grave.

Among the most honored and beloved names connected with the history of St. John's is that of the Dwight family. Samuel Dwight, the son of the Rev. Daniel Dwight and his wife, who was Christiana Broughton, married Rebecca Marion. He was generous enough to allow his son Francis to change his name to that of Marion, as General Francis Marion had no children and the name would otherwise have been lost to posterity.

Robert Marion, Esq., son of Gabriel Marion, resided at Belle Isle, and a part of this plantation was Burnt Savannah, where General Marion had his residence. Belle Isle also embraced the homes of Peter Couturier and Dr. James Lynah.

The Palmers were also connected with this old parish. Webdo was the residence of Joseph Palmer. He had one daughter, who married Peter Sinkler. Johnsrun plantation, the first settler of which is unknown, but which was once owned by a Williams, was purchased after 1793 by Capt. John Palmer, and in 1858 was the residence of S. Warren Palmer. Pollbridge, three miles to the south of Clay Bank, was settled by Peter Palmer after 1790. Gravel Hill was the home of John Palmer, Gentleman, whose successful enterprise in the collection of naval stores earned for him the name of "Turpentine John." It was his son John who lived at Richmond, and Peter who lived at Pollbridge. Ballsdam plantation, near the old Santee settlement of St. James, was the property of Dr. John Saunders Palmer.

Charlotte Rebecca, fourth daughter of John Palmer and Catherine Marion Palmer, of Cherry Grove plantation, St.

John's Berkeley, married Ellison Capers, who had a brilliant war record, and afterwards, in 1893, was unanimously elected Bishop of the Diocese of South Carolina.

"The Fair Forest Swamp is one of the principal features of the western branch of the Cooper River, into which it flows through Watboo Creek. It rises in the bays, within a few miles of Santee Swamp," and there it is, that a close connection between St. James, St. Stephens, Eutawville, and the headwaters of the western branch of the Cooper River is formed.

EUTAW SPRINGS AND VICINITY

The road to the "Congarees," on the old map called the "Charichy" path, ran directly to Nelson's ferry, over which the trade to the interior northwest passed. During the war of the Revolution it was the highway for the passage of the armed forces of both sides, and it was at Eutaw Springs, near this road, that the battle of Eutaw Springs was fought in 1781, which practically ended all British occupation of South Carolina outside of the City of Charleston and its environs, even though tactically General Greene and the American Army were repulsed. General Greene, in his letters to the Secretary of War, says:

"We have 300 men without arms, and more than 1000 so naked that they can be put on duty only in cases of a desperate nature. . . . Our difficulties are so numerous, and our wants so pressing, that I have not a moment's relief from the most painful anxieties. I have more embarrassments than it is proper to disclose to the world. Let it suffice to say that this part of the United States has had a narrow escape. 'I have been seven months in the field without taking off my clothes.' . . .

". . . . The brave men who carried death into the enemy's ranks at the Eutaw, were galled by their cartridge boxes, while a folded rag or a tuft of moss protected the shoulders from sustaining the same injury from the muskets. Men of other times will inquire, by what magic was the army kept together? By what supernatural power was it made to fight?"

138

UNITED HOUSE ADJACENT TO "BELVIDERE" PLANTATION

A monument to these brave men has been placed on the Battlefield of Eutaw Springs, which was on the Sinkler tract about a mile and a half from the house.

It is hard to make a distinction between Eutaw place and its sister plantation, Belvidere, to which it lies adjacent. Mrs. Harriette P. Gourdin, of Eutawville, a lady well over 80 years of age and a life-long resident of that section, writes in 1920, that "Henry Sinkler's home is on Eutaw plantation, and the house is built near the bank of a portion of Eutaw Creek which divides the place from Belvidere, another Sinkler homestead. Over this creek stands a narrow foot-bridge for the use of the two places. The house at Eutaw place was built by Henry's great-grandfather."

In Lossing's *Field Book of the Revolution* we find the following entry speaking of the action around Eutawville in 1781:

"While the British fell back a little, Greene quickly prepared for battle, and pressing forward the action commenced with spirit in the road and fields, very near to the present entrance gates to the seat of residence of Mr. Sinkler. . . ."

Of this place Lossing again speaks in describing his trip to the Southern battlefield:

"At 8 o'clock (Jan. 26, 1849) I arrived at the elegant mansion of William Sinkler, Esq., upon whose plantation are the celebrated Eutaw Springs. It stands in the midst of noble shade trees one-half mile from the highway. These springs are in Charleston district near Orangeburg line, about 60 miles north of Charleston."

The largest spring is at the foot of a hill 20 or 30 feet in height, from which it emerges after traversing a subterranean passage under the hill for 30 rods, and reappears on the other side. There is a tradition that an Indian made the successful attempt to follow the spring through the hill. The Santee River is reached about two miles below.

Ramsay says, relating to the battle of Eutaw Springs, that:

"the British were vigorously pursued, and upward of 500 of them were taken prisoners. On their retreat they took post in a strong brick house, and in a picquetted garden."

139

Mr. DuBose Seabrook, who is now living, tells of walking near the springs with his mother and being told by her that a pile of bricks adjacent to the spring which they found there were the remains of this house.

Charles Sinkler resided at Belvidere plantation in Upper St. John's Berkeley. His home life eminently represented that splendid type of Southern manhood—the flower of the patriarchal slave-holding civilization—which is but a memory to a few, and a tradition to the people at large. Mr. Sinkler was the grandson of Capt. James Sinkler, of the Revolutionary War, whose brother Peter Sinkler, of Marion's Brigade, died of typhus fever in the cellar of the Charleston Postoffice, a prisoner in the hands of the British. Charles Sinkler was born on Eutaw plantation, which partly covers the sight of the battlefield, and he inherited from his ancestors that intense love for the State which was the preëminent characteristic of the South Carolinian of the old regime. In March, 1836, he entered the United States Navy as a midshipman, was promoted, and soon after married Miss Emily, daughter of Judge Thomas Wharton, an eminent jurist of Philadelphia. While serving as sailing master of the United States brig Perry, which had just returned from the seige of Vera Cruz, he was wrecked on Sombrero Reef, about thirty miles from Key West, Florida, on a voyage from Havana to Charleston, and a graphic description has been written by a brother officer, Lieut. (later Rev.) R. S. Trapier, of the cyclone through which they barely escaped with their lives.

In February, 1847, Mr. Sinkler resigned and came with his wife, a lovely young girl, to his estates in South Carolina. Here he lived the life of the ideal Southern planter, and fortunately for him and for the many beneficiaries of his bounty, the war and its more direful results made no essential change in him or his belongings. Belvidere, his beautiful home, was the scene of the graceful and bountiful hospitality which had characterized the homes of his friends in better days. At his death it passed to his son, Charles St. George Sinkler, and his wife, Anne W. Porcher. Dr. Wharton Sinkler, of Philadelphia, who married a Miss Brock, of that city, was a brother of Mr.

Charles Sinkler, and his sisters were Caroline Sinkler and Mrs. Charles Brown Coxe, of Philadelphia, and Mrs. Charles Stevens, of Charleston.

Mr. Sinkler and his wife, Anne Wickham Porcher, have three daughters, all of whom have married and moved away, but the ancestral home is still the residence of Mr. Sinkler. His daughters are Mrs. Dr. Kershaw Fishburne, of Pinopolis, Mrs. Nicholas Roosevelt, of Philadelphia, and Mrs. Dunbar Lockwood, of Boston, Mass. Pictures are given of both of the Sinkler houses, much alike in construction and detail.

HANOVER HOUSE

A primitive wooden house of a type still to be seen in rural districts of South Carolina is pictured and described in "Ravenel Records" (intended for private distribution), issued in 1898 by Henry E. Ravenel, of Spartansburg, S. C., "Attorney at law; Master of Arts; Alumnus of the College of Charleston; one of the authors of 'Ravenel and McHugh's Digest,' etc.," so we may rely upon his work being good. The photograph and cut are both very defective, says Mr. Ravenel, but the house is very interesting in appearance and stands in a characteristic clearing of pine and oak trees, draped with moss. It is still in use after two hundred and five years.

Hanover House was completed about 1716 by Paul de St. Julien. As it is "roomy though small," one is not surprised at the fact that difficulty was found in supplying the brick for it when the extravagant manner of their use is seen. "The basement walls and cross walls are thick enough to hold a small Eiffel tower," and the basement itself is large enough to be used as a kitchen and pantry.

The chimneys to this house are most curiously constructed, being really two chimneys at each end of the building, one constructed outside of the other from the ground to the top. "The inside section must be about eight feet wide; the overlapping flue somewhat narrower." The legend "Peu a Peu" on the north chimney near the top remains perfectly distinct. It is deeply cut in the cement, and shows its excellent quality. There is, however, no date given.

141

Hanover was settled by Peter de St. Julien, third son of the Huguenot emigrant, Paul, who died there in 1741. He married Mary Amy Ravenel, youngest child of René Ravenel, the emigrant. Curiously enough there are still Ravenels living near Charleston possessing the characteristic looks, coloring, bearing, manners and achievements of their French forbears, and among them is found a René.

It is said that at Hanover "Peter de St. Julien designed to build a half story brick house," on the plan of the North Hampton House, so the builder made a kiln of brick to start with. When the foundation was completed to its present state, Peter discovered that he would not have bricks enough to carry out his designs of a brick house, but thought he would have enough for chimneys. In this he was again disappointed, owing to the curious construction of the chimney within the chimney, and the building ended by being made of wood, on a brick basement, three kilns having to be made to supply the bricks for even this much, so that "Peu a Peu," or "Little by Little" (said to have been put there in 1716) is literally true.

Hanover descended by inheritance to Mary St. Julien, the eldest daughter of Paul, who married Henry Ravenel, son of René Louis. A small book bound in calf is said to be the diary of this latter, and is in the possession of Mr. Thomas P. Ravenel. The following entry is taken from this old record:

"Henry Ravenel marryed to Mary De St. Julien the 13 of September, 1750. We came to live at home, called Hanover, the 13 of April, 1751, and went back to Pooshee the 9th of June, and my wife was delivered of a son on the 26th of said June. Then we came back home again the second time the 1st of October 1751."

The diary continues until about 1785, in which year Henry Ravenel died and was buried at Hanover, at the age of fifty-five years. The orchard became the family burying ground, and we find from the records that only six out of the sixteen children of Mary St. Julien and Henry Ravenel lived to maturity. Many of the children who died were buried at Hanover in the "orchard."

142

Another Henry Ravenel died at Hanover in 1823, aged seventy-two years and eight months. His age would indicate that he was born in 1751 and was probably the first son of Mary De St. Julien and Henry Ravenel, spoken of in the diary as having been born on the 26th of June, 1751. He too was buried in the family burying ground at Hanover.

In Ravenel Records it is stated that Stephen Ravenel, of Hanover (son of Henry and Mary), was married December 11, 1800, to Catherine Mazyck, daughter of William and Mary Mazyck, at the residence of Mr. Mazyck in Archdale Street. This residence still stands, as fine a house as one would wish to see. Stephen Ravenel was Secretary of State, but did not long continue in public office. Although he lived in Charleston, he spent much of his time hunting at the plantation, being devoted to the sport, and is said to have killed many deer. Later he lived at Hanover, where he and his wife are both buried, and as they had no children, the plantation was left to Stephen's brother, Daniel, better known in local circles as "Uncle Daniel."

"Uncle Daniel" was for many years Secretary of the famous "St. John's Hunting Club," whose Club House stood nearly opposite the Black Oak Church on the north side of the road. This Club House was built in 1800 by "Coll Senf, Engineer and Superintendent of the Santee Canal which runs through Wantoot plantation," and was pulled down by the negroes very soon after the first raid of the Yankee Army.

René Ravenel's Book says: "The original rules of the St. Stephen's Club are fair specimens of the rules of such societies of that day (1825) and section." These rules gave the name of the organization, time and place of meetings, and other regulations. Rule 3 specified that "Each member shall find a dinner in the order in which he shall become a member," and Rule 4 stated that "dinner shall be on table at half-past one o'clock." Rule 7 said, "The member finding the dinner shall be President of the day." It is to be noted that no sale, negro trial or card-playing was permitted at the club house on club days.

143

Dinner was the great event and as they used spits in those days, roasted meat meant that the meat was really roasted. The list of edibles suitable for club dinners specified:

"Roasted Turkey, Two Ducks, Two fowls or a dish equivalent to two fowls, one half of a shoat or sheep dressed according to the option of the finder, one ham or piece of salted beef, one peck of Rice, Two loaves of Bread, Mustard, Pepper, Salt, Vinegar, Eight bottles of Madeira Wine, Two bottles of Brandy, one of Gin, one of Whiskey, Twenty-five Spanish and Twenty-five American Segars (Cigars), Two dozen each of Plates, Tumblers, Wine Glasses, Knives and forks."

These club meetings were a prominent feature of the social life of the planters, and some lively anecdotes are told in connection with them. It is said that on one occasion a horse was ridden upstairs to the second story of a house, and difficulty was experienced in getting him down again. But passing by the excesses of those days, the clubs were undoubtedly effective in keeping alive the fraternal feeling, and contributed to the public spirit of the district.

Daniel James Ravenel ("Uncle") died at Hanover in 1836, leaving Brunswick and about sixty negroes to his nephew, Benj. Pierce Ravenel (son of Paul de St. Julien Ravenel and his second wife, Abigail Pierce, of Newport, R. I.). He left Hanover and about seventy negroes to his grandnephew, Henry LeNoble Stevens, a son of Charles Stevens and Susan Mazyck Ravenel (daughter of René, the son of Henry of Hanover). During the Civil War Henry was aide to Col. P. T. Stevens (late Bishop of the Reformed Episcopal Church) and was shot at the second battle of Manassas, August 30th, 1862, dying seven days later in a field hospital at Warrenton, Va. His body was subsequently brought on and interred at Black Oak churchyard. This Henry Le Noble Stevens had married Henrietta S. Gailliard in 1849 and their children are still large landholders in that section.

The Ravenels have built and occupied many beautiful and historic places both in country and town, and the history of Hanover has been given in full, because it is closely connected with the history of "St. John's," divided so quaintly by the inhabitants thereof into Upper, Lower and Middle St. John's.

These romantic houses of the past can never be created. To own one of them is to be not only the possessor of an historical house, but also of something entirely unique. In having a home of historical associations one is endowed not only with a thing of beauty, but with a possession which has a precious quality of its own wrapped up with its glorious history.

Architecturally speaking, these old houses display symmetry and real dignity; albeit it they are very simply constructed, they have a look of intrinsic power and strength which has come to them with the passing of the years. Mellowness is not to be bought with money. It is the gift of age.

WANTOOT

Among the numerous Ravenel properties was a plantation, Wantoot, once the home of Daniel Ravenel, who married Catherine Prioleau. Their son, Daniel Ravenel (1789–1873), was of Huguenot lineage not only through the Prioleaus, but through the emigrant, René Ravenel, of Bretagne.

Many of the Ravenels have been men of scientific achievement, including Dr. Henry Ravenel, to whom botany was subordinate to nothing. It was the constant all-absorbing passion of his life, the more so that serious deafness shut him off from the academic professions which would otherwise have appropriated him. A biographical sketch and somewhat incomplete bibliography of Dr. Ravenel in Professor Wilson Gee's "South Carolina Botanists," seem to be all the accessible published information in regard to him. The Charleston Museum is endeavoring to get together an interesting collection of letters written by him, which it purposes to publish from time to time as a contribution towards an ultimate biography. The most important are the generous gifts of the Misses Gibbes, daughters of Lewis R. Gibbes.

The Ravenel mycological herbarium, now owned by the Museum, was collected before 1853 during Dr. Ravenel's residence at Pooshee and Northampton plantations near the Santee Canal. From similarity of labeling, the specimens given by Miss Heyward, of Wappaoolah (or Wappahoola), seem to belong to the same period, or the Georgia ones possibly

10

after removal to Aiken, S. C. Dr. Ravenel's later, larger, and more valuable collection of fungi was sold to the British Museum. Correspondence shows his desire to have it deposited in the Charleston Museum, but circumstances prevented. The Ravenel herbarium of flowering plants from the Santee Canal region was rescued and remounted, and with the Stephen Elliott herbarium forms the classic basis for botanical work in this vicinity.

On July 5th, 1920, the St. John's Hunting Club, organized over a century ago, held one of its semi-annual meetings at Wampee plantation, with Mr. Thomas P. Ravenel, of Savannah, Georgia, in the chair. The semi-annual dinners of the club are events at which it is a privilege to be present; the delicious dishes, lively and entertaining table talk, and the delightful trysts beneath the ancestral oaks are golden links in the chain of life's enjoyments.

In the South we find a very distinctive style of house; high pitched, with dormer windows set in the roof. The chimneys are built at the gable ends of the house, but constructed entirely on the exterior of the building, and greatly resemble English chimneys in the way they widen at the bottom. Quaint little entrance porches are often found in these houses, and the materials used vary from native wood to imported brick. The gambrel roof is seldom if ever met with in this section.

Many old wooden houses are found in South Carolina up along the eastern branch of the Cooper River and into St. John's and St. Stephen's Parish, which all conform to the same simple lines of architecture found suitable for our southern type of life, and while the possibilities for decoration are never great these houses are entirely delightful, plain buildings. Generally they are of two and a half stories set on basements, and having wide piazzas for use during the long, hot summers. The halls are broad, with wide, low windows, lofty ceilings, and painted and paneled walls. Having once given a description of one, you have virtually described all of this particular type of Carolina colonial, which in its way is equally as perfect as any Colonial design of other sections.

146

Some one has used the happy expression "The Casual Artistry" of the past, and this applies with peculiar force to the old wooden buildings in St. Stephen's and St. John's, where time has mellowed their old walls, and the years have thrown an air of mystery and enchantment over these dear, plain old places, bestowing on them that gift of age and mellowness ever present in these quaint, old-fashioned homes, with their adzed beams, their regular and irregular windows, and their "off-center" chimneys.

But the houses are far from being frowsy or slatternly. They are fine and natural and dignified, so well expressing, in their old age, the builders' instinct for what was appropriate and fitting.

Mills' *Statistics* tell us that the upper and lower parts of St. Stephen's Parish were originally distinguished by the names of French and English Santee. The latter (what is now St. Stephen's) was situated about fifty miles to the northwest of Charleston; it was bounded on the northeast by the Santee River, on the southwest by St. John's Parish, and on the southeast by St. James Santee, thus St. Stephen's originally was a part of St. James Santee, and was divided from it about the year 1740.

The village of Pineville is in this parish. It began to be settled in 1794 as a retreat for health in summer and autumn by the families of the planters who lived on nearby plantations bordering on the rivers. In the beginning of 1784 St. Stephen's was one of the most thriving parishes in the State, and in proportion to its size one of the richest. It was provided with an educational institution called Pineville Academy.

Robert Marion, representative of Charleston district in the U. S. Congress, and Theodore Gailliard, formerly speaker of the House of Representatives of South Carolina and in 1826 one of the judges of the circuit court of law, both belong to this parish. But John Gailliard was perhaps the best known public man. Mr. Lawson speaks of Mons Galliare's (Gailliard) the Elder:

"who lives in a very curious contrived house, built of brick and stone which is gotten near the place. Near here, comes in the

Road from Charleston and the rest of the English settlements, it being a very good way by land, and not above 36 miles, although more than 100 by water. . . ."

On a piece of high land about a mile from Pineville there is a quarry of hard, brown stone, which is very heavy and has the appearance of iron ore. Some of this stone was used by Col. Senf, the engineer who constructed the Santee Canal. They were great on canals in these days. There was one projected from the Edisto to Ashley River, and one constructed from the Santee to the headwaters of the western branch of the Cooper River.

At the expiration of the first term of President Monroe and Vice-President Tompkins in 1821 John Gailliard of South Carolina was president pro-tempore of the sixteenth Congress and was duly qualified to have been acting President of the United States from noon on March 4th (the expiration of President Monroe's first term) until 1 o'clock the next day when Mr. Monroe commenced his second term. Gailliard's term did not expire with the end of the sixteenth Congress, and at that time the office of President pro-tempore was not construed as extending within "the pleasure of the Senate." The records of Congress show that Gailliard's formal reëlection as President pro-tempore did not take place until February 20, 1822, thus giving proof of his legal ability to serve as President for a day.

Thomas H. Benton, distinguished Senator from Missouri, says of John Gailliard, in a book published in 1856, that this gentleman from St. Stephen's Parish in South Carolina (born in 1769) had from the year 1804 been continually elected to the Senate, the first time for an unexpired term, followed by fourteen reëlections, in the course of the last of which he died. The years for which he had been elected numbered nearly thirty; and during this period of service he was elected President (pro-tempore) of the Senate nine times, and presided for fourteen years over the deliberations of that body, the death of two Vice-Presidents, and frequent absence of a third making long, continued vacancies of the presidential chair which Gailliard was called upon to fill.

He is described as being "urbane in manner, amiable in temper, and scrupulously impartial; delicate in manner when setting young senators right, facilitating transaction of business while preserving decorum of that body. There was not an instance of disorder or a disagreeable scene in the chamber during his long-continued presidency. He classed democratically in politics, but was as much a favorite of one side of the house as the other, and *that* in the high party times of the war with Great Britain, which so much exasperated party spirit."

Mr. Theodore G. Fitzsimons has in his possession at Wiltown a rapier worn with full dress by Mr. Gailliard; it was given by John Gailliard to his nephew, Samuel Gailliard Barker, who in turn gave it to his nephew, the present owner. The name of John Gailliard's plantation was Hayden Hill, on which the dwelling has been burnt. This plantation comprised several tracts, one of which was conveyed by the King to Thomas Farr. A list of all the Gailliard places, and there were many of them, includes Brush Pond, still used; the Wilson tract; the St. Julien tract; Newman and Godfrey tracts; the Rhett or Thompson tract, and the Oaks, near Eutaw Springs. Windsor was another Gailliard place, having been the residence of John Gailliard's father.

Perhaps the best known house in this family was that which belonged to Peter Gailliard, which goes by the name of "The Rocks." The register of St. James Santee carries this entry, probably in reference to the owner of the first plantation, and to The Rocks:

"David Gailliard of the Parish of St. Stephens, Bachelor, and Joanna Dubose of the Parish of St. Stephens, Spinster, were married at the plantation of Theodore Gailliard Senr of this Parish, by License, this Twenty-Third Day of September in the Year of our Lord 1773.

This marriage was
Solemnized between us
In the Presence of

David Gailliard
Joanna Dubose
James Rivers
Isaac Dubose."

The timber for The Rocks was selected during a freshet by Mr. Peter Gailliard, who took a canoe and went as far as Santee River, marking which trees he wanted; these were cut by slaves after the freshet, and the cypress allowed to season. The house was put up by his own carpenters, near Eutawville. It is likely that bricks for the foundation and chimneys, each of which give warmth to four rooms, being placed opposite the doors, were made on his own plantation. In some of the houses in this vicinity there was a queer little closet-like room at the rear, entered from the back steps. At The Rocks it was used as a store-room for cut glass and such things, and at Walnut Grove was used and furnished as a library.

Ruins of the Château Gailliard are in Normandy, placed on the summit of a projecting cliff, the castle rises up grandly, commanding a view of the River Seine for miles. According to tradition it was once the home of Richard Coeur-de-Lion, who is supposed to have been his own architect, and the skill shown in the construction of this fortress is considered masterly. The central donjon tower is of immense strength. It is the most perfect remaining part of the castle; the walls are from fourteen to fifteen feet thick. It may be that in some occult manner this spirit of engineering passed to Gailliard, the engineer who worked so faithfully for the benefit of America in making Culebra Cut in the Panama Canal, but whose name has been withdrawn and that of Culebra substituted.

There are several other houses in the vicinity of The Rocks, not yet mentioned, which are still standing, and which all conform to the same general plan of construction. Among them are Walworth, Belmont, Walnut Grove, and Springfield.

One of the Gailliards who served in the Revolutionary War had under his command a man by the name of Francis Salvador, who resided at Ninety-Six, and whose remains are interred in the old DeCosta burying ground in Hanover Street, Charleston. Mr. Salvador was a young Englishman who had come to Carolina about 1773; the Mesne Conveyance records show that he bought lands in this Province in 1774. His home was at Corn-acre Creek twenty-eight miles from Major Andrew Williamson's home. He was a member of the Provincial Congresses of 1775–1776, being one of the few Up Country representatives who had taken an active part in its proceedings. It was Francis Salvador who first brought word of the Indian uprisings at the time of the Revolution to Major Williamson. He was shot down by Williamson's side while attacking the savages, who unfortunately discovered him immediately and scalped him alive before he could be found by his friends in the dark.

To return to St. Stephen's and the settlement at Pineville, Mr. F. A. Porcher gives the following delightful account of a Pineville ball.

"Nothing can be imagined more simple or more fascinating than those Pineville balls. No love of display, no vain attempt to outshine a competitor in the world of fashion, governed the preparations. Refreshments of the simplest character were provided; such only as the unusual exercise would fairly warrant, nothing to tempt a pampered appetite. Cards were furnished to keep the old men quiet, and the music was such only as the gentlemen's servants could give.

"The company assembled early—no one ever thought of waiting until bedtime to go to the ball—and the dancing always began with a country-dance. The lady who stood at the head of the column called for the figures, and the old airs of *Ca ira, Money-Musk, Haste to Wedding,* and *La Belle Catherine* were popular and familiar in Pineville, even long after they had been forgotten in the city. . . .

"The evening's entertainment was always concluded with the *Boulanger,* a dance whose quiet movement came in appropriately to cool off the revellers before exposure to the chilly air. It was a matter of no small importance to secure a proper partner for this dance, for, by old custom, whoever danced last with a lady had the prescriptive right to see her home. No carriages ever rolled in the village streets after night; a servant with a lantern marshalled the way, and the lady, escorted by her last partner, was conducted to her home. And as the season drew towards a close, how interesting became those walks! how many words of love were spoken!"

ST. STEPHEN'S

Concerning St. Stephen's Parish, formerly known as Craven County, Dalcho's Church History gives the following information:

"This Parish was taken from St. James, Santee, and was usually called English Santee. It was established by Act of the Assembly May 11, 1754. The Chapel of Ease of St. James' Church fell within the limits of the new Parish, and was declared to be the Parish Church by St. Stephen's.

"The Revd Alex^d Keith, A. M., Assistant Minister of St. Philip's, Charleston, was the first Rector of this Parish. The Church had been the Chapel of Ease to St. James', was old and unfit for use from its ruinous condition, and became too small. The inhabitants petitioned for a new Parish Church. An Act was passed 19 May, 1762, appointing James Pamor, Charles Cantey, Philip Porcher, Joseph Pamor, Peter Sinkler, Peter Porcher, Thomas Cooper, Rene Peyre, and Samuel Cordes Commissioners to receive subscriptions, and to build the church on any part of the land of St. Stephen's then used for a church-yard. The Church is one of the handsomest Country Churches in South Carolina, and would be no mean ornament to Charleston. It is of brick and neatly finished. It is on the main river road and about twelve miles from the Santee Canal. Upon a brick on the south side is inscribed 'A. Howard, Ser. 1767,' and on another 'F. Villeponteux, Ser. 7, 1767,' the names of the architects.

"The Church was incorporated February 29, 1788. The family of the Gailliards lie here interred, as do the other old families of the neighborhood."

Connecting the settlers of English and French Santee was the fact that the Echaw, a branch of the Santee River, was settled by families of both, Louis Gourdin established himself there after his flight from his native place in the Province of Artois in France. He was a Huguenot, and like many others refugeed to the Province of Carolina in 1685. He died in 1716 and a mural tablet is found in the Huguenot church dedicated to him in 1860 by the fourth and fifth generations of his descendants.

Some of the Gourdin family moved over to what was afterwards Williamsburg district, among them Peter Gourdin, who married a Miss Singleton. Their daughter, Martha Gourdin, before her marriage to Wilmot G. DeSaussure, was

CHAPEL IN ST STEPHEN'S

known as "Martha, the Gazelle of the Santees." She inherited one-fifth of her father's estate under Act of the General Assembly passed 1791 for the distribution of Intestate Estates; and many interesting deeds bearing on this section of the country are now in possession of the family of the writer, a granddaughter of Martha Gourdin DeSaussure.

In investigating Pen Branch plantation, Williamsburg County, owned by Robert E. Fraser, of Georgetown; J. W. Hinson and J. D. Cummings, of New York, about to be purchased by N. T. Pittman, it is interesting to note, in further connecting Santee and Williamsburg, that this was an original grant to a John Gailliard, in three tracts, in 1768, and he transferred it to Philip Porcher in 1778. In the examination of titles it is stated that this was commonly called Porcher's Old Field lying on Pen Branch. Philip Porcher's father was Peter Porcher, of St. Peter's Parish, and the Porchers were described as owning land in St. Stephen's Parish in 1808. Peter Porcher had two plantations in St. John's Berkeley, Oakfield and Laban, and a tract of land in Prince Frederick Parish (Craven County), containing 1000 acres, bounded by lands of Theodore Gourdin on the northwest and east, and by the Santee River on the south. Peter Porcher's daughter Mary married John Corbett.

Samuel Dubose, Esq., in his Reminiscences of St. Stephen's Parish, written in 1858, says:

"A feature characteristic of this country, and one that deserves notice, is the family burying grounds. After the erection of St. Stephen's Church, the ground about it was the common cemetery, but many persons to this day continue to bury their dead in the old homestead, and chose to lie in death within the precincts of their ancestor's domain; even though perhaps they may have been strangers to it in life. The grave yard was near the house, usually behind the garden. As a precaution against the depredation of wolves, a large hole was dug to the depth of about five feet; a grave was then dug at the bottom of this hole, large enough to hold the coffin—after the coffin was deposited in this receptacle, it was covered with boards, and the whole then filled up. This practice continues to this day. I can hardly enumerate the several grave yards; those which have been latest used are that at Belle Isle for the

Marion's and their descendants; at Maham's for the descendants of Col. Maham; at the Old Field for the family of Philip Porcher; at Gravel Hill for the Palmers; at Hanover in St. John's for the descendants of the St. Julien's; and those at Pooshee and Somerton for the families of the Ravenels and Mazycks. It is not unlikely that there are graves on almost every old homestead in the country. . . .

". . . Some distance beyond the St. Stephen's line, and just below the Eutaw Springs, was another settlement, chiefly of Huguenot families, viz: the Couturier's, Marion's, Gignillat's, Chouvenau's, Gourdin's, &c., besides others of English descent, the McKelvey's, Ervine's, Oliver's, Kirk's, &c. All of these in the course of time were connected by intermarriage. The land was well adapted to the growth of provisions and Indigo, and in consequence of the fertility of the high lands, they escaped the full measure of the calamities with which their neighbors of Stephen's were visited, when the river became unsafe. The same picture of a prosperous and happy condition with which I have introduced this sketch, may be applied to this neighborhood also, and the happiness which is there described, continued to be the portion of the people, until in the course of the Revolutionary War, the British got possession of the State, and established their military posts over every portion of the country."

According to letters of John Rutledge, published in *Russell's Magazine* for June, 1858, Murray's Ferry was in St. Stephen's Parish.

CHAPTER VIII
ST. MARK'S PARISH

S T. MARK'S Parish originally included all the northwestern portion of the State of South Carolina. A list of delegates to Provincial Congress, 1775, "For District Eastward of the Wateree River" named Col. Richard Richardson, Joseph and Ely Kershaw, Matthew Singleton, Thomas Sumter, Robert Patton, William Richardson, Robert Carter and William Wilson. St. Mark's Parish was taken off from the western portion of Prince Fredericks by Act of Assembly 1757. Richard Richardson gave the lands for the church and glebe lands for a parsonage. This church was destroyed by the British soldiers. It was situated about ten miles from the place now known as Wrights Bluff, on the north side of the Santee River.

Camden, Statesburg and Columbia were in the original Parish of St. Mark. The Parish was again divided into Upper and Lower St. Mark's. Lower St. Mark's comprises much of the land in Clarendon County. One of the oldest homes in the Parish is the Col. Warren Nelson house, of which the chimneys have the date 1762 cut in them. The house is situated near Doughty Lake, a few miles below Nelson's Ferry and was the residence of William Doughty, lay reader in Lower St. Mark's. The grounds are set with many beautiful trees and the attitude of this old home is one of culture and hospitality. An extract from a letter of Brig. Gen. Sumter makes a mention of action of the armies in St. Mark's Parish.

". . . before I Return to the Congaree I think to move towards Santee—and endeavor to alarm Lord Rawdon to prevent his Crossing the River, or Removing the post from Nelson's ferry."

155

THE SAND HILLS OF SAINT MARK'S

MILFORD

The country house of John L. Manning, Governor of South Carolina from 1852 to 1853, was Milford, situated in Clarendon County, near Fulton, S. C., in what is called the Sand Hill region of old St. Mark's Parish. The place is sometimes called Manning's Folly, because of such magnificence being placed in such an out-of-the-way spot. To any one familiar with the history of this old settlement, however, the name is not at all applicable.

Laurence Manning, an Irish lad, came to this country with his widowed mother before the Revolution and settled in Virginia. He came to South Carolina as a lieutenant in Lee's Legion, and was distinguished in many battles and by many acts of personal bravery. His exploit of using a British officer as a shield for himself at the battle of Eutaw is the subject of a painting in the State House at Columbia. The South Carolina history of the Mannings starts when Susannah Richardson, daughter of General Richard Richardson and Mary Cantey, married this gallant young officer. After the Revolution, on the organization of the State militia, Laurence Manning was appointed Adjutant General, and held the office until his death in 1804. He also served the State in its legislature. The gallant Irishman and his aristocratic bride founded a family which has given many public-spirited men and women to South Carolina.

John Laurence Manning, the grandson of the founder of the family, and builder of Milford, was twice married, first to Susannah Hampton, and then to Sarah Bland Clark, of Virginia. The handsome home stands on a commanding slope and bluff overlooking a dense swamp, the tops of the trees in the swamp below are on a level with the lower sweep of the hill which Milford crowns with its massive structure of classic proportions and conception.

Inside, the beautiful woodwork of solid mahogany, and the very high ceilings, carry out the idea of elegance and space

156

"MILFORD," WEST OF PINEWOOD

Built by the Second Governor Manning, son of the First Governor Manning and uncle to Richard I. Manning, the Third Governor Manning

From a photo

evidenced in the exterior, and an additional architectural feature is the handsome circular staircase ascending from the front hall. The house is built with two long wings at the rear projecting on each side, so that the house forms a semi-circle, in the center of which, behind the main building, is a bell tower.

A most interesting entrance to the grounds is furnished by the porter's lodge from which a broad carriage road sweeps in a curve to the door of the mansion. Each outbuilding, including the lodge and spring house, is a miniature, minus the wings, of the large establishment, and the whole effect of Milford and its grounds is one of rare unity.

In his day Governor Manning was said to be the handsomest man in South Carolina, and he was a man of genial nature. His home reflected his taste, several massive statures retaining their proportion and beauty by reason of the excellent arrangement of the house. Entrance is gained directly from the portico with its broad columns into a beautifully proportioned hall, from which the circular stairway ascends, while folding doors lead to rooms on either side, giving an air of sumptuous spaciousness. On the left is the library, on the right the drawing-room, and in the rear the dining-room. In Governor Manning's time great alabaster vases of dazzling white stood in the front hall; indeed, the whole house enshrined many art objects of rarity and beauty.

Until after the Civil War the settlement around Milford comprised the families of Richardson, Brailsford, Manning, Nelson, and Cantey, all connected by marriage. Where there was once a flourishing community, and a great deal of political and social activity, there is now nothing but a few shut-up houses in the charge of caretakers. This condition has come about through the decay of the old slave-holding system, and the fact that the farms had to be abandoned for lack of labor, and although some of the men have retained their ancestral homes and acres, they make their residences in the adjacent towns and cities.

No better illustration can be found of the political significance of this now abandoned section than the history of Elizabeth Pierre Richardson. She married one of the Mannings, was a niece of Gov. James B. Richardson, an aunt of John Peter Richardson, Jr., wife of Governor Richard Irving Manning, Sr., mother of Governor John Laurence Manning, of Milford, and grandmother of Richard Irving Manning, the Governor of South Carolina during the world war.

Leslie's Weekly, March 16, 1918, in "Our Roll of Honor," says:

"Has any State in the Union more of a 'War Governor' than Governor Richard I. Manning, of South Carolina? Not only has he contributed in every way possible, officially and personally, to the winning of the war, but also every male member of his family wears the country's uniform (with the exception of his youngest son, a boy of fifteen)" . . . (six sons being in service) . . . "Capt. William Sinkler Manning is regimental adjutant of the 316 Infantry; Capt. Bernard Manning is in the 316 Regimental Field Artillery; Major Wyndham Manning is Major of Field Artillery, 156 Brigade; Burrel Deas Manning and John Adger Manning are in the Field Artillery, as is Vivian Manning."

Major William Sinkler Manning was one of the sons of Carolina who "paid the price" that Freedom's flag should remain unfurled. Mrs. William Sinkler Manning, who was a Miss Brodie, a granddaughter of Alexander Shepherd (former Governor of the District of Columbia), who now resides in the National Capital, received an official communication from the adjutant general of the American Expeditionary Forces saying that a distinguished service cross had been awarded posthumously to her husband, Major Manning, for "extraordinary heroism in action" near Verdun, France, November 6, 1918. Thus died gloriously, and for God, a noble son of a noble race.

ON THE CAMDEN ROAD IN ST. MARK'S PARISH

THE SINGLETONS AND THEIR HOMES IN ST. MARK'S PARISH

The Singletons were an old and honorable family in the low-country and were first found in the Scotch-Irish settlement in the Williamsburg District. They intermarried with

the old families, including the Richardsons, Canteys and Gourdins, and have been written up many times. "The State" for September 24th, 1916, carries a full and detailed history of them, and one of the most interesting things published in connection with the article is an account of the possessions of the family. These include Matthew Singleton's Commission issued under the crown, dated May 5th, 1770, his commission from the Council of Safety, dated October, 1775, his oath of allegiance, June 7th, 1778, and tax receipts reading —"1773 rec'd The sum of Four Pounds three shillings and 10d, Proclamation money; being for one years Quitrent due to the crown for two thousand and 94 acres of land held by him and situated in Craven County."

Mrs. Leroy Halsey, who was Decca Singleton, daughter of Richard Singleton of "Home Place," has in her possession a photograph of a part of a grant of land given to Matthew Singleton in 1756. This picture and other family relics are among Mrs. Halsey's most treasured possessions in her Charleston home.

MELROSE

"Melrose" is the oldest of the Singleton homesteads still standing. It is situated just off the public road, known in colonial days as the "Great Road from Charleston to Camden." This road led past the present town of Wedgefield through Manchester to settlements beyond. Mr. Thos. E. Richardson, Judge of Probate for Sumter County, says: "Manchester was a thriving little town, before the Revolution and was the head of navigation on Beech Creek for boats that plied between that place and Charleston after 1800. There were no places on the northeast side of the Santee and Wateree Rivers south of Camden where the river approached the high land except at Sumter's Landing near Hagood, and Wrights Bluff. Beech Creek unites with Shank's Creek near Manchester and this enlarged stream used to be navigable for canal boats; so Manchester was a sea port for this section of the country until the Rail Roads broke it up." The Singletons acquired their vast wealth by shipping indigo and later cotton by boat from Manchester.

"Melrose" is a small house but exceedingly quaint. A small one-story piazza extending across the entire front of the house shields two large rooms from the sun. At both gable ends are large chimneys, which are flanked on either side by long narrow windows. Through one of these windows James Singleton was fed by a faithful slave when the British were in this vicinity, he being ill with small-pox. Behind the large front rooms are found two smaller apartments with a hall dividing them and furnishing access to the rear. The hall contains a stairway leading to the rooms above. At the rear end of this hall a large arched doorway leads, by way of a "stoop," directly to the yard.

MIDWAY

The house on the "Midway" estate was a large one and was built by Captain John Singleton, who received the house as a wedding gift from his father, Matthew Singleton. It was named Midway because it lay midway between Melrose and Home Place, two other of the Singleton plantations. On either end of the house a large room was added the width of the house, the two being connected by a passageway. Tradition has it that Captain Singleton took great pleasure in entertaining members of the Legislature, who passed the house on horseback during Christmas holidays.

John Singleton married Rebecca Richardson, daughter of General Richardson. She was the widow of a Mr. Cooper, a man whom she had married at the age of sixteen, against the wishes of her father. Mary Singleton, daughter of John and Rebecca Singleton, married George McDuffie in 1829. McDuffie was left a widower with one child a year later. This child became the wife of Wade Hampton, Governor of South Carolina. Although George McDuffie died at the Singleton home, he owned a house called "Cherry Hill" in Abbeville District. McDuffie was one of the most brilliant orators of South Carolina. He was Governor of the State in 1834 and was a member of the United States Senate in 1842. Mr. McDuffie was never strong after his duel with Colonel Cunningham in 1820, but he did not die until 1851.

SINGLETON HALL

Irving, in his "History of the Turf in South Carolina," says that "Home Place" or "Singleton Hall" is situated on the line of the Charleston and Camden turnpike, which is skirted for many miles in front of the estate by a beautiful hawthorn hedge, the growth of many years. Fronting the house is a park of nearly fifty acres, with fine forest trees laid out in lines radiating from it to the public road. Nothing can surpass the picturesque beauty and effect of the partial views obtained through the vista of the trees of the massive columns which support the entablature of this splendid mansion, as seen from a distance. The approach to it is up through a broad avenue shielded on either side by "brave old oaks." Within this park the training course is laid out, an exact mile in circuit, so that the horses may be seen taking their exercise. One straight side of the course running parallel with the house is so near that orders can be given the trainers or jockies from the piazza.

"The racing stables are situated immediately in the rear of the house, with the paddocks on either side. Everything is substantially built and in perfect order, and there is no want of room, or convenience of any kind, manifest in the details.

"The elegant and refined hospitality of Singleton Hall, a noble mansion, as eminent for its beauty and the taste with which the extensive grounds are laid out, as for the courtesy and considerate kindness which characterizes the proprietor. Aside from the interest with which we regard this princely estate from its great extent, its high state of cultivation, the perfect order and good taste so apparent in its minutest details, and the associations connected with it as the time-honored seat of the distinguished family of its present owner, it had a peculiar charm as being the nearest approach to an American idea of the residence of

" 'The fine old English Gentleman
All of the olden time.' "

The house at "Home Place" (or as it was later called Singleton Hall), was built by Richard Singleton, son of John

11   161

and grandson of Matthew Singleton. He was a man of ample means and entertained royally. It is said that it took him two hours to dress in the morning, and that while he was adjusting his cravat and combing his hair, a la pompador, his wife read the Bible and newspapers to him. Upon being twitted by his neighbors for being late to business, he replied, "It did not matter when you started, but what you did after starting." He was evidently a man of strong personality and was loved by all who knew him.

Richard Singleton owned several other plantations in addition to Home Place, among them were Gilman's; Headquarters or Kensington, near the Acton station; The Fork; Scott; Gadsen; and True Blue, the name of the latter having been derived from the fact that this was once an indigo plantation.

"Home Place" was the scene of the marriage of Angelica Singleton, daughter of Richard, to Col. Abram Van Buren, son of President Van Buren. At this wedding the rare and beautiful Singleton silver was used, as was also the glass and china. It is said that Richard Singleton was the first to introduce silver forks in the family, and that the children always spoke of them as "Uncle Singleton's Split Spoons."

The following interesting story is told of how Angelica Singleton met her husband; "To complete her education, as was fitting her station, she was sent to school to Mme. Greland's in Philadelphia. In 1827 she spent a portion of her holiday in Washington with her kinswoman, Mrs. Dolly Madison, who took pleasure in introducing her to President Van Buren. As she was a girl of rare beauty and charm, she at once became a reigning belle and one year later was married from her home 'Home Place,' to Major Abram Van Buren, eldest son of the President, a graduate of West Point, an officer in the army, and who at the time was acting as his father's private secretary. Mrs. Van Buren made her appearance as mistress of the White House on New Year's Day, shortly after her marriage (1838). The newspapers of the day spoke of her as bearing the fatigue of the three house levee with patience and pleasantry which must have been inexhaustible." Mrs. Van Buren was a very beautiful woman, a portrait of her shows her with her hair piled high, bunches of curls clustered on each side of her face, and a number of ostrich feathers towering above all this. Her descendant, Mrs. Helen Coles Singleton Green, of Columbia, possesses many interesting relics of her distinguished ancestress.

"Kensington" or "Headquarters," was willed by Richard Singleton to his son Matthew, who built a home there, which is now one of the handsomest places in Richland County. It was saved during the Civil War by the intrepid and courageous appeal of Mrs. Singleton's mother to a young northern soldier who had been sent to fire the building. She saved the home and possibly the life of the youth, as Hampton's Scouts heard of the proposed burning and came riding hard upon the heels of the would-be incendiary. The house is built in the shape of a cross, with wings on either end and the wing in the rear being balanced by a *porte cochere* extending from the roof of the front porch.

Matthew Singleton is described as being "a spirited and accomplished young gentleman, who inherits a large portion of his father's taste for fine horses, and who, we trust, will one day succeed him on the Turf." As Halsey children will inherit Singleton trophies, brief extracts concerning their paternal ancestry are given.

Thomas Olney, the ancestor of the Olneys in America, had his birthplace in Hertford, Hertfordshire, England. He received a permit to emigrate to New England April 2nd, 1635, and came to Salem, Mass., by the ship *Planter*. In January, 1636, he was appointed a surveyor, and granted 40 acres of land at Jeffrey Creek, now known as Manchester, near Salem. He was made a freeman the same year and early associated with those who accepted the peculiar views of Roger Williams. With a number of others he was excluded from the colony March 12th, 1638, and with Roger Williams and eleven others formed a new settlement at the head of Narragansett Bay which they named Providence, in grateful remembrance of their deliverance from their enemies. They thus became the "Original Thirteen Proprietors of Providence," having purchased their rights from the Indians.

George W. Olney, son of Captain Olney (named for George Washington, under whom his father had served), passed his childhood and early manhood on his father's farm at Providence. After the war of 1812 he made several business ventures to Southern ports, which led him to think so favorably of Charleston, S. C., that he made it his permanent home. His wife was Olive Bartlett, of Williamstown, Mass., and their daughter, Maria, married Capt. E. L. Halsey in 1870.

Concerning Captain Halsey's ancestors we find among the records of the town of Lynn, Mass., which have survived a fire, that in 1638 Thomas Halsey was allotted one hundred acres of land. His coming to America was apparently connected with the colonization enterprizes of which John Winthrop became leader. In the history of New England from 1630 to 1649 Halsey's name is mentioned frequently in connection with the religious upheaval in the colony at the time.

Captain and Mrs. Halsey had a large family, members of which are now identified with Charleston's social and business life. One of the sons, Leroy Halsey, married Decca Coles Singleton, who has in her possession a decanter which was used at Melrose plantation, Sumter County, in 1760, and later was in use at Midway, then at Home Place and Black Woods, all of which were plantations of the Singleton family.

ON THE ROAD TO STATEBURG AFTER LEAVING THE SINGLETON ESTATES

After leaving Wedgefield, on the road to Stateburg, the following houses are found: The first is Argyle, recently the home of Miss Mary McLaurin, where General Greene had his headquarters just before the battle of Eutawville. Number two is found on the same side of the road, the right, and is known by the name of The Oaks. It is a tall wooden house set on a hill quite a distance back from the public road, which forms a fine approach to the structure and sets off the colonial portico that adorns the façade of this building. The house has fine woodwork inside, although very plain.

The situation of this home is particularly interesting, as it is built on the crest of a hill on the watershed of the Santee and

Black Rivers, the waters from the front flowing west to the Santee, and those from the back draining east to the Black River. Mr. Screven Moore now owns this property, the house having been built either by a Bracey or a James, probably the latter, as the place was once known as James Hill, but has since been changed to The Oaks.

The next house above The Oaks is built in the same style, set on a high brick foundation with two stories above, and belongs to Mr. William Flood. In the vicinity of these three houses already mentioned, and on the other side of the road, was the old Richardson house, at which Dictator Rutledge stayed when he made his quarters in the high hills of Santee. This place is called Bloomhill, and is now in the possession of Mr. Thomas Richardson, Judge of the Probate Court, Sumter, S. C.; Mrs. Mary Ellen Alexander, and Mrs. H. Pinckney.

Continuing the journey from Wedgefield north, there is a very interesting house north of the Flood place which was, for many years, the home of the Reese family. It is a mellow old house, placed close to the ground, the lower rooms being used by the family as living-rooms.

A little above the Reese house comes in the road from Sumter. Upon this road about six miles distant are found the residences of the Nelsons, Andersons and Friersons, a portion of the Frierson place being a very old house. The place is known by the name of Cherry Dale. The Frierson family came to South Carolina about 1730 and formed a part of the Scotch-Irish settlement in Williamsburg Township. One of the locks of the Santee Canal bears the name of John Frierson. Mr. James Nelson Frierson, recently elected dean of the University of South Carolina Law School, is a grandson of the builder of Cherry Dale.

Leaving Cherry Dale and returning toward Stateburg, on the right-hand side of the road is found the Reynolds house, for many years the home of Mr. Mark Reynolds, of Sumter Bar. The parsonage intervenes here, a bleak old wooden house set on a bare hillside, while to the west of the place stands the home which goes by the name of The Ruins, which place very much resembles Hopseewee in general appearance. It is the home of the Pinckney family, Mrs. Marion DeVeaux Pinckney being the present owner. Mr. Harry Pinckney, a member of this family, was also the owner of a handsome old house in Stateburg neighborhood, which he left to his godson, Ioor Tupper. This house was built by Colonel John Russell Spann, who married the widow Broun (originally Harriet Richardson Singleton). Mr. Pinckney inherited the property through the Spann connection.

This brings us again to the Camden road, and at this juncture the Church of the Holy Cross is found, opposite which is Hill Crest, the home of the Anderson family. Beyond Hill Crest and the church are the following plantations, none of the buildings on which, however, possess any historical interest. They are as follows: Marshton, belonging to William Saunders; Acton, a Ravenel place; the house already mentioned as belonging to Mr. Pinckney; and the plantation of Mr. DeSaussure Bull, adjacent to which is found the Bradley house.

Just where the road turns eastwardly from the Bull place going to the Bradley house is the Sebastian Sumter house. Here is to be found a monument erected to General Sumter bearing the following inscription:

West Side
This stone marks the grave of one of South
Carolina's most distinguished citizens,
T H O M A S   S U M T E R.
One of the founders of the Republic.
Born in Va., Aug. 14, 1734.
Died June 1, 1832.

South Side
Erected by the General Assembly of S. C.
1907.

East Side
He came to South Carolina about 1760
and was in the Indian Service on the
Frontier for several years before settling
as a planter in this vicinity.
Commandant of 6th Regt., S. C. Line,
Continental Estab., 1776–1778.

Brig. Gen. S. C. Militia, 1780–1782.
Member of Continental Congress, 1783–1784.
Member U. S. Congress, 1789–1793, 1797–1801.
U. S. Senator, 1801–1810.

North Side
Tanto Nomini Nullium
Par Elogium.

Beyond the Sebastian Sumter house are a few other old plantations, among which is The Terraces, a Boykin residence, but the house is of no special note. Rembert Hall, in Sumter district, is still standing, and there are also some old, if not antique, houses found in the vicinity of Bradford Springs. St. Philip's Church, at Bradford Springs, St. Mark's Parish, was built in 1843 through the efforts of Mrs. Esther Holbrook, daughter of Theodore Gourdin. Among the contributors were John A. Colcolough, William Burrows, John Bossard, James Gailliard, Porcher Gailliard, Thomas W. Porcher and Charles Sinkler, whose summer homes were in this neighborhood.

HILLCREST

"Hillcrest" is at Stateburg, S. C., and is on the old mail coach road from Charlotte, N. C., to Charleston, S. C., just fifteen miles below Camden. The house is built on the crest of a majestic hill amid a bower of trees and is still in a good state of preservation and replete with associations, relics and legends pertaining to colonial days, the Revolutionary War, the War of 1812, the Mexican War, the war between the States and now sadly connected with the World War, as it was the home of Captain William Harrison Saunders, who was killed in an airplane accident in the fall of 1919. Captain Saunders was an honor graduate of West Point of the class of April, 1917, and went to France in July of that year in the aviation service. He was the first American in observation aviation to go over the German lines on a mission and the first man from our army to be both a pilot and an observer. That he survived this dangerous service is almost a miracle, for the Boches nearly had him twice. It was while he was at Fort Sill, after his return from France, that he met his tragic death.

167

The beautiful sweet-scented gardens at "Hillcrest" are a tangle of shrubs and groups of pyramidal cypress. There one may rest in the portico of the old library, which is a separate building in this garden, or linger beside the old sun dial. There is a large oak on the sloping lawn known as the "Spy Oak" with the girth of two centuries or more and the gnarled "bumps of knowledge" holding fast the secrets of the Tory spies who were hanged from its branches, lending a sinister air to the place. Here Cornwallis established himself, making "Hillcrest" his headquarters while in this vicinity, harassing that gallant and determined band, which, led by the intrepid Sumter (a resident of the high hills of the Santee), carried on their guerilla warfare with such telling effect.

At another period of the Revolutionary War, the American patriot, General Greene was so favorably impressed with the charm and healthfulness of these high hills that he selected this neighborhood in which to encamp his army when rest became necessary, bringing his men here several times to recruit. He made his headquarters on one occasion in this same house which, a short period before, his enemy had appropriated. General Greene left a lasting memorial of his visit by having one of his men brand the opposite doors of the large entrance hall with the letters "C. A." (Continental Army). One of these doors already bore a mark which still remains, which was caused by a blow with the butt end of a musket in the hands of a British soldier during the occupancy of Lord Cornwallis. It was when General Sumter's home in this neighborhood was burned by Tarleton's men that Mrs. Sumter took refuge under the roof of Hillcrest.

Although Hillcrest was for many years the home of the Anderson family and is now in the possession of Mrs. William Saunders (who was before her marriage Katie Anderson), the Revolutionary owners of this historic home were Thomas Hooper, Esq., brother of Wm. Hooper, signer of the Declaration of Independence, and Mary Heron Hooper, his wife. Thomas Hooper died in the year 1795 and his wife in 1820. Their niece and adpoted daughter, Mary Jane Mackenzie, was the daughter of Elizabeth Heron and John Mackenzie, of

"HILLCREST," STATESBURG

Scotland. Her maternal grandfather, Benj. Heron, was for twenty years an officer in the royal navy. His fine portfolio of maps bearing the date of 1720 is well preserved among the relics in the Anderson family. At the time of his death, which occurred in 1770, he was one of his majesty's councilors of North Carolina.

Mary Jane Mackenzie was married January 30, 1818, to Dr. Wm. Wallace Anderson, who was from Montgomery County, Md. He was the son of Col. Richard Anderson of Revolutionary fame and Ann Wallace, whose descent traces back to a brother of the heroic Scotch commander, Sir William Wallace.

Dr. William Wallace Anderson settled at Hillcrest, practicing his profession during a long and honored life. Here was born his sons and his daughters, among whom were General Richard Heron Anderson and Dr. William Wallace Anderson, respectively the ranking officer and the ranking surgeon from South Carolina in the war between the States. Capt. Edward Mackenzie Anderson, another son, was killed in the bloody battle near Williamsburg, May 5th, 1862, while serving as an aid to his brother, General R. H. Anderson.

General Richard Heron Anderson, called "Fighting Dick Anderson," graduated from the United States Military Academy at West Point, July 1st, 1842. He was then sent to the cavalry school for practice at Carlisle, Pa., where he remained until 1843. In 1850 he married Sarah Gibson, daughter of John B. G. Gibson, Chief Justice of Pennsylvania.

Dr. William Wallace Anderson graduated from the South Carolina College in the class of 1846, and later from the University of Pennsylvania in 1849. In 1855 he married Virginia Childs, daughter of Brig. Gen. Thomas Childs, a distinguished officer from Massachusetts.

At Hillcrest died that eminent statesman, diplomat, scientist and botanist, the Hon. Joel R. Poinsett, LL.D., while on a visit (1851) to Dr. Anderson, who was his devoted friend. Though LaFayette never visited here, one of the most cherished possessions of this home is the LaFayette bed, with its eagles and flags and stars. It is a quaint old bed in which

Marquis de LaFayette reposed when he visited Charleston. It was afterwards brought to "Hillcrest" where it remained for many years, being called by the servants "The King's Bed." Speaking of other relics, Mrs. Saunders (writing of her ancestral home) says: "Each child in the family has sipped from General Washington's spoon, and viewed the candles, yellow with age, taken from the stores of Lord Cornwallis after his surrender at Yorktown. The small Bible lost by General Childs during the seige of Fort Erie in 1814 and found at Fort Niagara in 1816, the gaily embroidered priest's robe (the gift of grateful nuns for protection during the Mexican War) and the swords and sashes are all valued by us as family heirlooms."

The fine library contains gems of rare and ancient books, which it has been possible to collect, as this home has been for years owned by a family of scholars. One of the Dr. Andersons, who lived at Hillcrest, was the first person on record who successfully removed the jaw bone for cancer, his patient living for many years in the enjoyment of health and strength. Surgeon William Anderson (son of Dr. Anderson) inherited his father's tastes for natural history and science. While stationed at posts in Texas and New Mexico he became interested in making a collection of rare plants and birds; his finest specimens of the latter were sent to the Smithsonian Institute at Washington, D. C., where his contributions were appreciated as of unusual interest and value. He also discovered and forwarded to Washington an entirely new species of bird, and in the grounds of the old home in South Carolina still bloom fragrant shrubs which he sent there from the West so many years ago. As a voluntary observer for many years, his meteorological records were of great value and service to the Weather Bureau at Washington in its research work.

"Hillcrest" is a large brick building so constructed that the ground floor is nearly level with the outside, and follows the colonial plan of placing a building, situated on an elevation, low to the ground in order that the view should be unobstructed. This house is true to this tradition and the observer may stand in the rear door of the living room and on a clear

CORNWALLIS HOUSE, THE OLD KERSHAW HOMESTEAD, CAMDEN
From an old painting

day gaze out over the intervening miles, and behold the smoke rising from the factory chimneys in the city of Columbia, thirty miles away.

Primitive flagstones still form the flooring to the lower piazza of Hillcrest and to several quaint old passages which serve to connect the different parts of this delightfully rambling place, the fitting shrine of so many relics of colonial history. The adjective of mellowness is one that applies with peculiar fitness to "Hillcrest" and "exclusive," carries with it the identical atmosphere produced by this fine old home.

THE CORNWALLIS HOUSE

On an elevation south of the town of Camden, South Carolina, stood a handsome old residence, which was highly prized as an interesting relic of the Revolutionary War. The house was built with materials imported from England, by Colonel Joseph Kershaw, an enterprising pioneer of central South Carolina, several years before the Revolution. It was his elegant and comfortable residence until shortly after the fall of Charleston, in 1780, when the British troops overran the State. Lord Cornwallis, upon his arrival in Camden, took possession of this house for his headquarters.

Col. Kershaw was at this time a prisoner in the Island of Bermuda, and Mrs. Kershaw was subject to the many trials and indignities inseparable from the circumstances. Each fresh arrival of British officers in Camden, among them the merciless Lord Rawdon, brought a repetition of the same indignities. Mrs. Kershaw, unable to endure these any longer, sought refuge in a small house, called "The Hermitage," owned by the family and built in the swamp of the Wateree River.

The mansion fronted to the west, and immediately south of it, only a few hundred yards distant, in the thick pine grove, stretched the long line of American fortifications, the remains of which are still to be seen. Tradition says that an American sharpshooter, hidden in the thicket aimed at a party of British officers, who were playing cards in the southeastern room of the second story and killed one. A spot of blood on the floor

171

(said to have been the Englishman's) always remained an object of interest to visitors.

After the evacuation of Camden by the British, the old mansion house was again occupied by its owners. General Greene's wife, who was then passing through the country on horseback, protected by a detachment of cavalry, became an inmate of its hospitable walls for several days. Upon the slope in front of the house General LaFayette was received on his visit to Camden, in 1825, by a large concourse of citizens; and upon this lawn were held the military reviews on the 4th of July and other public gatherings.

The name of the old residence, "Cornwallis House," and its history, together with the remains of the old Revolutionary cannon, which had been planted in front of the house, were ever a source of interest to strangers visiting Camden. The Cornwallis House was burned to escape Howard's corps of Sherman's army when these vandals passed through Camden in 1865; it having been fired by John Devereaux, C. S. A.

To revert to the early history of the house; it stood on a tract of one hundred and fifty acres, which was surveyed for William Ancrum on June 12th, 1758. An oil painting in the possession of Rev. John Kershaw, rector of St. Michael's Church, Charleston, S. C., only son of General Joseph Brevard Kershaw, shows the house as commanding a view of the parade grounds, while a muster is in progress. Mrs. Royal in her "Southern Tours" writing of the place in 1830 says, "One of the trees, planted as a stake to direct their center march" (reviews of the red coat troops were held in front of the mansion) "is now green and flourishing." Another writer of the same time, says, "The very hawthorn trees by which Lord Rawdon and Col. Balfours ranged their scarlet lines of war are yet among us." In the dining-room of this old home Cornwallis, Rawdon and Tarleton discussed over their grog their wicked schemes and their bloody fingers signed orders for needless executions in the nearby prison pens. Many ghostly stories gather around this house. It is said that American prisoners were hung from the second story windows in the northwest room. The tragic tale of the love of Agnes of Glas-

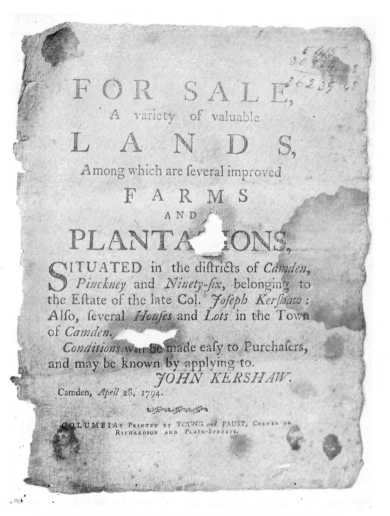

FOR SALE,

A variety of valuable

LANDS,

Among which are several improved

FARMS

AND

PLANTATIONS,

SITUATED in the districts of *Camden*, *Pinckney* and *Ninety-six*, belonging to the Estate of the late Col. *Joseph Kershaw*: Also, several *Houses* and *Lots* in the Town of *Camden*.

Conditions will be made easy to Purchasers, and may be known by applying to.

JOHN KERSHAW.

Camden, *April* 28, 1794.

COLUMBIA: PRINTED BY YOUNG and FAUST, CORNER OF RICHARDSON AND PLAIN-STREETS.

HANDBILL ISSUED IN 1794 ADVERTISING SALE OF KERSHAW LANDS

gow, a Scotch maiden, is as shadowy as it is haunting. It, too, figures in the story of the house that was the headquarters of Cornwallis, whom it is said she loved and followed to America only to find the grave she now occupies near Camden.

The furniture in the house at the time of its confiscation by the British was pitched out of the windows and broken to pieces. The few articles saved had been previously buried, among them a grandfather clock, now in the possession of one of the members of the Kershaw family. The Kershaws have intermarried with the Langs, Shannons, deLoachs and deSaussures and are descended from the Canteys, Douglas and Debose families. Rev. John Kershaw, of Charleston, and his son, Dr. T. G. Kershaw, of North Augusta, South Carolina, and several grandsons are the only descendants of General Joseph Brevard Kershaw now bearing the name.

LAUSANNE

Lausanne, the old Chancellor DeSaussure homestead, is described as being on the Wateree River, near "Camden-town," the site of the famous battle of the Revolution where Lords Cornwallis and Rawdon led the English forces and the gallant De Kalb stuck to his guns until outnumbered and killed. Those were stirring times for Camden, and years after, when the country was becoming prosperous, the town elected to put up a monument to the fallen hero. When the unveiling of the monument took place, LaFayette, who was in the country at the time, was invited to attend the ceremonies. Lausanne was then the show place of the neighborhood; moreover, it had sheltered the most distinguished chancellor, and was famous for its hospitality as well as for its beautiful rose gardens and stately magnolia trees. LaFayette was entertained at Lausanne mansion, and a certain yellow-thumbed manuscript once in the possession of the De Saussure family stated that the aide-de-camp was so struck by a famous portrait of Washington that hung on the wall, that he exclaimed in French: "My friend, God guard you!"

The history of this portrait concerns Lausanne, the home of the DeSaussure, whom Washington appointed director of the mint at Philadelphia, and who afterwards became chancellor. Under his direction and jurisdiction the first gold coins used in the United States were minted. The very first gold coin ever issued used to be treasured at Lausanne, and was kept in the male line of the family until one day a young lady of the family got possession of it and decided to change its form. She thought it would be much nicer to have a ring than a coin to keep, so the old souvenir was merged into a circlet just as the girl's name was afterwards merged into another family name than DeSaussure.

President Washington and Mr. DeSaussure were warm personal friends, and when the latter in 1795 resigned his directorship and prepared to return to the practice of his profession in his native State, he desired a likeness of Washington to take with him. He therefore persuaded the great general to sit to Rembrandt Peale for a picture, which he subsequently carried with him to his South Carolina home. He took with him also the younger Peale, who was himself an artist, that he might find new patrons in Charleston, the then fashionable and prosperous city of the South. This portrait, painted but four years before the death of Washington, hung upon the walls of Lausanne from that time on, narrowly escaping a bayonet stab during the Civil War. Among the yellow documents which are laid to its account is Peale's description of the sitter at the time it was painted, as told by him in a series of lectures which he delivered in various cities of the country in the winter of 1857 and 1858.

"Washington sat to my father and me together," he says, "for the portrait desired by Mr. DeSaussure. He gave us three sittings from 7 to 10 in the morning, and by that means I had the opportunity of seeing him with his hair arranged in a more natural manner than after the barber had arranged it in fashion later in the day. Washington shaved himself before coming to me, and when the powder was washed from his whiskers and the front of his ears the dark brown showed beneath."

The younger Peale goes on to say that there was something in the upper part of the original face painted by his father that he preferred as a likeness, and an expression about the lower

174

"LAUSANNE," THE De SAUSSURE HOME, CAMDEN

Named for the French home of this family. Now a portion of the Public School

part, the mouth and chin, as expressed in his own work, that he judged better. Some years afterward he took the two and worked out a blended likeness with the conception he had kept for years in his own mind as something to aspire to, he having always felt that the first likeness which he painted was not as perfect as he could make.

During the war between the states evil days fell upon old Lausanne. A company of impetuous and war-hardened soldiers, in no very good humor, tramped over the place and stuck their bayonets through such articles of furniture or ornaments as could be stuck through without too much inconvenience. There were a number of good pictures on the walls, some ideal paintings, some portraits, among which was an old gentleman with a benign face. A soldier who was idly lunging at everything on his side of the house, and had let through two or three portraits broad streaks of daylight, felt his arm arrested as he was about to let fly at the dignified old man with the powdered head and the ruffled shirt front.

"Hold on there, you fool; don't you see who that is?" exclaimed a comrade. The vandal looked up at the portrait and his arm dropped to his side.

"By jove," he said, "if I wasn't going to slash old George. I beg your pardon, mister," and making a feigned obeisance he passed on. Thus was saved the portrait, which was later sold.

Although the Civil War was over, terrible times prevailed in Camden and thereabouts. Eleven years after the war the descendants of the old chancellor De Saussure were in sore straits. Lausanne was about to be sold; the cherished acres and associations alike had to be parted with. The plantation further out in Kershaw County was retained to be planted, but the old homestead was given up, and has become a part of what is now known as "Court Inn," in the town of Camden.

MULBERRY

Mulberry, one of the handsomest homes in South Carolina, was the home of the Chestnut family, who located near Camden.

Jasper Sutton, who was a member of a company of frontier rangers, after Braddock's defeat in 1755 moved to South Carolina. The Indians devastated Virginia to such an extent that many families moved south, and with his wife and family, including the Chestnut stepchildren, Jasper Sutton traveled southward. They halted a year in North Carolina, but finally landed in South Carolina on "Granny's Quarter Creek," in what is now known as Kershaw County. John Chestnut was then a lad of thirteen years. About two years later he entered upon an apprenticeship under Joseph Kershaw. The year 1767 found John Chestnut possessed of a considerable amount of land, having risen rapidly to an independent merchant and land holder. The end of the Revolution found him in possession of much property.

In the Revolutionary War, John Chestnut served as a paymaster with the rank of captain, but resigned as unfitted for service, suffering from rheumatism after the battle of Purrysburg. Upon his recovery he entered the militia and served in the Georgia campaign. He commanded the Camden militia in Charleston when that city was besieged, and when the British occupied Camden, John Chestnut was taken prisoner and put in the Camden prison. He was, it is said, chained closely to the floor and to the day of his death bore the marks of iron on his ankles.

James Chestnut, brother of John, owned the property on which Mulberry now stands. James died unmarried and without a will, but had intended that the land go to James Chestnut, 2nd, son of John. John Chestnut, thus inheriting it, left it at the time of his death to his son James.

Through purchase and inheritance James Chestnut, at the time of his death, was the owner of a vast amount of land, an area of about five miles square, extending from the southern edge of Camden down to Daniels' Branch and bounding on the river all the way. His slaves numbered several hundred. Mr. Chestnut not only managed his estates, but he was active in public affairs, being for many years a member of the House of Representatives, and holding various other public offices.

176

"MULBERRY," NEAR CAMDEN

The old home of the Chestnut family, now owned by Mr. and Mrs. David R. Williams

In 1820 Mr. Chestnut built "Mulberry," two miles south of Camden. He used it as a winter residence, the river swamps being so near that it was not considered healthy during the summer months. He would therefore move his family in summer to his Sandy Hill place, three miles east on the uplands. Sandy Hill was burned about 1885. The roads between Sandy Hill and Mulberry were a bee line and were kept in excellent condition, and it is said in order that Mr. Chestnut might ride at a swift pace—his coach was always attended with outriders.

Mulberry, the old manorial hall, is a four-story brick and stone mansion. It is approached by an avenue of oaks and is surrounded by beautiful laurel trees. The exterior of the house is simple, but the interior is quite out of the ordinary, the woodwork being particularly interesting. The state and style of life proceeding in the South can have no better illustration than this old home and the manner in which it was conducted. It is said that Mary Cox, the wife of James Chestnut, although the mother of thirteen children, found time each day to teach her retinue of slaves. The school is supposed to have been held in one of the brick outbuildings.

Mulberry is now the home of Mr. and Mrs. David R. Williams, descendants of the Chestnut family.

CHAPTER IX

FROM DOVER TO CALAIS VIA THE PARISHES OF CHRIST CHURCH AND ST. THOMAS

CHRIST CHURCH PARISH

IN Christ Church Parish many large plantations and interesting places are found. On one of these stands a brick pillar, one of two, that marked the northern boundary of William Hort's plantation. Northeast of this the corresponding pillar stands and is found deep in the woods. In olden times there was also a town called Tarleton nearby Mr. William Lucas' plantation, which was called "Barrack's Old Field," because at one time this place contained the remains of some old cavalry barracks built of lime and shell such as constitute the remains of the Greenwich Village Mills seen in that locality.

Out from the town the larger plantation houses are located at or near the waters that make this body of land into a peninsula. A few houses have been mentioned in connection with the upper reaches of the Wando River as being situated in the Parish of St. Thomas. The planters nearer the sea coast desired and had a parish of their own, with a church building erected thereon conveniently placed for the use of themselves and families. This was called Christ Church Parish and the church is about six miles out from Mt. Pleasant village. There is nothing very remarkable about it except its age. It is a small square brick edifice surmounted by a cupola. It is surrounded by graves that are older than the church itself. Miss Mabel Webber has published in the *South Carolina Historical Magazine* interesting extracts from the Parish Register. The inside of the church is in no way remarkable, the chief feature being the simplicity of its furnishings. Jacob Motte, Esquire, in

1763 gave the communion plate, a chalice and a paten, still in use at Christ Church.

This parish was established by Act of Assembly November 30, 1706; and its boundaries defined by an Act of December 18, 1708, as follows: "to the North east by a large creek or river, commonly called Awindaw Creek or Seawee River, being the bounds of Craven county, to the South-East by the sea, to the West by Wando River, and to the North-West partly by the said River, and partly by a line drawn from the Cowpen of Capt. Robert Daniel, or the Swamp at the head of the Wando River exclusive, to the Cowpen of Joseph Wigfal, on the head of the said Awindaw Creek or Seawee River inclusive."

The first church was begun in 1707, but was not completed for some years. This church was accidently burned in February 1724/5, but was almost immediately rebuilt, and was again burned by the British in 1782, the present church was built after 1800. The following advertisement fixes an approximate date for the rebuilding of the church. It is headed: *Christ Church Parish April 21, 1787*, and says, "Whereas the Vestry and Church wardens of the Episcopal Church in the parish of Christ Church, have resolved to rebuild the church and vestry house, as speedily as possible; therefore public notice is hereby given to any person or persons that are inclined to undertake the rebuilding of the same." Signed by the Church wardens.

Near the Church on Wando River side, reached by an avenue of fine old oak trees, stands Boone Hall plantation which contains a quaint old house built in the early eighteenth century. It has been considerably altered during the lapse of years, the chief architectural feature, however, being found in its unusually well constructed slave quarters. The place gets its name from the Boone family, and in the family burying ground adjacent to the house a Daniel Boone lies buried.

This plantation passed into the hands of the Horlbeck family and Miss Marie Horlbeck (whose father was a nephew of Major Horlbeck) is authority for the statement that Boone Hall was bought by the Horlbecks on account of the great number of slaves the Horlbecks possessed and the capacity this plantation had for accommodating them. Color is given to the theory by the fact that a description of this place mentions "miles of pasture upon which fine stock is raised, brick and tile works on Horlbeck Creek, the gin houses, stables, barns and dozens of little cottages where the several hundred slaves have their home—not in a negro quarter but dotted about over the country, each with its little patch of land for the tenant."

This description bears out a statement published in *The New York Sun*, concerning negro education, which says:

"It will perhaps astonish a great many complacent and unsuspecting persons in this part of the country to hear it said that a very considerable number, if not a majority, of the old-time great Southern slave-holders were heartily opposed to the 'institution.' Such is the truth, nevertheless, as every one familiar with the inner history of that section knows full well . . . To put it briefly, we may say that before 'Uncle Tom's Cabin' saw the light, and while as yet the great slave-holding magnates of the south regarded slavery as an establishment beyond the reach of social agitation or political vicissitude, wise and kindly members of the ruling class had conceived and set in operation a system whereby slavery could be robbed of all its most repulsive aspects and transformed into an agency of exaltation. Thus it came about that schools were established on hundreds of plantations; nothing like our modern schools, of course, but just plain simple agencies of experiment and observation. The idea was to disclose the special gifts and tendencies of the pupils and having ascertained them, perfect and develop. So it followed that thousands of slaves became bricklayers, carpenters, blacksmiths, tailors, engineers, sugar boilers, artisans of every kind, even musicians, and were permitted to pursue their vocation in perfect freedom, merely paying to their masters a small percentage on the assessed value of the individual earnings after graduation."

Miss Horlbeck stated that there were thirteen Horlbeck brothers; that the persons who bought Boone Hall were the generation following John and Peter Horlbeck, identified in local history as the men in charge of altering the post-office.

Interesting history is given concerning this family in an account of the Fusilliers by John A. Moroso. "Mr. John Horlbeck, one of the privates in the original Fusilliers, who did such valiant service for America and Charleston during the Revolutionary War, particularly at the siege of Savannah, when the corp after heroic action reached home (under the command of Lieuts. Strobel and Sass) sadly diminished.'' Soon after these events, 1780, Charleston fell into the hands of the British. The Continental Fusilliers were compelled to disband and relinquish one hundred superior muskets which had been presented to them by the British officers in control. Mr. Horlbeck had carried his gun in the seige of Savannah and did not relish giving it up, so he hid it by dropping it between the wainscoting of his home and the wall. He then surrendered another gun and this historic fussee has been in possession of the Horlbeck family ever since. As an instance of logevity given in Mills statistics is found the name of Mr. John Horlbeck, ''born in Saxony, lived in Charleston 44 years and never took a dose of medicine in his life, died at the age of 80.''

The last owner of Boone Hall was the late Major Horlbeck, whose grandfather had planted a few pecan trees around Boone Hall. Finding these to have flourished they were left when other trees were cut down. From this small beginning and a great expenditure of time, trouble and money, Major Horlbeck developed a large industry and had the satisfaction of seeing his experiments succeed. In 1904 he was credited with owning the largest pecan grove in the world.

OAKLAND

Oakland Plantation, in Christ Church Parish, Charlestown County, is eight miles out from the village of Mt. Pleasant, on the Georgetown road, and was granted in a tract of one thousand three hundred acres, by the Lord Proprietors in 1696 to Captain George Dearsley but was settled by John Abraham Motte as agent for John Perrie (a later owner) then of Antigua, formerly of Youghal, Ireland. It was named Youghal in honor of Perrie's birthplace and this name was retained through the successive ownerships of Cleland, Benison and Barksdale, only to be later renamed Oakland.

As Thomas Barksdale in his will dated July 2nd, 1850, refers to ''my plantation called Youghal, my residence,'' the name must have been changed to Oakland by his son-in-law,

James Macbeth, next owner. This was done in recognition of the magnificent avenue of live oaks, which was either planted or extended by one of the Mrs. Barksdales, perhaps Mary, wife of Thomas the First. An old slave named Cain Bryan, who was living on the place when it passed from James MacBeth to Philip Porcher, said that in his boyhood he remembered going into the woods with his mistress to select the trees to transplant from the forest to the avenue.

At the time that Mr. Porcher came into possession, Oakland was a thoroughly equipped plantation and country estate, comprising in its grounds extensive gardens and an orchard. The outside buildings included the regulation plantation kitchen with brick oven in the side of the chimney, a brick smoke-house and a brick dairy (which flanked the house at the head of the avenue), a carriage house, a barn and gin house, poultry houses, extensive negro quarters, and last but not least a day nursery for the little slave children, who were left there during the work hours of their mothers in the care of an old "Maumer."

The dwelling house at Oakland is an unpretentious but fine example of an eighteenth century plantation home, with quaint Dutch roof and large living-rooms, with chimneys in the corner of each room, and odd seats in the upstairs dormer windows. The timbers of this building are hand-hewn black cypress and the woodwork indicates that it was done by skilled carpenters among the slaves. The low foundation on which the residence stands is of brick made from oyster-shell lime. The age of the house can only be surmised, but it is apparently the oldest in the parish and was probably built by George Benison or his successor, Thomas Barksdale, about the year 1750, although the exact date cannot be announced. The gable end of this house, with its Dutch roof, is similar to another Motte place, near Monks Corner, which is significant in connection with the fact that a Motte settled Oakland for John Perrie.

The ghost at this fascinating old place is described as a gentle wraith who comes to pray at the bedside of those who sleep in the "Ghost Room," but it is said that she comes very rarely and no one knows who she is or was.

OAKLAND PLANTATION, MT. PLEASANT, FRONT AND REAR VIEWS
A Colonial house now owned by A. K. Gregorie

An interesting story told of the Revolutionary days is that just as the Barksdales were about to dine, a British soldier spurred his horse into the dining-room and carried off from the table, on his sword point, a roasted fowl. Another tradition connected with this historic house is that General Sherman while stationed at Fort Sumter prior to the War of the Confederacy was a welcomed visitor as he was in other homes in and around Charleston. The cause of the general's feeling against South Carolina is said to have had its origin in an affair of the heart. He fell in love with a beautiful Charleston girl, who did not, however, reciprocate his affections but coquetted with him in an obvious manner. This attitude on her part so offended him that he revenged his feelings on the entire South.

The window panes of the dining-room have long been used as a guest's register. Among many other is the signature "I" or "S," William Bull. The oldest inscription is ascribed to Thomas Barksdale and is dated December 21, 1802, but the most interesting pane of glass is no longer in its place. Joseph Pillmoor, one of John Wesley's Missionaries says in his journal that on March 9, 1773, he was at Mrs. Barksdale's where he was kindly received and spent the evening worshipping God and rested in peace. Before leaving he wrote on one of the window panes at Oakland in very clear and well-formed characters:

"Jos. Pillmoor, March 10, 1773.

Exalt Jehovah our God." Followed by the quotation repeated in Hebrew.

This frail memorial went through the perils of two wars and survived in its place more than a hundred years. In October, 1877, it was presented by Mr. Porcher to Wofford College, where it is now framed and hangs in the library.

During the troublous days of the Confederacy while Mr. Porcher was with the army, his young wife and children took refuge with her parents and the plantation, being abandoned, fell on evil days and the house stripped of its belongings. The large wall mirrors were set out on the roadside and used as targets by Union soldiers, while books and book cases were carried away with other furniture. Fences around the place were used as firewood, and goats and cattle destroyed the shrubbery.

At the close of the war during the Federal occupation of the country, Oakland had a narrow escape. Col. Beecher of the Union Army and his wife visited the adjoining plantation, Laurel Hill, then owned by Dr. Peter Porcher Bonneau, one of the signers of the Ordinance of Secession. The house was the handsomest in the parish, but they burned it to the ground, and it is said that Mrs. Beecher set fire to the place with her own hands. Not content with this it is said that they came on to Oakland and Mrs. Beecher had lighted her torch to serve it in like fashion, when some of the slaves on the place begged her to give the house to them to live in instead of burning it. Thus she graciously bestowed it on them, and when Mr. Porcher returned after the war he found each room occupied by a negro family. A "meeting" was in progress in the dining-room, where the sideboard served as a pulpit. The negroes refused to give him possession, saying the house was theirs and he had to appeal to Gen. Sickles, the Union Commander in Charleston, then living in the house on Charlotte Street now occupied by Mr. Sottile, who sent soldiers to clear the house and restore it to the rightful owner.

The dwelling survived the poverty-stricken days that followed the war and though building after building subsequently went down in ruin until of all the buildings, only the smokehouse, dairy and kitchen were left, this dwelling withstood two wars, storms and earthquakes.

In 1917 Mr. Porcher sold Oakland to his daughter Anne, Mrs. Ferdinand Gregorie, and it is now, in the possession of her family, emerging from ruin, and taking again its rightful place as a typical southern home.

The Porchers of Christ Church Parish are descended from Philip E. Porcher, who came to the parish from St. Stephen Parish in 1859, and all of the Porchers are descended from the emigrant, Isaac Porcher.

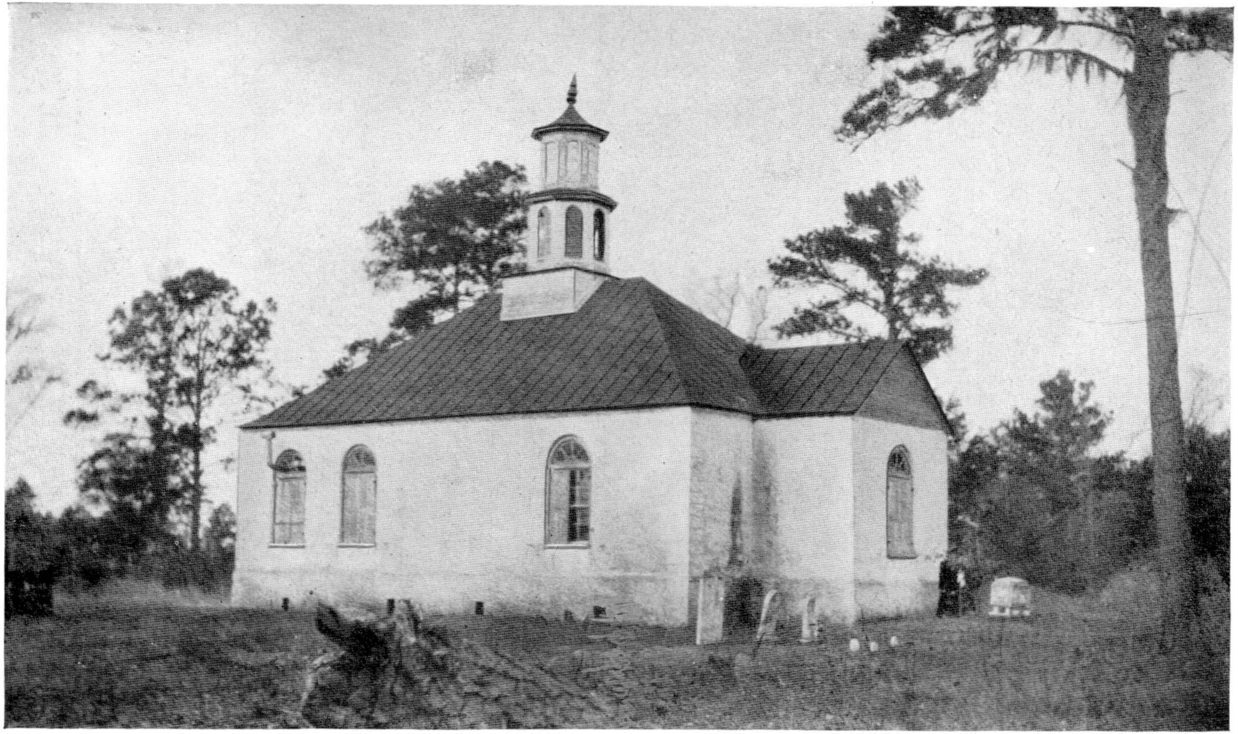

CHRIST CHURCH, CHRIST CHURCH PARISH, NEAR MT. PLEASANT

St. Thomas' Parish lies above Christ Church Parish and adjacent to many of the plantations on the headwaters of the eastern branch of Cooper River. The principal settlement in the Parish of St. Thomas is Cainhoy. Between Oakland and Cainhoy, however, are found several interesting places which are briefly mentioned in the following pages.

ST. THOMAS' PARISH

At Cainhoy is a large old wooden house, one room of which has been converted into a chapel as the few remaining members of the old church find it too difficult to reach the "Old Brick Church," which is three miles away in a southeasterly direction on the Clement's ferry road that leads from the Cooper River to the Santee settlements. Next to the brick church was a place owned by the Sanders family. This place, with several others, is mentioned in a poem written in 1804 by Edward Othmel Gale Brale, describing a trip up the Cooper River, via Wando. He says that where:

> "Cainhoy's stream its silvery waters roll
> Arrive at Williams wharf, with setting day,
> Then to the village soon we bend our way
>
> *   *   *   *   *
>
> Six Buildings stand that grace this silent place
> And dignify its banks with rural grace;
> The dwelling first as sailing up the stream
> Is shut now constant to Sol's golden beam;
> The next just as the other clos'd up fast,
> The Door too fasten'd likely so to last;
> The third now open to Sol's cheering beam
> And near the door a Willow hangs all green;
> Oft have I seen the master of this house
> Walk near this tree in converse with his Spouse;
> They seem'd to live in lonesome, silent love
> With all the fondness of the turtle dove;
> 'Twas he that gave this little Village birth
> And tryd to make it rise to real worth;
>
> *   *   *   *   *
>
> The fourth a Mansion Mrs. Pinckney owns,
> 'Twas there I first did rest my languid bones;
> The fifth the house of Mr. L. Wigfall
> Lays open to the Goats and comers all;
> The Six the property of Miss Gailard

185

> Out buildings numerous with a spacious yard;
> (To me this Mansion did she freely lend,
> To her my heart felt gratitude I send
> Accept the loan and thank my unknown friend);''

The poet remained at Cainhoy for four months, when leaving he waved farewell and,

> "Old Saunders quick return'd it with his cap;
> His House stands near to Cainhoy Cooling Stream.''

The Wando River has no prettier spot upon its banks than the little green gem of a peninsula upon which stands the buildings of the Beresford Bounty, over which seems to brood the very spirit of quietude and calm loveliness, typical of the charity which has existed here for nearly two hundred years. On March 17, 1721, died Richard Beresford, Esq., who bequeathed the net profits of his estate to the vestry of St. Thomas' Parish in trust until his son, then eight years, should reach his majority. One-third of the interest was to be paid to schoolmasters and the rest to support and educate the poor children of the parish. The sum amounted to £5200. In 1739 the school was built. In 1763 the Rev. Alex Garden, as rector and schoolmaster, reports the school as flourishing. This continued until the Revolution, when the fund had accumulated to £12,800, but was reduced by the general bankruptcy that followed. By careful management it had increased to $70,000 in 1861, when it was again dissipated by the disastrous ending of the war. The population of the parish is now much reduced, the Legislature has relieved the vestry from the necessity of boarding, housing and clothing the children, but instruction is still given in the school house, the rector of the parish being the principal. The public schools have superseded this fine charity.

Near where School House Creek makes into Cooper River stood a two-story house made of cypress cut out of the nearby swamps by the slaves. This old mansion was set on a high brick foundation arched underneath. The negro quarters and outhouses are built of brick, nearby on the Grove plantation is the part of an old wine house.

There is on the Wando River only one old house of any importance which is still habitable. Most of these plantation houses were burned during the Civil War, or have been destroyed since by fire. Charleywood Plantation, seven miles out from Christ Church Parish, immediately adjoins Chantilly. The Charleywood property belonged during a period antedating the Civil War to the Wigfalls, but very little of its early history is known.

Lachicotte's place is found near Guerins Bridge, in Berkley County, which bridge crosses a branch of the Wando River. This place was near Charleywood and Chantilly, nearer in towards Mt. Pleasant. Right back of Daniels Island on the mainland in the Parish of St. Thomas on Mt. Pleasant side is a Shingler place. On this place used to reside Mr. Elfe, who married a Miss Lucas. One of his daughters still lives in Charleston. Very little can be ascertained of the history of this old home.

Another old house used as a refuge for soldiers during the Revolution stands on the mainland in Berkley County, behind Daniels Island, on a plantation called Hartford, owned by W. L. Venning, Jr., who resides in the Court House Square in Charleston. The house at Hartford has an avenue of oaks leading to it that is especially beautiful. A double row was set out about one hundred and fifty years ago, says Mr. Venning, with spikes driven into the heads to make the trees spread out. The limbs now touch the ground. The house is fully as old as the avenue. The bricks of which it is built came from England.

Several fine old houses used to be found on Daniels Island, a part of the Parish of St. Thomas lying west of the Wando River. One place in particular was said to have been built by Robert Hazelhurst, (whose town house on Lower Meeting Street has recently been remodeled by Dr. A. E. Baker). It contained mahogany floors as well as doors, mahogany beams and closets and paneling, which dated from the days when Robert Hazelhurst traded with the West Indies. Another old place found on this island is ''Yellow House,'' its name being taken from a nearby creek of that name.

CHAPTER X

ON THE ASHLEY RIVER AND IN SAINT ANDREW'S PARISH

THE GIBBES HOUSE ON CHARLESTON NECK

COLONIAL place commonly known as the Gibbes house on Charleston Neck is the house still standing on the bank of the Ashley River. According to Judge H. A. M. Smith, on March 2nd, 1701, a grant was made to Patrick Scott for one hundred and ninety acres on Charleston Neck, the boundaries showing that it included all of the Joseph Dalton grant lying to the west of the part held by Joseph Blake. Scott must have therefore acquired from the transferees of Jane Lawson all this remainder and taken out a new grant to himself. In addition to other legal matters connected with this and other adjoining lands in a deed from Patrick Scott to Richard Cartwright dated 31st of October, 1710, it is recited that this one hundred and ninety acres was a parcel of a greater quantity of land formerly granted to Joseph Dalton.

Some time later, under the will of Richard Cartwright, who had acquired a great deal of that land, much of the property passed to his three sons, Daniel, Richard and Hugh. A greater part of the one hundred and ninety acres, with additional land to the north fell to the portion given to Daniel Cartwright, who conveyed it in 1738 to John Braithwaite. It then passed to John Gibbes, but from whom John Gibbes acquired it has not been ascertained. It was certainly in his possession in 1769 when he obtained a grant of the marsh land fronting on the river. Gibbes' property has been generally known as the "Grove" farm or plantation and embraces the area between Congress Street and the Creek north of the farm lately owned by Captain F. W. Wagner and which was long known as

188

Lowndes' Grove and The Rose Farm. Lowndes Grove was famous as a field of honor and many famous duels took place there, the most noted being a duel with swords between General Christopher Gadsden and General Howe.

Some of the most noted duels of the nineteenth century were between Wilson and Simons, Hunt and Ramsey, Craft and Boy, Reynolds and Brawley, Robertson and Waring, Cohen and Moise, and other encounters of a later date well known to the old inhabitants of the community. The last duel in the State occurred in 1880, but did not take place in Charleston. A famous book written by John Lyde Wilson and published in Charleston in 1858 was an acknowledged authority in matters of honor in the State as long as the practice continued. The book is an interesting contribution to the ante-bellum literature of the South.

According to popular tradition a favorite meeting place was upon that rise of land now included in Hampton Park just to the rear of the new citadel. The Washington race course was upon a portion of this tract and after 1794 the old course at " New Market " was abandoned and the Jockey Club held its races on the new course. The present Hampton Park which included the race course is on the "Grove" plantation. At the entrance to the old race course stood some interesting brick pillars which were taken down in 1902. Replicas of these are to be found marking the entrance to Hampton Park Terrace, and all of this tract was held by John Gibbes in 1769.

The John Gibbes who owned the Grove tract was not the first man of that name, for it is found on a highly colored memorial tablet on the wall of Goose Creek Church " Under this Lyes the late Col John Gibbes/Who deceased on the 7th of August 1711/Aged 40/"

Col. John Laurens reported that his battalion had been posted near this old place during the Revolution to "watch the enemy and prevent too sudden an approach. As soon as I received notice of their advance I went forward with Major (Hyrne) to reconnoitre them. We went rather too near, for single horsemen, to the yagers, who fired from behind trees on each side of the road. The Major was unfortunately wounded in the cheek. . . . The violence of the blow dismounted him, and I had barely time to cover his retreat and drive off his horse. A Hessian seized the Major's hat, but did not enjoy the trophy long, being killed in the skirmish which ensued, and the trophy was recovered.'' Other extracts establish the fact of a ferry being opposite the house and that this place was the scene of several sharp encounters during the Revolutionary War.

Peter Timothy, who was posted in St. Michael's steeple as a lookout for the Americans and who made daily reports of what he saw through his spy glasses, had given as his report on March 24th that tents had been taken from T. Horry's house and carried beyond E. Horry's, and he had kept a pretty strict watch for he says that ''the redout begun at the latter's landing last night (March 23rd) and was completed by 10 this morning and at half-past ten Lord Cornwallis and a Hessian general, with the usual attendants, with spy glasses, etc., viewed the several works and seemed to pay particular attention to Gibbes' place.'' Later on Gibbes' place is described as being ''Up the Path,'' an idiom meaning the main path from the city through the forest precincts.

John Gibbes at the outbreak of the American Revolution had extensive gardens and greenhouses and a pinery on the Grove, but when the British under Prevost advanced and threatened Charleston in May, 1779, they crossed the Ashley River at Ashley Ferry and advanced down the Neck to Gibbes' settlement at the Grove, and during the occupation the terraces and greenhouses were destroyed.

Mrs. E. H. Pringle, Chairman of the Colonial Exhibits held in this building in 1902 at the time of the West Indian Exposition, in a contemporary account of exhibits of the Colonial Dames of America is an authority for the statement that this house was built by Mr. Gibbes.

''They have an appropriate background or setting for this exhibit in the old colonial house, which will form a part of the woman's building. This house was built before the Revolution by Mr. Gibbes and the grounds were beautiful with many rare flowers and imported plants. The British soldiers wilfully

THE GIBBES HOUSE, CHARLESTON NECK, SOMETIMES CALLED THE LOWNDES HOUSE

laid waste this lovely garden, and this so affected and distressed Mr. Gibbes that he died in consequence. There is no trace now of the fine garden, but some old oaks remain near the house. . . . Three rooms and a large hall have been devoted to the colonial exhibit. These rooms remain as originally built, with wainscoting and the old high mantels. A colonial dining-room and bedroom will be represented, with the fine old furniture of that date. . . . A large committee has been formed and Mrs. Drayton-Grimke, with the assistance of twelve ladies, will have charge of the furnishing of the drawing-room. Mrs. Langdon Cheves, with twelve others, will present a picture of the dining-room of our forefathers. Mrs. Arnoldus Vander Horst, with a score of helpers, will furnish forth the great wide hall.''

An account of the exhibit given by the Daughters of the American Revolution furnishes interesting data concerning this place and from it we learn that at the southeast corner of the house is one of the handsomest rooms, that the walls are beautifully wainscoted with black cypress and that it is in as sound a state of preservation as the day it was placed in position. The house itself is built entirely of black cypress and cedar put together with old-fashioned hand-made nails. The paneling in all the rooms is very beautiful and the house itself is built on the square colonial style, having an inclosed loggia in the brick basement which forms the first story of the house. Big fireplaces with finely carved mantels are found through the house. At the time of the Exposition a fine portrait of Washington and a portrait of his kinsman, Col. William Washington, and one of Col. Joseph Habersham, the first Postmaster General of the United States, hung over the colonial mantels. Among other pictures gathered together at this time was a curious engraving showing General Marion inviting the British officers to share his dinner of sweet potatoes, and another of the General crossing the Pee Dee River with his men in flat boats. There was also a copy of the General Proclamation of Peace (1783), and one rare engraving showed Washington being blessed by his mother before departing for battle.

191

In this old house at the time of the Exposition there were numerous pieces of historic furniture, duplicates of which will only be found in the collection at Mt. Vernon.

The house is now in the possession of Mr. and Mrs. James Sottile, and Mrs. Sottile in restoring this place, which had fallen into disrepair, has treated the Gibbes house with the respect that its history demands. She has sought to preserve in every way the simplicity of the original lines both inside and outside the house. Wherever possible, she has left the original work, notably in the instance of the rooms on the second floor and the beautiful circular stairway and skylight above. The massive front door still presents the appearance of being able to fulfill its function of withstanding attacks that it had seen many times in Indian days, as do also the heavy wooden shutters to the windows of the lower floor. In the inside lintels of the front door are still to be found the iron rests on either side used to hold in place the stout oaken rods that barricaded the door. The interior decorations are all of the Adam period, and "The Grove" has been restored very carefully, and as far as was possible in exact duplicate of its original woodwork and carvings.

DORCHESTER AND BEYOND

"About twenty-six miles from the city of Charleston, on the north bank of the Ashley River, and about six miles in a southwestwardly direction from the railroad depot in the present town of Summerville can be seen an old church tower with an overgrown disused graveyard around it, and some two hundred paces farther on—on the edge of the river—are the walls of an old fort, constructed of that mixture of shells in lime mortar formerly called 'tapia' or 'tabby.' These two conspicuous objects, with some scattered and shapeless masses of brick at irregular intervals, marking the sites of former houses, are all that remain of the town of Dorchester, once a comparatively flourishing hamlet in the Low-Country of South Carolina, but which with the lesser hamlets of Jamestown, New London or Willtown, Jacksonborough, Purrysburgh and Somerton, and the still lesser, or only projected, villages of

192

Radnor, Ashley Ferry, Childsbury and Chatham, has so long been deserted that its story has been nearly forgotten, and its very site nearly obliterated." So says an extract from "A Sketch of the History of Dorchester," which was published in the *South Carolina Historical Magazine*.

St. George's Church was built about the close of the Proprietary Government and commencement of Royal Government, 1719. The tower or steeple of this church is built after a design by Sir Christopher Wren, "that little bird who was fond of putting up large nests," and on April 9, 1734, an act was passed for "repairing and enlarging and pewing the Parochial Church of St. George's Parish in Dorchester."

THE VICINITY OF DORCHESTER

Above and beyond Dorchester, near the road to Bacon's Bridge, was Fair Spring, another Izard residence, situated on the old grant to William Norman, and sometimes called "Burtons." Above this again was the site of the original grant to Benjamin Waring, the ancestor of the Waring family and during the Revolutionary War was owned by Dr. David Oliphant, a member of the Council of Safety and Surgeon-General of the Continental forces in South Carolina. Contiguous to this lay the old grant made to Col. Andrew Percival and known as "The Ponds" (the chief pond now being "Shulz's Lake").

Of all the places in this vicinity, however, that containing the best outbuildings, and most pretentious mansion house was at "Newington," the old Axtell settlement, which descended through Lady Axtell's daughter, Lady Elizabeth Blake, to Col. Joseph Blake. The Newington house was said to have been one of the largest brick houses built in lower Carolina at that period, and with its double avenue of live oaks and wide gardens was at the time of the Revolutionary War one of the "show places" of the countryside. Ralph Izard, who married a daughter of Col. Blake, settled, after his marriage, about a mile and a half from Newington, and a straight avenue led from one house to the other.

West of Newington, across the swamp and within a few

13

yards of the public road (now called the Orangeburg road) was the brick mansion of ''Mount Boone,'' said to have been devised by Lady Axtell to another daughter, Mrs. Joseph Boone. By his will in 1733, Mr. Boone directed himself to be buried at Mount Boone, and his broken gravestone is still there adjacent to the foundations of the house, with inscription dated 1733.

The ruins of '' Archdale '' are below Dorchester, but '' Pinckney Plains '' and '' Pine Hill '' are marked by old graves with characteristic cherub face, or else the substantial marble slab on a brick foundation. These places were formerly homes of the Waring family of Tranquill Hill, another Waring plantation near Dorchester.

Some land which seems to have been granted originally to Peter Slan, from whom Slan's Bridge takes its name, passed to Richard Waring in whose family it continued for many years. Four hundred acres of that land was sold in 1818 (as the property of Thomas Waring, of Pine Hill) to Dr. Fabricius Perry and was then known by the name of ''Clay Hill.''

From about 1790, little by little one planter after another made a summer settlement and built homes in what is now known as the town of Summerville. They abandoned the decaying houses of Dorchester (from which material, and especially brick, were removed) forming the basis and furnishing the foundation of the new town, until nothing but crumbling piles of broken fragments of brick were left to mark the site of the old town. But before parting company with this charming and once flourishing place, let us copy an advertisement appearing in the *South Carolina Gazette* of November 2nd, 1738, which gives us an idea of the dress of the women of that day:

"Lost on the 17th of last March, between Dorchester and Charlestown, a Linnen Bagg with sundry Things therein, *viz.,* one Womans Suit of Cloaths of Sattin strip'd with red, green and white, one Suit of all white Sattin, one Yellow Night Gown faced with red Taffety, one yellow Suit of yellow Peiling, and one blue Night Gown faced with white, a red Callimanco Night Gown faced with Brocade, one child's stiffen'd Coat of an Ash Colour'd Damask, and sundry other Womans wearing Apparel,

"ARCHDALE HALL," LAMBS, NEAR DORCHESTER
The Baker homestead, 200 years old

with Head Dresses and shifting Linen, one Sampler with the Child's Name and Age and Date and Place of her abode, a piece of work embroider'd for a Top of a Table, and two Paper Gloves, and a Hatt Band from a Funeral, directed for Wm. and Mrs. Mary Baker, and sundry other Things. Any one that can give any Information to me in Dorchester or to Wm. Linthwaite in Charleston, or to the Printer so that they may be had again shall have from either £10 reward paid on sight.''

There are the remains of a number of old houses in Dorchester County, particularly in the vicinity of Summerville. There is an antebellum residence near Bacon's Bridge and two very old houses in Stallsville. It was in the country in and around Dorchester, that the legion of "Light Horse Harry" during the Revolutionary War was posted when General Greene and the American Army occupied the territory around Charleston after the battle of Eutaw Springs.

Lee's legion was for a long time stationed at the "Villa" plantation, a portion of the Ketelby grant then owned by the Izard family. Lee says that "the first day's march brought his detachments to the country settled by the original emigrants into Carolina. The scene was both new and delightful. Vestiges, though clouded by war, everywhere appeared of the wealth and taste of the inhabitants. Spacious edifices, rich and elegant gardens, with luxuriant and extensive rice plantations, were to be seen on every side." He continued later, "during our continued marches and counter-marches, never before had we been solaced with the prospect of so much comfort. Here we were not confined to one solitary mansion, where a few, and a few only, might enjoy the charm of taste and the luxury of opulence."

Long before Lee's occupany, as far back as the year 1722, Susannah Baker, the then owner of the "Villa" tract, filed her memorial stating that it was composed of a part of a grant to John Cooper, dated 29 September, 1710, and part of a grant to Charles Craven dated 9 April, 1714, and had been conveyed to her by Thomas Cutliffe in 1722 and then was described as being bounded northwest "on lands laid out to Major Edward Jukes." But the land on this boundary had been granted to

Landgrave Ketelby and was included in a vast tract of land lying adjacent to Dorchester to the west and called "Ketelby Barony." The probable inference is that Landgrave Jukes came out to the Province in 1709; had lands surveyed out preparatory to a grant, died in 1710 before any grant was issued and his lands were then granted to others. Ketelby Barony is now of no particular historic value, except that in this vicinity the Wragg family once occupied a homestead and owned vast areas of land. The mansion house of this family was destroyed in 1865, but the remains of the graveyard are still to be found situated on high land between the site of the old dwelling and the river. There a broken monument is seen, which when pieced together says:

"Under this Marble
lieth the Body of Samuel Wragg Esquire
who
Having in 1717 purchased the Tract of Land
called Ashley Barony
and
dying.....day of November 1750"

Later the Signiory of St. Giles was split up into many tracts and plantations among which we find Wragg's, Uxbridge (the residence of Hon. John Matthews, Governor of South Carolina in 1783), Salt Hill, Haggatt Hall, The Laurels, Wampee and the Gadsden lands. These plantations remained practically intact as estates until the close of the Civil War, that cataclysm which completely broke up the landed and labor system as well as the feudal form of society previously found in the low-country of South Carolina.

To the north of the Ketelby grant lay the "Westo" plantation on Westo Savannah near the head of the Ashley River, for which a grant (1697) of 1000 acres was made to John Stevens, of Dorchester. Under the will of John Stevens the lands at Westo Savannah went to his son, Samuel Stevens, who with his brother John were directed by the will to be brought up "at the Colledge in New England to good learning." At the death of Samuel Stevens in 1760 the Westo plantation was by his executors in 1762 sold to Henry Smith,

196

ST. GEORGE'S CHURCH, DORCHESTER
Designed by Sir Christopher Wren

a son of the second Landgrave Thomas Smith and by Henry Smith was devised to his son Thomas Smith in the hands of whose descendants it continued until the war of 1861–1865.

TONGUEWELL

The Perry house, called "Tonguewell," after its builder, is located at the settlement of Tongueville between the Ashley and Edisto rivers, thirteen miles out from the town of Summerville. According to information obtained from Mrs. Jennings Waring Perry, mother of Mrs. J. H. Haskell, and a water color owned by Mrs. Hampton Perry of Charleston, this old mansion was built in 1789 by Edward Tongue, it is said, of pine, cypress and brick, the latter of which was imported. The other materials were native and prepared by the slaves, who built the house. The present piazza and steps are not the original ones, but were added later. The house is square in shape and has a "hipped" roof covered by shingles. The building is elevated from the ground by a brick basement, which allows space for a cellar beneath divided into four rooms with cement floors, and there were stored in the good old days all the wines, provisions, etc., for a plantation home, as well as affording protection in time of attack. From the front and back of the house steps lead to the grounds; one set of steps fronts the avenue of oaks, leading to a bridge which crosses a creek and an old sun dial that stood near the bridge. The steps from the rear lead to a garden and to the big kitchen and outbuildings, part of the equipment of a well-constructed place in those days.

The house at Tongueville was not the only establishment possessed by the Perry family, for Edward Perry had bought from William Wragg a portion of the Ketelby Barony known as "Poplar Hill" plantation and he also purchased 620 acres from William Bull and another 147 acres which had been granted to Bull in 1716. From his three purchases he formed the three plantations known as "Mansion House," "Old House" and "Poplar Hill," which places continued in the possession of himself and family until late in the nineteenth century. It is not certain at which of these places Dr. Benjamin

Lucas Perry resided, who died in 1792. At the outbreak of the Revolutionary War Dorchester, although still a mere village, was, next to Charles Town and George Town, the largest village in South Carolina.

INGLESIDE OR THE HAZE

Ingleside Hall on Goose Creek, not far from Dorchester, was formerly the residence of Hon. John Parker, a member of the old Congress (1774–1789) who was born in 1749, married Miss Susannah Middleton and died in 1822. It was bought afterwards by Professor Francis S. Holmes, a descendant of Landgrave Smith, and developer of the phosphate deposits of Carolina, and an existing picture presents the interior of the house and shows Prof. Holmes in his study.

Francis Simmons Holmes (1815–) was the son of John Holmes and his wife, Anna Glover. While a youth of about fourteen years of age he visited England with a maternal uncle by marriage, a Mr. Lee, of England. Returning to America he engaged for a number of years in mercantile pursuits, in which, however, he was not successful, so removed to St. Andrew's Parish and devoted his attention to agriculture. Experience taught him that a knowledge of the science of geology was essential to an intelligent planter. In the pursuit of this study he obtained the friendship of the leading geologist of the country, Professor Agassiz, a letter from whom is found in the scrap book of F. S. Holmes, a great-nephew of Prof. Holmes. A similar friendship was also formed with Count Pourtales, an engineer, who came to this country about the same time that Agassiz and Dr. Holmes became intimates. He became connected with and was assistant to Prof. Price, U. S. Coast Survey, and visited Prof. Holmes for six weeks with Agassiz at Ingleside.

Prof. Holmes is best known in connection with the discovery of the commercial value of South Carolina phosphate rock for fertilizing purposes, and that he was no ordinary man is manifested by the fact that the boy who left school at the age of fourteen, by his own application, energy and perseverance fitted himself for a professor's chair in Charleston College

THE PERRY HOUSE AT TONGUEVILLE (SOMETIMES CALLED TONGUE WELL), NEAR DORCHESTER

From an old painting

which he held until the Confederate War, when he was appointed to office in connection with coast defenses and became chief of the Nitre and Mining Bureau in South Carolina and Georgia. Upon his withdrawal from the professorship at the College of Charleston he generously left in the museum his entire collection of fossils, said to be among the largest and most valuable in the country. The commercial prosperity of Charleston in the field of fertilizer industry rests largely upon the scientific achievements of Professor Holmes, whose knowledge was ungrudgingly given to his fellow-citizens, and who received from abroad and at home many marks of appreciation of his genius and position.

Ingleside, a colonial country house, is described by Mrs. Deas as being "situated on the crest of a gentle elevation; a square, hip-roofed brick dwelling having two stories and an attic; and sufficiently high from the ground to admit of rooms beneath." These rooms, however, did not form a basement, as the floor was some steps below the level of the ground and really constituted a crude fort.

The front door opened directly from the porch into a large room, and from this a door gave entrance into the other and smaller front room. The back rooms were separated from each other by a narrow hall, in which the staircase with its heavy balusters were placed. Under the stairway was a flight of steps leading down to the basement.

There were four rooms on a floor, those on the first floor being connected in pairs by the "Thoroughfare closets" so common in old houses. The rooms were wainscoted halfway up, and had deep, low window-seats; the window sashes were broad and heavy, and the shutters of paneled wood. The back door was unusually thick and heavy, being built, so tradition says, to resist Indian attacks in the early colonial days.

The view from the front windows was over a level field stretching off to the woods. Near the end of the field a clump of trees marked the family cemetery where stands the Parker shaft. Ingleside was for many years the property of the Parker family, its original name being "The Hays."

199

At the time of the Revolution, when the plantation was owned by Mr. John Parker (whose wife was a Miss Middleton), the British were marauding near Ingleside one day, and while Mrs. Parker was sitting near a window sewing a party of these marauders came up the avenue and fired at her. Fortunately the ball missed Mrs. Parker, but struck the wall, and the hole it made could be seen for many years.

A gentle slope leads from the back of the house to the "lake," where a double row of towering cypresses makes a romantic walk on the very edge of the water. The lake was used as a reservoir for irrigating the rice field. Following the causeway along its banks and crossing a field brings a traveler to a giant live oak known in tradition as "Marion's Oak," but someone has facetiously remarked that if Marion dined under all the oaks under which he was supposed to have given his famous sweet potato dinner he would have had no time for fighting, but would have spent his time as uselessly as popular tradition would have us believe George Washington did, *viz.,* in sitting in the numberless "Washington Pews" and sleeping in the numberless "Washington Beds."

The birthplace of General Marion has been disputed by many people, but, according to General Irvine Walker, Mr. Philip E. Porcher, aged 88 years, of Christ Church Parish, was told by his granduncle, Francis Cordes, that Marion was born at Goatfield plantation opposite "Chacan gate," not far from Cordesville. The remains of Marion repose at Belle Isle, a plantation near Ingleside. His grave was for many years neglected, but was later cared for through the efforts of Shirley Carter Hughson, of Sumter, S. C., now better known as "Father Hughson."

Another fine old house formerly in this neighborhood was Woodstock, a spacious dwelling, with lofty columns supporting the roof of the portico. Still another "low-country" home was Fontainebleau, the residence of the late Alonzo J. White. This house like most of the others has disappeared. An old brick wall encloses two tombs, those of Joseph Hanscom and his daughter. And last, but not least, Mount Pleasant on

"INGLESIDE" OR "THE HAZE," GOOSE CREEK

INTERIOR AT "INGLESIDE," GOOSE CREEK
Professor Francis S. Holmes in his library

Goose Creek was once the hospitable mansion of Mr. Wm. Withers, who died there in 1778.

BELLINGER'S FERRY OR BEE'S FERRY

The River Road which crosses the Ashley River at Bellinger's Ferry follows the stream along its western bank, just west of the plantations lying between the river and the road only to recross the Ashley many miles above and enter "Dorchester"; thus there were in those days two ways to get to this old town (a river road on either side of the Ashley). It is of more than passing interest to note the type of vehicles which passed over the ferry and the rates charged in those old days. According to the acts published in Grimke's collections there were several persons exempted from paying passage money. The Public Laws of South Carolina, A. D. 1754, No. 848, tells us that the several sums following were to be paid "in proclamation money, or the value thereof in other money current in this Province.

For every coach, charriot, landau, berlin, chaise, chair, calash, or other vehicle drawn by 6 or more horses, the sum of 3s. proclamation money,

For every coach, charriot, landau, berlin, chaise, chair, calash, or other vehicle drawn by 4 horses, the sum of 2s. 6d. like money,

For every coach, charriot, landau, berlin, chaise, chair, calash, or other vehicle with 4 wheels, drawn by less than four horses and more than 1 the sum of 2s. like money,

For every chaise or chair drawn by 2 horses and not having 4 wheels, the sum of 1s. 6d. like money.

For every chair or chaise and single horse, 1s. like money.

For every wagon drawn by 4 horses or oxen, the sum of 2s. like money.

For every cart, 1s. like money.

For every horse, mule or ass, laden or unladen, and not drawing, 3d. like money.

For every foot-passenger whatsoever, 2d. like money.

For every man and horse, 4d. like money.

For every drove of oxen or neat cattle, the sum of 3d. per head, like money.

For every drove of calves, hogs, sheep or lambs, the sum of 1½d. per head, like money."

MAGWOOD'S GARDENS

Just below St. Andrew's Church is found the Old Magwood Gardens which contains nineteen acres of japonicas, azaleas, holly, mistletoe, ivy and hundreds of other trees of Japan and native to South Carolina. The gardens have passed from the possession of the Magwood family, but Bishop Moreland, of California, whose grandmother was a Magwood, writes from England, while at the Lambeth Conference as a guest of the Archbishop of Canterbury, that Simon Magwood built as a town house the place (now owned by Mr. Henry C. Williams) at the southwest corner of King Street and South Battery. It was built as a wedding present to his daughter, Susan C. Magwood, upon her marriage to Andrew Moreland, grandfather of Bishop Moreland. Simon Magwood was a rich Charleston merchant who owned a cotton plantation in St. Andrew's Parish as well as the gardens.

DRAYTON HALL

Of all the beautiful manor houses which formerly stood on the estates lying in St. Andrew's Parish, contingent to Ashley River, "Drayton Hall" alone is left. The first site of Charleston was over in that vicinity and the settlements along the Ashley River were made by wealthy cultivated English gentlemen and their families. Among them were the Draytons, although not holding lands originally granted their family, but early acquired from former grantees. Like the Bulls they acquired valuable properties to the southward in Granville County, but continued to make their homes on their estates on the Ashley River. Thomas Drayton, son of the Honorable John Drayton, toward the end of the eighteenth century largely increased his holdings on the river, which were again disposed of by his grandson, the late Reverend John G. Drayton, so that their present holdings are restricted to the Drayton Hall property and a portion of Magnolia.

The letters of Eliza Lucas abound in reference to festal days at Drayton Hall and other mansions on the Ashley, and

"DRAYTON HALL," ST. ANDREW'S PARISH, ON ASHLEY RIVER NEAR CHARLESTON

SIDE VIEW OF "DRAYTON HALL"

it is said that it was at Drayton Hall that she first met the man who later became her husband, Chief Justice Pinckney.

Perhaps the most distinguished of the family of Draytons was William Henry Drayton, who was born at Drayton Hall, and who became first Chief Justice from the Independent State of South Carolina. He went to England when he was a boy, in company with Charles Cotesworth Pinckney and Thomas Pinckney. These three lads attended Westminster School in London, and afterwards went to Oxford University. Then they returned to South Carolina to work and fight side by side against that unjust ruler, King George the Third. Concerning Chief Justice Drayton, a most amusing incident is narrated in a letter of Honorable Richard Hutson:

". . . . New Battery, which General Lee has entirely demolished excepting three guns. His first question upon seeing it was, what d——d fool planned this Battery? A bystander replied that it had been planned by Mr. Drayton, our present Chief Justice. Says he, he may be a very good Chief Justice, but he is a d——d bad engineer, for if the enemy had had the planning of it, they could not have fixed it in a better place for the reduction of Fort Johnson."

Drayton Hall was built in 1740 by Thomas Drayton, father of William and Henry, and named after the family residence at North Hamptonshire, England. This home is built of brick, with large columns of Portland marble and is said to have cost ninety thousand dollars, much of the fine material having been imported from England. The wainscoting, which at a later date was repainted, extends from the floor to the ceiling. Over the large, massive mantles are frames set in the wainscot for pictures or coats of arms. The fireplaces are adorned with colored tiles. In one of the cellars there were at one time a number of marble columns lying on the ground, this giving rise to the story that the old mansion was never completed.

It is said that Chief Justice Drayton designed one side of the great seal of South Carolina, the other side having been contributed by Arthur Middleton, his neighbor, signer of the Declaration of Independence. Drayton died at the early age of thirty-seven, while attending Congress in Philadelphia in 1779.

A visitor to South Carolina gives the following account of Drayton Hall:

"We stopped to dine with Dr. Drayton, at Drayton Hall. The house is an ancient building, but convenient and good; and the garden is better laid out, better cultivated and stocked with good trees, than any I have hitherto seen. In order to have a fine garden you have nothing to do but to let the trees remain standing here and there, or in clumps, to plant bushes in front of them, and arrange the trees according to their height. Dr. Drayton's father, who was also a physician, began to lay out the garden on this principle; and his son, who is passionately fond of a country life, has pursued the same plan. The prospect from the garden is like all other views in this part of the country."

At the death of this last Charles Drayton in 1820 he devised to his son Charles—another Charles Drayton, M. D.—"his place called Drayton Hall situate on the Ashley River," and the property still remains in, and is occupied by the descendants of the name, *viz.*, the heirs of the late Charles H. Drayton.

MAGNOLIA GARDENS

At one period Magnolia Gardens and Drayton Hall comprised a single estate, but this property later was divided into two tracts, when one of the Drayton brothers acquired Drayton Hall and the other Magnolia Gardens.

Below we quote from a description concerning Magnolia Gardens on the Ashley, written by Miss Constance Fenimore Woolson in *Harper's Magazine* for December, 1875:

"Next above Drayton Hall is beautiful Magnolia. In the spring the steamer carries tourists to this enchanting garden, where they wander through glowing aisles of azaleas, and forget the lapse of time, recalled from the trance of enjoyment only by the whistle of the boat which carries them back to the city. The old mansion at Magnolia was burned by a detachment of Sherman's army, as were nearly all the homesteads in the parish of St. Andrew's, but a pretty modern cottage has been erected on its site."

TOWN HOUSE OF THE BULL FAMILY, WHOSE COUNTRY ESTATE, "ASHLEY HALL,"
LAY IN ST. ANDREW'S PARISH
Now owned and occupied by Mr. H. Ficken

Speaking of the gardens, she says:

"Seven persons touching fingertips can just encircle the sylphide rose-tree seventeen feet in height by twenty feet wide. There are also many rare trees and shrubs, among them the sacred tree of the Grand Lama, Cupressus lusitanica. But the glory of the garden is the gorgeous coloring of the azaleas, some of the bushes sixteen and seventeen feet through by twelve feet high, others nineteen and twenty feet through by thirteen feet high, solid masses of blossoms in all the shades of red, from palest pink to deepest crimson, and now and then a pure white bush, like a bride in her snowy lace. It is almost impossible to give a Northerner an idea of the affluence of color in this garden when its flowers are in bloom.

"Imagine a long walk with the moss-draped live oaks overhead, fairy lakes and bridges in the distance, and on each side the great fluffy masses of rose and pink and crimson reaching far above your head, thousands upon tens of thousands of blossoms packed close together, with no green to mar the intensity of their color, rounding out in swelling curves of bloom down to the turf below, not pausing a few inches above it and showing bare stems or trunks, but spreading over the velvet and trailing out like the Arabian Nights. Eyes that have never had color enough find here a full feast, and go away satisfied at last. And with all their gorgeousness, the hues are delicately mingled; the magic effect is produced not by unbroken banks of crude red, but by blended shades, like the rich Oriental patterns of India shawls, which the European designers, with all their efforts, can never imitate."

Thomas Nelson Page pays the following tribute to this magnificent garden of which every South Carolinian should be proud:

"It was the most magnificent display that I have ever seen. It cannot be described. It is beyond expression. I have seen a great many celebrated gardens, including those at Cintra, near Lisbon, and the Kew Gardens in England, and while the natural conditions at Cintra, where the gardens placed up a mountain, are better and more favorable, there can be no doubt at all that the floral display at Magnolia is the more beautiful."

Magnolia on the Ashley is now in the possession of Mr. Norwood Hastie, whose mother was a Miss Drayton. The Hastie family are particularly generous in that they open, for a short period in the springtime, these gardens to visitors.

RUNNYMEDE

One of the most beautiful old places on the Ashley River is "Runnymede," which adjoins and is just above Magnolia Gardens.

It was settled before the Revolution, but no incidents of historic or romantic interest are, during this period, connected therewith. Soon after the Revolution, it was the home of Hon. John Julius Pringle, who was Speaker of the House of Assembly in 1787, and Attorney General of the State for many years from 1792. The Duke de la Rochefoucault Liancourt spent some time with him as a guest at his home in Charleston, and it was with Mr. Pringle he made his trip up the Ashley. In his account of this trip he makes the following reference to Runnymede.

"Hence" (*i.e.,* from Ashley Ferry) "we crossed the river, and stopped at a plantation lately purchased by Mr. Pringle, the former name of which was Greenville, but which he has named Susan's Place, in honour of his lovely wife. This plantation is likewise without a house, that of the former occupier having been consumed by fire; on the foundation of this building, which remains unhurt, the new mansion is to be erected, which will be finished this summer. . . . The situation is much the same as that of Fitterasso, except that the morasses, covered with reeds, lie on the other side. The river flows close to the garden, and the ships, which continually sail up and down the river may anchor here with great convenience."

The new mansion was completed in due time and the plantation was by Mr. Pringle ultimately named "Runnymede" by which name it has ever since continued to be known. Thomas Fuller conveyed to John Julius Pringle 637 acres off the adjoining plantation which was added to Runnymede. Under the will of John Julius Pringle who died in 1841, the Runnymede property passed to his son, William Bull Pringle, who added an adjoining tract of 450 acres. The entire tract was thereafter acquired by the late C. C. Pinckney who for years mined off the phosphate deposits. The mansion house built by Mr. John Julius Pringle was destroyed by the enemy in 1865. The present residence was built by the late Mr. C. C. Pinckney.

MIDDLETON GARDENS

Above Runnymede stands the old Pinckney place, which is noted for its beautiful formal gardens and velvety lawns. A house is found upon this property, said to have been constructed around the remains of the old brick kitchen.

MILLBROOK

The name "Millbrook" appears to have been given to the place above Runnymede, now owned by J. Ross Hannahan, during the ownership of John Alleyne Walter. By Abraham Ladson, to whom a deed for the property had been executed in 1786, it was conveyed to Honorable Thomas Middleton in 1786. The deed does not appear on record but the boundaries in deeds of the line of adjoining places show that Thomas Middleton owned it, and for some reason, probably to fortify his title, Thomas Middleton on 17 September, 1786, took out a warrant for a new grant which appears to have been issued. He also purchased the Vaucluse property lower down the river and does not appear to have ever made Millbrook his residence. Possibly the residence house had been burned. He died in 1795 and the property remained in his estate until 1838 when it was conveyed by his heirs and representatives to J. Pinckney Clements as Millbrook plantation containing 338 acres.

CHAPTER XI

JOHN'S ISLAND AND EDISTO ISLAND, THE PLACES AND THE PEOPLE

ST. ANDREW'S PARISH AND ST. PAUL'S

N Stono River are found many historic spots, some of which will be subsequently discussed in connection with John's Island. On the mainland, however, adjacent to Charleston, was the Eliza Lucas plantation commonly known as the Bluff, on old Wappoo Creek before Elliott's cut was made. It was on the trucking place lately in the possession of John N. Voorhees. Here Eliza Lucas sat in her "little study," and planned such wonderful things for South Carolina.

On the Stono also lived Martha Ferguson Blake, who married William Washington, and both are buried in the old Elliott private cemetery on "Live Oak," St. Paul's Parish, not far from Rantowles bridge. There in the sadly neglected graveyard are also buried Colonel William Washington and his wife, Jane Riley Elliott, and the only inscription on the stone which covers them both is "My parents Dear Lie Here."

This is on the mainland, and is a little above John's Island Ferry, which has long been in operation.

JOHN'S ISLAND HOUSES

During the Revolutionary War many stirring scenes were transacted in the neighborhood of John's Island, and Mrs. Ellet's Domestic History of the Revolution tells many of the most interesting of these, including the incident of a Fenwick child being rescued by a Miss Gibbes. A miniature of the latter is owned by Miss Anna Gibbes, the subject being Mrs. Alexander Garden, *née* Mary Anna Gibbes (The Heroine of the Stono), who saved the life of an infant cousin during the

ST. ANDREW'S CHAPEL, IN ST. ANDREW'S PARISH, ON ASHLEY RIVER, NEAR CHARLESTON

Revolution when the British were firing upon the house. The infant afterwards became Major Fenwick, of the War of 1812.

This story is often erroneously ascribed to the house called Fenwick Castle, but Mrs. Ellet says that "Fenwick Place," still called "Headquarters," was three miles from "Peaceful Retreat," the Gibbes home. From the fact that the graves of Robert Gibbes and Sarah, his wife, are found in a graveyard about three miles beyond Headquarters, it would seem that Peaceful Retreat was adjacent to that cemetery.

Near the Ferry stood the Laurels, built by Mr. Turnbull, on a high bluff now called Simmons Bluff. The house was constructed of black cypress, held together by hand-wrought nails. It stood on a high brick foundation, and was three and a half stories high, containing 32 rooms. In the old burying ground adjacent to the home site are found the names of Mrs. Edith Matthews and several of the Simmons family, while another graveyard about two miles distant on the roadside contains tombstones bearing the names of Barnard Smith Elliott, Barnard Elliott, Robert Gibbes (died July 4, 1794, aged 64 years) and his wife, Sarah Gibbes (died 1825, aged 79 years).

Letters from Kinsey Burden to Micah Jenkins (of Woodland and Capes plantations), about roads on John's Island, speak of the "Old Ridge Road" as a "man and horse way— 'a foot way for my people to and from Church,' " and describe the east end of the Old Ridge Road, from "your middle gate on said road where it enters the pine barren through to the lower or River Road." Kinsey Burden also says that Micah Jenkins had attempted to move the public landing from the place of Mr. Jenkin's son-in-law, Mr. Gervais. John Louis Gervais was an intimate friend and companion of Henry Laurens, and his descendants are still extant.

FENWICK CASTLE

At what date the first Fenwick came to South Carolina is not known, but it was about the beginning of the eighteenth century. During the French Invasion in 1706 he commanded a company of militia. In South Carolina we find Edward Fenwick, sometimes called Honorable, as a member of His

14

Majesty's Council in 1747. He was married twice, his first wife being Martha Izard, daughter of Honorable Ralph Izard. Their only child, Elizabeth, married John Barnwell, but she died within a year and left no issue.

In 1753 Edward Fenwick married Mary Drayton, daughter of Thomas Drayton, and by her had many children. After her husband's death Mrs. Fenwick married William Gerard de Brahm, an engineer officer in the service of the colonies of South Carolina, and removed to Philadelphia. Her will is dated 1805.

Edward Fenwick's children were as follows: Edward Fenwick, John Fenwick, Sarah Fenwick, who was twice married, first to John MacCartan Campbell, of Charleston, 1777. Mr. Campbell bought from his brother-in-law (the Hon. Edward Fenwick) a residence on Lower Meeting Street in Charleston, now known as the Calhoun Mansion. After her husband's death Sarah married Dr. George Jones, of Savannah. Another daughter of Edward Fenwick, Mary, married Walter Izard, son of Ralph Izard, but died shortly after her marriage, and in 1758 was born her brother Thomas, of whom very little is known, which is true also of Robert, born 1761.

Martha Fenwick, another child of Edward, married in 1778 Thomas Gadsden, a captain in the first regiment South Carolina Continentals, a son of General Christopher Gadsden. The daughters seemed to have contracted brilliant marriages; one of them, Charlotte Elizabeth, was twice married, her first husband being William Leigh Pierce, of Virginia, a captain in the Continental Army, who was voted a sword by Congress for his good conduct at the battle of Eutaw Springs. William Pierce and his wife settled after the war in Georgia and we find him as a delegate from that State to the Constitutional Convention. After his death his widow, Charlotte, married Ebenezer Jackson, of Massachusetts, a lieutenant in the third Continental artillery. Their daughter, Harriett Jackson, married her first cousin, Commodore Tattnall.

Of the next two Fenwick children, Selina and Matilda, little is known, except that Selina was appointed sole executrix of her mother's will and Matilda married Robert Giles. Edward

"FENWICK CASTLE," JOHN'S ISLAND

Fenwick seems to have been fond of repeating names in his family, or to have followed the fashion of naming a living child for one that had died, as we find a Robert William Fenwick, born in 1765, as we also find a John Roger Fenwick, born in 1773. This John became a second lieutenant in the Marine Corps, rising from that to a captaincy. From this service he resigned to enter another branch of military life and died in 1842 as brevet brigadier general. He is the last child, genealogically speaking, but his sister Harriett, who was younger than himself by four years is more interesting to us. She married Josiah Tattnall, Jr. (second son of Josiah Tattnall and Miss Mullrayne), who was born at his grandfather's place, Bonaventure, in Georgia. Harriett's husband became Governor of Georgia, and her son, who married his cousin, Miss Jackson, became Commodore Josiah Tattnall.

There was one other son, George Fenwick, of whom we learn very little, suffice it to say that when the Hon. Edward Fenwick, a member of the King's Council in South Carolina died in New York on 7th of July, 1775, his widow and sons chartered the sloop *Commerce* for the voyage to Charles Town, whither they carried his remains for interment.

When Edward Fenwick's will was read Robert Gibbes and John Gibbes were found to be qualified executors, although Robert alone served. There was a close kinship between the Gibbes and Fenwick families, the Hon. John Fenwick, of South Carolina, who died about 1747, having married Elizabeth Gibbes, a daughter of Gov. Robert Gibbes, of South Carolina. Although the Fenwicks elected to drop their titles of nobility, the records in England clearly show them to have been of noble origin, and it is doubtless due to this fact that Fenwick goes by the name of Lord Ripon. A partition in the Court of Chancery, the original being in a collection of Prof. Yates Snowden, of the University of South Carolina, shows that they were a family of immense belongings, and much other information is set forth. It is with interest that we read in Rice's Digested Index that "in 1796 Miss Fenwick was allowed to bring certain negroes into the State."

The Fenwick mansion is a beautiful home built of brick and erected in a substantial and dignified way. The façade of this building reveals a two-story structure erected over a deep brick basement employed as a fort in primitive times.

Within the basement is found an old well used to supply the garrison with water in case of seige, and an underground passage which extends about a hundred yards to a little gully at the rear of the house. It is a brick passage large enough to permit a man to crawl through on hands and knees, make his escape, and give the alarm of Indian attacks. In addition to these measures for protection the note of defense is again struck in the substantial inside shutters of the windows. The house has a hipped-roof upon the top of which is erected a small observation platform which commanded a view of the country for miles around.

The interior decorations of the building are unusually beautiful, the paneling of the up and down stairs rooms being of cedar, and the wainscoting of pine. The mantels are very highly decorated, the pattern of the wall of Troy occurring frequently. The railings of the staircase are of mahogany, and the style in which the entire house is finished can be realized from the fact that the latches of the windows are all of solid silver. The rooms measure sixteen by eighteen feet, with unusually high ceilings. The carving around the mantel in the largest sitting-room is extraordinarily beautiful, being a combination of the St. Andrew's Cross with the Greek Key and Acanthus leaf.

Fenwick Castle has many romantic stories connected with it, perhaps the most interesting being that concerning the love affair of a daughter of the house with one of her father's grooms. Fenwick was sometimes called Lord Ripon, and was noted for the fact that he had a private race course laid out in front of his house. It is doubtless true that one of the girls did fall in love with some handsome young Englishman who came to bring some thoroughbred racers to her father's estate.

However, the father would have none of the marriage, and we can picture the unhappy scene which transpired in this old house with its magnificent furnishings when the girl pleaded

"BRICK HOUSE"
The old Roper-Stanyarne Home on John's Island, near Charleston

in vain to be allowed to marry her lover. Consent being refused, it is said that the couple ran away and were married, whereupon the father pursued them, with very tragic consequences. He is said to have hung the young man while the latter was seated on his horse, causing the girl to lash the horse from under him, resulting in her lover's death and her broken heart.

The same sternness of character was exhibited by Edward Fenwick, as he was among the Loyalists in South Carolina, and his estates were confiscated. Nothing is known of the life of the Fenwick family after the Revolution except what information was found in legal papers pertaining to the estate. Their genealogy is given in full in the *South Carolina Historical and Genealogical Magazine.*

The only other really old place on John's Island is the old Roper place down near Legareville, known as Brick House. Although deserted, it is still standing, and is closely connected with the history of the Hext and Roper families, while graves of Stanyarnes and Freers are found in the little overgrown burying ground not far distant from the house. The place now belongs to the wife of Bishop Knight, who came into possession of it through her first husband, the gallant Captain William Yates. On Kiawah Island stands a handsome house belonging to the Vanderhorst estate.

EDISTO ISLAND AND ITS HOMES

The first mention concerning Edisto Island is found in a history of the baronies of South Carolina when "On the 18th March, 1675, a formal grant for 12,000 acres on Ashley River was issued to Anthony, Earl of Shaftsbury, but for some reason the Earl of Shaftsbury did not seem at first to have taken very kindly to his signiory on Ashley River and inclined to establish himself elsewhere." On the 23rd of May, 1674, the Earl wrote to Maurice Matthews: "My thoughts were to have planted on Ashley River, but the people tooke soe little care to allow or provide for me any accomodacon neare them having taken up for themselves all the best conveniences on that river and left me not a tolerable Place to plant on nearer than two Miles from the Water that I am forced to seeke out in another place and resolve to take me a Signiory at Edisto River.'' The place selected by him was on Edisto Island (then called Locke Island), and the person selected to take it up was Mr. Andrew Percivall. Percivall seems to have been some sort of connection of the Earl of Shaftsbury as in the letter to Matthews the Earl describes Percivall as one ''Who hath a Relacon to my Family.''

Percivall was not only to take up a signiory for the Earl, but was to make a settlement there for the Lord Proprietors, and to be independent of the Government at the settlement on Ashley River. Mr. Henry Woodward was directed to treat with the Indians of Edisto and buy it of them, but this projected settlement of Edisto Island seems to have been abandoned.

In South Carolina until 1716 the Indian trade was conducted solely under the auspices of individual enterprise. Next to the traders were the burden bearers, who frequently consisted of boys, under the direction of an experienced ''voyageur.'' The place of Peter St. Julien, near Dorchester (a town near the head of the Ashley River) was a great camping ground for these traders, as from this place the trails to the Congaree and Chickasaw diverged. A caravan, for instance, on the latter route leaving Charleston would stop first at St. Julien's, thence proceed to Wasmasaw, thence to ''The Ponds'' and on to Edisto, thence to Fort Moore, or Savannah Town, a short distance below Hamberg, opposite Augusta, Ga. Nearly the entire railway system which had been constructed up to 1859 followed almost precisely on the routes of the old Indian trails of her infant commerce.

An Act dated June, 1714, is entitled ''An act for continuing the road to Edisto Island and making a bridge over Dawhoo Creek, and finishing the road to Port Royal, and making a bridge over the South Edisto River.'' Some of the names of the inhabitants of Edisto Island are found in an Act dated 1751 in which commissioners were appointed for ''cutting, clearing and cleaning 'Watt's Cutt' '' and all the male inhabitants, from the ages of 16 to 60 years, living and residing from

VANDERHORST HOUSE, CHAPEL STREET, CHARLESTON

VANDERHORST HOUSE ON KIAWAH ISLAND

the plantation of Captain William Eddings, to the plantations of William Adams and Joshia Grimball, inclusive, and Jehossey Island "shall work on the said Cutt."

During the Revolutionary War Edisto Inlet was particularly infested by privateers, "refugees' boats," and Row-Galleys, coming up from St. Augustine, seeking cattle for the garrison there, plunder of indigo and rice, and revenge. These "refugee boats" were long, low, uncovered pettiaugers, carried from 40 to 50 men, armed with muskets and boarding pikes, and manned each with 24 oars, 12 sweeps to the side, and carried each a six-pounder in the bow and a four-pounder in the stern; they were rigged with sliding gunter masts and latteen sails, very like the pirate galleys of the Mediterranean, and were usually manned by refugee royalists who had fled from the State, and by Mediterranean sailors from the Greeks at New Smyrna.

Edisto Island is bounded, roughly speaking, on the north by the North Edisto River, spoken of as Edisto Inlet; on the south by the South Edisto River; west by Dawhoo River, which connects these two large rivers; and on the east by the Atlantic Ocean. This island has been facetiously called "The Independent Republic of Edisto," because, at the time preceding the Civil War, she threatened to secede from the State of South Carolina, unless the State seceded from the Union.

Although the main industry of the island was the planting of Sea Island cotton, many of the planters were college graduates, and not a few could show university degrees from famous European universities, for example, Theodore Gaillard Thomas, M. D., who was born on Edisto Island, S. C., 1831, and was the son of Rev. Edward Thomas and Jane Marshall Gaillard, daughter of Judge Theodore Gaillard. He received his early education at the College of Charleston and was a graduate of the Medical College of the State of South Carolina, subsequently went to Europe and studied medicine in the great scientific centres of the world. After serving as interne at Belleview Hospital he became professor of obstetrics and diseases of women in the College of Physicians and Surgeons in New York, and consulting physician to the Nursery and

Child's Hospital at St. Mary's Hospital, Brooklyn. He was also surgeon and one of the founders of the Woman's Hospital in New York. He was president of the American Gynæcological Society, and an honorary member of the Obstetrical Society of Berlin. Dr. Thomas was twice married, his first wife being his cousin, Mary Gaillard, and his second wife, a Miss Willard, of Willard's Academy, N. Y., one of the noted sisters of that name. He was the author of numerous books and pamphlets touching subjects connected with his profession, of which some have been translated into French, German, Italian and Chinese.

Edisto lands being ill adapted to rice cultivation, the islanders early turned their attention to the indigo plant. Their product was in great demand and sold for a higher price than any other grown and manufactured in the State, but the culture of indigo ceased to be remunerative and in 1796 experiments were made with the cotton plant.

From a register kept by Mr. Murray, some years previous to 1826, it appears that in the course of sixteen years, there were among the white inhabitants sixty-six marriages, two hundred and twelve births and one hundred and seventy-seven deaths. The following are mentioned as owning plantations: Rev. McLeod, Ephraim Mikell, James Clark, William Eddings, Daniel Townsend, William Seabrook, William C. Meggott (Meggett), Dr. Chisolm, Gabriel Seabrook, and Norman McLeod.

Mr. Mills, in his Statistics, says that "It does not appear that any establishment similar to that of a tavern was ever attempted on the island; strangers and visitors are hospitably entertained in private families and are sent about on horseback, or in carriages as their cimcumstances or exigencies may require." Mr. Mills speaks with authority, as many of his boyhood days were spent on the island. He goes on to say that "two ferries were early established but such was the infrequency of the intercourse that these ferries have been discontinued." Contracts were, however, made in Mr. Mills' time (1826), for the construction of a causeway and ferry from this island to the mainland, which has ever since been in use.

Several old homes are found in the interior of the island situated near the old public roads, but the ferries were for many years abandoned and passage was made only by boat, thus most of the old settlements are to be found on the rivers or on the three bold creeks that cut deep into the island. The one known as Steamboat Creek comes in from the North Edisto River. There is a similar large creek sweeping in from the South Edisto River, called Pierre's Creek, which divides into two branches known as Fishing Creek and Big Bay Creek.

THE WILLIAM SEABROOK HOUSES

The William Seabrook House on Edisto, according to Judge Smith, the present owner, was built about 1808 by Mr. William Seabrook, of Edisto Island, who was a very wealthy planter and acquired a great deal of property. He died about 1837, and the property continued to be occupied by his widow until after her death, about 1854 or 1855; when it was sold, and purchased by Mr. J. Evans Eddings, then a very wealthy planter, by whom it was sold some time near the year 1875.

This is a very handsome house. The foundations are of brick, and the outside weather-boarding is of cypress, of which the greater portion of the house is built. It is a substantial three-story dwelling, the chief architectural feature of which is the interior stairway in the rear hall which ascends to the second story by a double flight, broken half way up by a landing on which a beautiful colonial window with a double arch occurs. The only other similar set of steps is in the Brown residence in Charleston, on Ashley Avenue. Unlike the majority of houses on the island this place does not display the usual double piazzas on the front, but has a double portico, up and down stairs.

When the house was bought by Judge Smith there was no furniture in it of any value; nothing but a few old broken pieces. The tradition is that a raiding party of Northern soldiers, during the Civil War, entered the house, threw nearly all of the furniture then inside out of the windows and from the upper piazzas, wrecking most of it, and destroyed a great many of the banisters and railings of the front stairs and piazza.

Prior to the acquisition of the property by the elder Mr. William Seabrook, the land was owned by the Townsend family for many years, which family is fully discussed in connection with Bleak Hall, one of the few "dead houses" on Edisto Island.

William Seabrook was, as has been said, a man of large means, and the Seabrook family has spread to the surrounding islands and to the mainland. Mr. Seabrook was formerly the owner of Sea Side plantation on Edisto, part of which, lying on the west side of the middle road, joins lands of Mr. Eddings the elder. His first will was made in 1836, in which the Charleston house of the Seabrooks is described as being on the south side of Broad Street, and the east side of Logan. In 1837 Mary Ann and Sarah Seabrook (who married James Legare) conveyed this property to Andrew Dibble.

In this Seabrook home on Edisto, not far from the steamboat landing, LaFayette was entertained at a great ball. Just before the affair a female infant three weeks old was brought in and christened. LaFayette took her in his arms and named her Carolina for the State, and LaFayette for himself. This was the lady who subsequently lived in the Hopkinson house, having married a Mr. Hopkinson, and it is curious to note that she was born on Washington's Birthday, February the twenty-second. The old home of the Seabrook family is at present unoccupied, being in the care of R. T. La Roche, who married Ruth Seabrook.

OAK ISLAND

An interesting old wooden house is found at Oak Island, now owned by Mr. E. Mitchell Seabrook, grandson of William Seabrook the younger. Judge Smith says that the elder Mr. William Seabrook (whose place is now the property of Judge Smith, the house on it having been built about 1808), also had a son, William Seabrook, who owned a plantation about two miles away called Oak Island. There are some very pretty photographs of this place and the garden, which were taken, it is believed, by some Northerner during the war. Concerning these pictures Mrs. George E. Hazlehurst, who was Miss

THE WILLIAM SEABROOK HOUSE, EDISTO ISLAND
Now owned by Judge H. A. M. Smith

Jennie Mikell, of Edisto, relates that upon one occasion a Miss Whaley, who was attending a function in Washington, met during the evening an officer who had been stationed on Edisto Island when it was occupied by the Federal troops. Finding that she was from Edisto he went on to describe to her the gardens at Oak Island as being the most beautiful he had ever seen. He may well have said so then, as the place boasted of the finest natural features with which the imported English landscape-gardener could wish to work.

This gardener had been brought over to this country for the purpose of laying out the gardens at Oak Island. He utilized the lakes and little islands much in the style of a Japanese garden of to-day, and connected these charming little retreats with rustic bridges. Formal fish ponds were placed at either end of the garden, and on several of the islets aviaries were established, while sacred lilies of India were planted in the waters of the little lakes.

Oak Island went to John Edward Seabrook, who married Elizabeth Baynard Whaley, and years after the Civil War it passed to Mitchell Seabrook, in whose possession is found also Seaside, one of the largest plantations on Edisto Island, which is situated near Big Bay Creek, and is adjacent to McConkie's Beach and Eddingsville Beach. Near this latter place, on Frampton's Inlet, an old settlement formerly existed, which has now been swept into the sea.

William Eddings was one of the most prominent men of this section, and one of the founders of the Presbyterian church on Edisto. The Register of the Circular Church in Charleston contains the following entry:

"William Eddings and Theodora Law, Widow, were Solemnly Married together Septemb^r: 1733, by me, I being well assured by a Testimonial to me produced, from under the hand of the Rev^d: M^r: —— Moore, Min^r: of a Congregation at Edisto in this Province (where both parties are well known) that the purpose of the said Marriage was duly published in the Meeting-House, and in the Hearing of that Congregation, on three several Sabbath-days, immediately before Divine Service; and no Objection being made . . ."

Below Eddingsville Beach, to the south, is McConkie's Beach, the last beach on the island. Between McConkie's Beach, Big Bay Creek, Fishing Creek (a branch of St. Pierre's Creek) and the road which leads around the creeks lies a large body of arable land which contains several plantations, Seaside being one, and Crawford's (on Store Creek) another. In this vicinity is found a splendid old house of the island type, built by an Eddings, inhabited by a Whaley, and now occupied by Mr. James Whaley. Beyond Big Bay Creek lies Bailey Island, the Baileys being a family closely connected by marriage to all the Edisto people. Adjacent to Crawford lies a place called Freedman's Village, a residence of the freed negroes of the island.

TOM SEABROOK HOUSE

The Tom Seabrook house is up in the "Burrough," as it is called in local parlance, being a name applied by "Edistonians" to a certain portion of the island lying in its center, to distinguish it from portions contingent to the North Edisto River. The house is now in the possession of Mr. Arthur Whaley, a son of William B. Whaley, and grandson of Edward Whaley; into whose possession it came by inheritance, the house having been built about the year 1780. It was bought later (1840) by Edward Whaley for his son William.

This house is a quaint old-fashioned wooden structure, built, like the majority of island houses, rather high up from the ground, on a brick foundation. There is a piazza around it on three sides, and a hall running through the center with rooms on either side, and sleeping rooms in the second story.

It was at this place, during the Civil War in 1864, that eight Confederate soldiers were captured by the Federal forces and the house bears marks of the bullets fired at that time by the invaders. There are several branches of the Seabrook family (to which this dwelling belonged probably at one time, as it has always gone by the name of the Tom Seabrook house), all of which are connected and presumably descended from one ancestor. As anciently written, the name was Seabrooke; the family at present is widely scattered.

THE HOPKINSON HOUSE, EDISTO ISLAND

BRICK HOUSE, EDISTO ISLAND
Built by the Hamiltons but identified with the Jenkins family
Used as a fort in olden times

THE HOPKINSON HOUSE

Of this place Mrs. Julia H. LaRoche, who was a Miss Hopkinson, says that the Hopkinson house is not over 72 years old, and was built by her father, James Hopkinson. He married his neighbor, Carolina LaFayette Seabrook, whose christening has been described in connection with the history of her father, Mr. William Seabrook. On their extensive wedding trip, which included a journey to Europe, Mr. and Mrs. Hopkinson were entertained while in Paris by the family of General LaFayette, the general himself being dead.

This visit later resulted in an "affaire du coeur," as a sister of Mrs. Hopkinson, a Miss Seabrook, met (through the acquaintance Mrs. Hopkinson formed on her wedding trip) and later married the Count de Lastaigne, thereafter making her home in Paris. This connection, and the fact that Mrs. Hopkinson was named Carolina LaFayette, seems to have exercised a deal of influence over the destiny of herself and family, as George LaFayette visited America afterwards and stayed at the Hopkinson house on Edisto Island. What excited his greatest interest at the time was said to be the existence of slavery, and he would say wonderingly to Mrs. Hopkinson, who continued to point out to him the advantages these people enjoyed, "But, my aunt, they have not liberty."

The house is described as a wooden building conforming to the square colonial type, and set upon a high brick foundation. Its wide veranda, festooned with rose vines, is reached by a hospitable looking set of steps ascending from a circular drive cut into the front lawn.

The term "livable" is one that fairly fits this place, and gives in a word the whole atmosphere of the Hopkinson family residence. As so much has been told concerning LaFayette and his family in connection with this house, it may not be amiss to conclude this brief account of the charming place with an account of the departure of LaFayette from America upon passing Mount Vernon, General LaFayette having expressed a desire to see this sacred spot where reposed the remains of his foster-father, George Washington.

221

A correspondent of *The National Intelligence* says that when the boat, bearing LaFayette down the Potomac, came abreast of Mount Vernon the General went on deck with his son, and while the band played Pleyel's hymn he stood viewing the home of Washington, tears coursing down his bronzed cheek. With one arm around the neck of his son, and the other on the shoulder of Trench Ringgold (then Marshall of the District of Columbia) he took farewell of Washington's home.

Concerning the Hopkinson family, little is known in this section of the country, but it is eminent in Philadelphia. One of this name was a celebrated writer, and his son was the composer of "Hail Columbia." The former, Francis Hopkinson, was born in Philadelphia in 1738. His father, Thomas, was an Englishman who emigrated to that city, having secured, it is said, government patronage through his marriage with the niece of the Bishop of Worchester. Francis Hopkinson married Anne Borden of New Jersey; represented that state in the General Congress of 1776, and signed the Declaration of Independence. His son, Joseph Hopkinson, who wrote the song, "Hail Columbia," was also associated with the City of Philadelphia.

BLEAK HALL

John Townsend was born at "Bleak Hall" on Edisto Island, the home where generations of his ancestors had lived and died. Bleak Hall was so named from the fact that it is exposed to the gales and breezes of the Atlantic Ocean. John Townsend was the son of Daniel Townsend (styled in the old legal family documents "gentleman and planter") and Hepsibah Jenkins his wife. These ancestors were of Anglo, Norman and Welsh descent, the American progenitor being a younger son of the Norfolk family of England, of whom the Marquis Townsend is the head.

The boyhood days of John Townsend were spent in the regulation plantation life of the South, which gave him a vigorous physique and training, enabling him "to ride and shoot and speak the truth." When fifteen he was sent to the South Carolina College, with "Daddy Sam," the body servant who

"BLEAK HALL," THE TOWNSEND HOME, EDISTO ISLAND

delighted to enlarge upon his use and importance and would say, "I keep all his money and look after tings." In death these two were not long parted for in old age they passed away near together.

While at the College of South Carolina, John Townsend had a severe illness. After his recovery he entered Princeton College where he graduated in a class said to be of note for the brilliant gifts of some of its member. Among them was R. I. Breckinridge, of Virginia, his ardent and life-long friend. It is said that at a dinner party given to the parties marking the line between Canada and the United States, when Breckinridge was asked by the English envoy what was his family coat of arms, replied, "A gallows erectant, a rope pendant and a man at the endant," which showed that American rebels were still "persona non grata" in England. Breckinridge is also credited with the witty remark, "That stars might fall, moons fail to give their light, ere Townsend ceased to be polite."

When Townsend returned home, after his college days were over, he studied law in Charleston, but left this to take charge of his father's planting interests on Edisto and Wadmalaw Islands. He was elected to the State Legislature before attaining his majority and his father had to await the son's twenty-first birthday to give him the land on which to qualify for the office. He represented the Parish of St. John's Colleton for many years in the House and Senate, took great interest in educational problems, and was trustee for the public schools, doing much for their promotion.

At the age of thirty-five John Townsend married Mary Caroline, daughter of Richard and Phoebe Waight Jenkins, of Wadmalaw Island. About this wooing it is told that he crossed five miles on the North Edisto River and rode eleven miles on land through all weathers to visit his "Lady Love," who called him the "Knight of the Golden Crest." She became the guiding spirit in their home at Bleak Hall. When he would make weekly business trips a lamp was placed in the cupola of his home by which his boat might find a beacon star on its return.

During the Civil War Bleak Hall was confiscated and the cupola was used as a signal station for the Federal fleet.

Finally the home was burned and the lands divided among the negroes. It is to be noted that the attitude of the negroes on Edisto Island toward their masters was remarkable. They were content with the "forty acres and a mule" which was given them and did not pillage their master's homes as did many of the negroes of the other sections of the country. They regarded themselves as guardians of their master's property. Bleak Hall became the victim of the flames of the Federal Army during the reconstruction days. The house has been rebuilt, and is very much like the first one. The picture presented is taken by a pastel sketch done by Miss Phoebe Townsend, daughter of John Townsend, and by whom the above information was given.

In the vicinity of Bleak Hall are to be found, on the North Edisto, the plantation known as Swallow Bluff, now owned by Mr. Julian Mitchell, and "Grimball's Point of Pines," often mentioned in the Acts for establishing roads and ferries, the Grimballs being an old and distinguished family.

Adjacent to the Townsend plantation, separating it from the sea, is found Botany Bay Island, and further south, behind Eddingsville Beach, are Shell House plantation, Seaside, and several other large places. Sea Cloud is also situated not very far distant from this neighborhood; a quaint old house named "Sea" for Seabrook, and "Cloud" for McLeod, when a man of the first name wedded a maiden of the last.

PROSPECT HILL—EDISTO ISLAND

Prospect Hill house on the South Edisto River is only about eighty years old, and was abandoned for many years as a wreck, but the present owner now intends to restore it to its proper condition. The chief historical interest connected with the place is found in the title deeds, which are very old, and have been kept in a bank vault in Columbia for a long period of time.

Mr. Mikell Whaley, who moved from Edisto Island to Columbia, becoming a distinguished physician of that place, was the son of Mikell Whaley, of Edisto, and his mother was Miss

Baynard, of Prospect Hill. Closely connected with this family also is Judge Marcellus Whaley, of Columbia.

The present owner of this dwelling, P. H. Whaley, a son of the late Reverend Percival Whaley, plans many and extensive improvements at Prospect Hill. The house is beautifully situated on a little bluff overlooking the waters of the South Edisto, and is a three-story structure of fine proportions. An entrance on the ground floor leads to a basement, floored with flagstones, which contains several beautiful rooms constantly used in earlier days by the residents of the establishment. The floor of the piazza on the second story is reached by a broad flight of steps (in the center) with iron railings, and this floor forms an agreeable veranda to the basement. Although the house is not a hundred years old, its air of antiquity, combined with its dignity of construction make it a beautiful place in spite of its disrepair.

Inside the house the ceilings are very high, and the cornices very simple. The doors are large, and the wainscoting, and the woodwork around the mantelpiece, and above the windows are fine examples of the period immediately following that known as the Adam period.

Mr. Whaley, now connected with the Whaley-Eaton Service, Washington, D. C., is a brilliant writer, and was for many years on the editorial staff of the Philadelphia *Ledger*. He will find no more fitting setting for his reconstructive abilities than the renovating and restoration of the spacious and gracious house at Prospect Hill on the Edisto.

There are three houses which bear this name—the present house, the house near Georgetown, and Mr. Bissell Jenkins' house (formerly Manigault-Barnwell) near Wiltown on Pon Pon River.

LITTLE EDISTO

Little Edisto Island is owned almost exclusively by Mr. J. Swinton Whaley, and his home there is called "Little Edisto." Some of the land on the island is owned by Julian Mitchell, but it is only a very small portion. The house on Little Edisto was built by Mr. J. Swinton Whaley's father, Mikell Whaley,

15   225

and is a magnificent frame house built on a high brick foundation. Mr. Whaley is one of the progressive men of the State and is a representative of the well-known Whaley family, whose genealogy can be traced in the *South Carolina Historical Magazine* files.

At a recent exhibition in the Charleston Museum, showing the life on the plantations, Mr. J. Swinton Whaley, who is one of the trustees of the museum, brought from his plantation "Little Edisto," the old hand corn mill, the log rice mortars, and the fanner baskets, which were put into use for what might be the last time. A negro over eighty years of age, expert in the by-gone industry, demonstrated the work. Corn was ground in the mill and separated with the fanner basket into the meal, the fine and coarse "grits" or hominy, and the husks. South Carolina golden rough rice was pounded in the old log mortar and again the fanner basket was used to separate the finished rice, the hulls and the rice from flour. These operations were a part of the daily routine of the old South Carolina plantations in preparing both the food of the master's family and that of the hands. There was a corn mill for the use of the master's house and another in the plantation street where the negroes ground the corn that was issued to them as rations. The use of the fanner basket is rapidly becoming a lost art. Rice has almost ceased to be planted in South Carolina and examples of the old plantation implements are becoming rare. The corn mill consists of two very fine French buhr stones that have been in the family of Mr. Whaley for many generations and that were presented by him to the museum several years ago.

Across Russell's Creek, opposite Mr. J. Swinton Whaley's place, lies the Ephraim Baynard place, now owned by Charles Whaley Seabrook (son of E. Barnard Seabrook). The house is one of the old landmarks of the island, although it is of no particular significance, architecturally speaking.

Little Edisto and the C. W. Seabrook house, as well as Old Dominion are found near a place known to the Edistonians as the Borough, the origin of the name being entirely unknown.

226

It is in the interior of the island between St. Pierre's Creek and the Dawhoo River.

FROGMORE

The Edward C. Whaley house, Frogmore, is exactly opposite the Edisto school house, on the public road. It is an old wooden building on a brick foundation, and was built by Dr. Edward Mitchell, of Waccamaw when he married Miss Elizabeth Baynard.

Another nearby place was Brooklines, the Ephraim Seabrook plantation, which lay inland in the immediate vicinity of Frogmore, between it and Laurel Hill. This latter has on it a substantial old dwelling which belonged to one of the Edward Seabrooks, but the place is now partitioned between Edward Bailey and Charles Seabrook by right of purchase.

PETER'S POINT

On St. Pierre's Creek there is a fine peninsula formerly known as Peter's Point, which for years belonged to the heirs of John J. Mikell, and is now owned by Mr. J. Townsend Mikell. There is also an old house called Pierre Point House, constructed in 1840. The front piazzas are found on both floors, but in the rear these extend only on the lower story. The timbers for this place were specially cut, being unusually long, to resist the strain and swing caused by storms. The rooms are large (18 by 20), there being two on each side of the hall, and two smaller ones in the rear. Almost the entire second story is enclosed in glass, and resembles a conservatory. There is a most interesting double stairway in the rear hall, which affords an ascent to the second story and shelters a descent into the basement.

It is a remarkable fact that with but few exceptions the old houses on Edisto (and there are many of them) are nearly all still standing.

POPE HOUSE

Above St. Pierre's Creek, in the same neighborhood as Prospect Hill and Laurel Hill, is found a quaint house which may perhaps be considered in some ways the most interesting place on Edisto Island. It is called the Pope House, better known in history as the Old Middleton Place, it having been the home for many years of Oliver H. Middleton. Although the house is known in history as the Old Middleton Place, the names of John and Joseph Pope are to be found signed as "commissioners" in the records of the Episcopal church after the year 1792 along with the names Jenkins, Fickling, Bailey, Wilson, Seabrook, Simmons, Grimball, Murray, Hannahan, Crawford, Eddings and Beckett. The distinguished jurist, Daniel Pope, is of this family. The name of O. H. Middleton does not appear until about 1841, according to Mr. Seabrook's sketch of the Episcopal church on Edisto.

Oliver Hering Middleton was the third son of Governor Henry Middleton. His first venture in life was as a midshipman in the United States Navy, but presently he resigned this office and returned to his estates in South Carolina, where he later shared with unbroken spirit the ruin that overwhelmed his class during the Civil War. He married Susan Matilda Harriet, only daughter and heiress of Robert Frail Chisolm, M. D., of Edisto Island, and by her had a son, Oliver Hering Middleton, who was killed in the Confederate service at Matadequin Creek. His second child was Mary Julia, who married Benjamin H. Read, of Rice Hope, on the Cooper River, and his third child, Susan Middleton, died unmarried at St. Catherines, Canada. His daughter Eleanor married Benjamin Huger Rutledge, Esq., colonel of the 4th S. C. Cavalry, C. S. A., and his other daughter was Olivia, who married Mr. Frederick Rutledge Blake, late captain of the C. S. A.

It is through this branch of the Middleton family that we are interested in this house, although it is of significance also, because of the Hamilton holdings on Edisto, that Governor Arthur Middleton's eldest son married Elizabeth Hamilton, a daughter of the Honorable James Hamilton. It is of note concerning the Chisolm family that Mr. Alexander Chisolm, a merchant of Charleston, married a Mrs. Sarah Maxwell, of Charleston, who was the widow of William Maxwell, Esq., of Edisto.

The building itself is a handsome affair, rather more elaborate than the usual island houses. The rooms are particularly spacious and airy, and the ceilings unusually high, the colonial idea of square rooms being everywhere evident. The lower story of the house displays elaborate hand-carved cornices and woodwork over the door and windows. In many respects the place differs from the general run of the island houses, one strange feature being a circular stairway. In some of the rooms the mantels are of Italian marble, and the chimneys are constructed with five flues. The brick basement is arched, and the foundation timbers very large and heavy.

A ghost story concerning the Middleton place is connected with the Chisolm owners, and it is said that Mrs. Chisolm's spirit is often seen at twilight down by the big gate; she stands in the shadow of one of the brick posts that separate this old domain from the public road. Mrs. John Andell, of John's Island, who was a Miss Seabrook and lived in this old house for many years, says that the negro tenants refuse to pass the place after dark for fear of meeting this "Haunt."

BRICK HOUSE

The "Brick House" property was granted to Paul Hamilton by the Lord Proprietors about the time of the first settlers in and around Charleston and vicinity. Mr. Edward J. Jenkins has in his possession papers dating back to 1703, which prove that Brick House and its outhouses were built before this date, though the exact year has not been established. It is thought that the house was ereceted some time between the years 1670 and 1680. Four hundred and thirty acres of land and one hundred and eighty-one acres of marsh were granted to Paul Hamilton. The property was bounded on the north by Russel Creek, on the south by lands of Capt. William Bower, on the east by lands of Thomas Sachwerell, and on the west by lands of Lewis Price. With the exception of Paul Hamilton, these names are not remembered on the island, there being no descendants.

Concerning the Hamilton family Mr. A. S. Sally, Jr., writes: "In the office of the Historical Commission in Columbia there is a small manuscript volume, 'A Booke for Recording of Cattle Markes & others Given by Hono. Thomas Smith Esq. Landgrave & Govern'r in Sept 1694.' " Previous to this time a few marks had been recorded at random in other volumes. Some of the first record of Cattle Markes & others refer to "Mr. John Hamilton of Edestoh Island in Colleton County & Recorded his marke of Cattle Hoggs. &c: being as followeth, In each Eare two Half Moones. The Topps of both Eares Cropt & Soe Slitt down to bottom of each Eare this Brand Marke as per Margent. This day came Mr. John Hamilton of Edestoh Island in Colleton County and Recorded; His daughter, Mary Hamilton,. . . his Sonn Paul Hamilton . . . and his daughter Anna Hamilton."

Mr. Edward J. Jenkins, the present owner of "Brick House" says, "The property reverted to James and Harriett Maxwell and was purchased from them by Joseph Jenkins, my great-grandfather, who willed it to his son, Col. Joseph Evans Jenkins (my grandfather) from whom the property passed to my father, John Micah Jenkins, and from him it came to me. As I am the father of four boys and four girls, it probably will remain in our possession until the house crumbles into dust."

The brick from which the house is built came from Holland. The house is Dutch colonial, the walls are two feet thick and the facings on the corners and under the windows are of concrete. The panelings of the rooms are cypress and some are painted in oil by a master hand. All the lumber used was the best and was seasoned for years. The work was done by carpenters brought from England.

THE MORTONS AND THE WILKINSONS

The present Ed. Wilkinson house on Edisto Island was said to have been built by one of the Jenkins family. It is a conventional wooden structure rising upon a high brick foundation, suitable for the climate of the Sea Islands. Its chief architectural feature is its front piazza which has unusually large and beautiful columns. The house is adjacent to the Murray homestead and has near it the family burial ground.

OLD HOUSE AT "WILTON BLUFF."

The family of Wilkinsons is a very old and honorable one in the State. Landgrave Joseph Morton came to the colony about 1681 and is said to have married a Miss Blake. His son Joseph Morton married Sarah Wilkinson, who, becoming a widow in 1721, married two years later, Honorable Arthur Middleton and died in 1765, leaving a long and interesting will, the first bequests of which relate to her own kindred. She gave Christopher Wilkinson, son of her "Cousin" Francis Wilkinson, deceased, a plantation on Wadmalaw Island, "Commonly Called Bear-Bluff Ladinwah and Morton Town"; gave Edward Wilkinson, son of said "Cousin Francis," a plantation or island opposite to Willtown (there are several Wilkinson graves in the burying ground at Willtown on the Bluff) and the lots in Willtown which she had bought of her "Cousin" Joseph Wilkinson and Robert Yonge, deceased, and the buildings thereon and a tract of land in the upper part of Beech Hill, St. Paul's Parish; gave Morton Wilkinson, son of said "Cousin Francis" two plantations called Tooboodoo (Toogoodoo) and Juniper's in St. Paul's providing that if said Morton Wilkinson should die without male issue that the said plantation should go to her grandson, John Middleton.

The Wilkinson family is connected by marriage with the Jerveys and with many of the other old low-country families. The Morton connection has, however, vanished and we look into the records of the past for further facts of interest. One of the earliest bits of information concerning Landgrave Morton is found in a letter of Edward Randolph to the Board of Trade (1698–1699) "In year 1686, one hundred Spaniards, with negroes and Indians landed at Edistor (50 miles to the Southward of Charles Town) and broke open the house of Mr. Joseph Moreton, then Governor of the Province, and carried away Mr. Bowell, his brother-in-law, prisoner, who was found murdered two or three days after; They carried away all his money and plate, and 13 slaves, to the value of £1500 sterling, and their plunder to St. Augustine."

An inventory of the estate of Mr. John Morton in 1752 reveals some choice belongings for these early days, among them being "eleven mahogany chairs, two elbow chairs and a couch, a mahogany book case, two long sconce Glasses, card table, a round Tea lavee, pictures of the twelve months in proper dress and the Rakes and Harlots progress, also a harpsi-cord and a pair of Red and Green enameld china bowls; showing culture and good taste." The inventory included the names of many books and carried also a goodly number of guns and swords.

The direct descendants of the Wilkinsons are lineal descendants of Landgrave Morton. Representatives of the family are not only found on Edisto Island but on other adjacent Sea Islands. The old homestead is situated on the high road that crossed Edisto in a diagonal direction.

CHAPTER XII

BEAUFORT—INCLUDING COMBAHEE AND CHEE-HA DISTRICTS—WITH TWO PICTURES OF WILLTOWN HOUSES AND ONE AT BARNWELL

BETWEEN CHARLESTON AND BEAUFORT

 JOURNEY from Charleston to Beaufort in 1785 or 1786 is most delightfully described in the diary of Timothy Ford; who begins the account thus:

"Friday 4th Ap. This day set out in a chair with Mr. De Saussure for Beaufort about 70 miles where the circuit court is to be held. We rode through very heavy sandy roads with fatigue and difficulty until we reached Ashley ferry (Bee's ferry), and after crossing it had very good roads causways only excepted which are frequent in this country & generally bad. As our rout was for some distance on the side of the river we were often entertained with the prospect of country seats of which there is a number and some of them fraught with taste and magnificence. In the evening we reached the plantation of Mr. Waring. . . . We stay all night at this mansion & are most hospitably entertained. In the morning we set off at 8 o'Clock upon our journey. . . . We ride Eleven miles to Pompon ferry. . . ." (at Jacksonboro settlement).

The old places on the Combahee deserve notice, even if fragmentary; there are three men now living who can supply probably better than anyone else the history of this once prosperous and now deserted region. One of these is Capt. William Elliott, over eighty years of age, who served in the war between the States, now of Yemassee, S. C. He lived many years at Ball's, on Chee-Ha, upper Chee-Ha neck, and is familiar with the local history. Another authority on the subject of Combahee matters is Mr. Daniel J. Chaplin, now living at

Walterboro, whose mother owned Fields' Point, the last plantation on Combahee, next to the sound. Mr. Ambrose E. Gonzales, of Columbia, S. C., also knows a great deal of the history; he used to live on Chee-Ha, his father having been General Gonzales of the "Bluff" plantation, who married Mary Elliott, daughter of the Hon. William Elliott of this locality.

Mr. James Henry Rice, Jr., tells us that the only houses left below Bonnie Hall are those of Oaklands (Col. Lowndes), Rose Hill (Mr. Theodore D. Ravenel), and negro streets at Cypress (Col. William C. Heyward), with overseers' houses at Paul and Dalton. Combahee had no mansions on it at any time, so far as is known, only frame structures; this was generally true of Chee-Ha as well, whose history is infinitely more interesting and valuable than Combahee. More has been heard of the latter merely because rice continued to be planted on it after the war, and still is planted, whereas Chee-Ha was allowed to go down.

Brick House, the present home of James Henry Rice, is on Chee-Ha, and belonged at one time to Colonel B. F. Hunt, a friend of Petigru, Webster, and other celebrities. It is said to have been the first place settled, and to have on it the first house built in that part of South Carolina.

To quote Mr. Rice, "Combahee flows roughly southward; to the west are marshes and low islands, dividing it from Wimbree Creek and lower down still comes Willimon Creek, back of Willimon Island; settlements on Combahee, after leaving Combahee Ferry (situated on Nieuport plantation— Henry Cheves) with the exception of two, one of which belongs to Cheves and the other to Dr. Wilson, of Savannah, are on the east side. Facing the ferry on the east are Cypress plantation (Col. W. C. Heyward before the war) and Oakland, Colonel Lowndes; then comes Hickory Hill, Rose Hill (Ravenel), Longbrow (F. Q. O'Neill), Paul and Dalton, Magwood, Old Combahee (properly Woodburn plantation) Middleton . . . Tar Bluff (Fripp family), and Fields' Point, composed of two small plantations, Walnut Point, facing Chee-Ha and Fields' Point, facing Combahee.

234

"Former Governor Heyward, the irridescent and cloud-massing Clinch, occupies with his associates, the Du Ponts, the upper stretch of Combahee, where it is formed by the junction of Cuckold Creek with Saltkehatchie. . . .

"The scenery along the river is picturesque, with a haunting appeal, such as far countries make when first beheld, much as Australia and Patagonia, for example. There is nothing on the coast exactly like it. The bold bluff, from Fields' Point to Old Combahee is without parallel in the entire South.

"It is crowned with magnolias, palmettoes, giant live oaks, and with a few large pines that the vandals have not cut yet. At intervals sharp and deep ravines cut through it, just as they do in the mountains, the sides of which would keep a botanist, a mycologist and musicologist busy for months. Far away to the southeast the smoke of the Beaufort factories may be seen, and, in the immediate foreground, lines of palmettoes look so much like date palms that one fancies the Nile just above Cairo when looking toward Ghizeh."

In 1768 the third Landgrave Bellinger sold 977 acres he had inherited from his sister Elizabeth to Barnard Elliott, in whose hands it became known as Bellevue. It was on this plantation that Colonel Barnard Elliott erected, before the Revolutionary War, the "Temple" of which Mr. William Elliott in his Carolina Sports gives an account in the chapter "A Day at Chee-Ha."

"The traveller in South Carolina, who passes along the road between the Ashepoo and Combahee rivers will be struck by the appearance of two lofty white columns, rising among the pines that skirt the road. They are the only survivors of eight, which supported in times anterior to our Revolutionary War, a sylvan temple, erected by a gentleman, who to the higher qualities of a devoted patriot, united the taste and liberality of the sportsman. The spot was admirably chosen, being on the brow of a piney ridge, which slopes away at a long gun-shot's length into a thick swamp; and many a deer has, we doubt not, in time past, been shot from the temple when it stood in its pride—as we ourselves have struck them from its ruins."

It was at the headwaters of the historic Chee-Ha River, which is second only to the Ashley and Cooper, that Colonel Barnard Elliott erected the Temple. The next place is put down in Mills' atlas as Marchland, and just below it was Hutchinson, named for a noble family. Mr. Hutchinson hired a tutor from the North named March, who made the most of his opportunities and married Miss Sallie Hutchinson, who had long been classed as an old maid (they were considered old maids when youthful in those days). On the first visit of the newly wedded couple to Beaufort in a rowboat the negroes improvised a chorus, thus "Miss Sallie, she got husbon'; shum dar, shum dar." All the way down and back this "epithalamium" resounded. One of their daughters married a physician of Philadelphia, but they were later separated, and she afterwards married in Paris Count Tedini, an Italian, cousin of the King of Italy. For many years she and the Count lived at March plantation, by which name Hutchinson was then known. The house there has fallen down, but the grove is one of the noblest on the coast, and still remains.

Stock plantation, which adjoins March plantation, has a noble house site, overlooking miles of marsh down Chee-Ha, with enough large live oaks left to add all needed picturesqueness. The old house is gone, but it was here that John Laurens spent the last night of his life. He was buried the next day in the graveyard at Stock, but his body was later removed by his father, Henry Laurens, to the plantation of Mepkin. The next place below, and on the west side of the Chee-Ha, was bought by Shaffer, for some time sheriff of Colleton County, and it is held by his son, E. T. H. Shaffer, of Walterboro. The adjoining plantation is the Baring place, later known as the Farmer place, when acquired about the time of the war by a member of Judge Farmer's family. Both of these last two places, however, were cut from the original Minott tract. The next plantation on the same side is Whaley, owned formerly by the Whaleys of Edisto Island. Then comes Brick House, and lastly Riverside, on which there was a frame house, near which was the cemetery. Over this cemetery the Savannah River Lumber Company has erected its saw mill plant.

236

"PROSPECT HILL," NEAR "WILLTOWN" (OR "WILTON")

Formerly a Barnwell-Manigault House, now owned by Mr. Bissell Jenkins

On the east side of the Chee-Ha the first place belonged originally to Colonel Barnard Elliott and was later bought by Mr. Robert Chisolm. It is at present cut into two places owned by a Mr. Boynton and a Mr. Savage. Below this, on both rivers (the Chee-Ha and Ashepoo are here close together) everything was owned by Thomas Rhett Smith (born 1800) whose ancestors had owned it from earliest times. His daughter married William Elliott (author of "Carolina Sports"), and from her brother, Thomas Rhett Smith, Jr., she inherited an additional twenty thousand acres, all of which passed to the Elliott descendants. The greater portion was acquired by Ambrose Elliott Gonzales, whose mother was Mary Elliott, and whose father was General Ambrose Jose Gonzales, one of the Confederate and Cuban Armies.

Thomas Rhett Smith, Jr., was a man of culture and travel. He had many visitors from different parts of the world, especially from England and France, as did William Elliott, who enjoyed a wide acquaintance in those countries. One of the most conspicuous names was William Makepeace Thackeray, who spent a month at the Bluff, on Social Hall, with Mr. Elliott. The lower place was known as Airy Hall, and there was a Concert Hall above, the exact location of which cannot be determined. Mr. Thomas Rhett Smith, Jr., kept a French gardener to look after his flower garden and his rosary, the latter containing ten acres. He had an English gardener for his vegetables. Mr. Smith had a large library, and a nearby hill where he used to retire to study is known as "Study Hill." Chee-Ha neck shows signs of Confederate fortifications from end to end, these having been designed by General Pemberton and Captain William Elliott, of Yemassee, who has been previously mentioned.

Timothy Ford writes: "The planters all fix (live) at a distance from the road with avenues cut through the woods leading up to their houses. The negro houses are laid out like a camp & sometimes resemble one."

Edwin De Leon, writing in *The Southern Magazine* on "Ruin and Reconstruction," says:

"One of the most curious and attractive sights on a Southern plantation used to be this negro quarter, with its regular rows of small cabins grouped together, with narrow streets between, and as fresh and smart-looking as whitewash could make them externally, and compulsory scrubbing and sanded floors could make them within. Generally remote from the planter's mansion and outhouses, contiguous to the fields under cultivation, these cabins had allotted to each a small patch of land, on which the negroes could raise their own vegetables, poultry and pigs, which were their private property, and from which, when industrious, they could earn pocket-money by selling the surplus to the master, or to outsiders, at will. Their regular supplies of food, or rations, were regularly supplied, irrespective of the products of these small patches—which were considered and treated as their private property—so that the chance even of accumulation was given them, of which, however, they seldom availed themselves. Attached to these cabins was always a large hospital or infirmary, with a regular physician visiting it at stated intervals; so that the infirm or sick were promptly and properly cared for and cured—an advantage shared by no other class of laborers anywhere. . . . Disabled or aged slaves were, until death, the pensioners of the slaveholders, who could not, if they would, shirk the charge.

"The negro quarter was the little world wherein the slave lived and moved in his hours of leisure. . . . From the cabins from nightfall until midnight might be heard the sound of banjo, 'bones,' or violin, the loud laugh or the peculiar sounds of negro minstrelsy, and the dance was as frequent as the song. With a quick air for music, and sweet, clear, though uncultivated voices, the negro race everywhere enjoys melody, and used to indulge freely in it, both of a religious and secular character. The voice of prayer and praise used to ascend from those cabins, for the negro women were great psalm-singers and the men great exhorters; and their masters encouraged religious exercises among them."

But "over master and man the tide has swept," and in the great rice planting regions, near Beaufort particularly,

". . . . the eye of the visitor roves over great tracts of cultivation, semi-tropical in outward aspect, where the planter's lordly mansion stands (in some few instances), embowered among evergreen live-oaks, magnolias and cedars, whose hedges of Cherokee rose and jessamine fill the air with perfume, and the fig, banana and orange are flourishing in the open air, laden with their luscious fruits. Long reaches of marshlands, as flat and as fertile as those of the Egyptian delta, which they strikingly resemble, stretch out as far as the eye can reach; and the great rice-grinding buildings, crammed with their costly machinery, tower aloft and give a fictitiously busy air to the deserted plantations.''

Concerning Combahee Mr. Langdon Cheves writes briefly. ''There must have been a good house at Sheldon from early times, as the Bulls were one of the leading families of the Province and kept some state in their domestic affairs. The Yemassee Indians delayed development in this section and such plantations as were owned there were held by non-residents. It was not until after the Revolution when tide water cultivation of rice came in, that large plantations were developed by resident owners on both sides of the river and good houses built. There were large houses at Bonny Hall, Tomotley and many other places, down to Clay Hall in later times. Although most of these places were burned during the Civil War their history is worthy of preservation.'' Mr. Timothy Ford's diary (1785) tells of his arrival late in the evening at the ''widow DeSaussure's, where we are regaled with a dish of tea and spend the night. This is a very pleasant place but very solitary, no neighbors in less than 4 or 5 miles w^h induced me to recommend to Miss DeSaussure to get married in self defense.''

Daniel DeSaussure, the oldest son of Henry, was born at Pocataligo in 1735. His father, of an old French family of Lorraine, which left France on account of religion in 1551 and moved to Switzerland, came to Carolina in 1731 from Lausanne and settled near Coosahatchie. Daniel moved to the town of Beaufort and took an early and active part in the Revolution. In 1778 in command of a company, he captured, near St. Helena, a British transport with troops and two captains. During the seige of Charleston, he bore arms and was sent a prisoner to St. Augustine and was liberated in 1781. He was appointed president of a branch Bank of the United States at Charleston, and was president of the Senate of South Carolina in 1798, when he died. He lost two brothers in the Revolution and his only surviving son was the distinguished Chancellor, Henry William DeSaussure.

After the visit at the DeSaussure's, Timothy rides into "the little village of Beaufort. It consists of about 30 houses—stands on an arm of the sea very pleasantly & is stiled a very healthy place. The inhabitants are almost all connected by marriage." He proceeds to give his impressions of the town, which differ but slightly, with the exception of the number of houses, from what would be said about it to-day. Beaufort has always been famed for the beauty of its women and the culture and bravery of its men.

The earliest mention of the name "Beaufort" in connection with the town is found in the minutes of a meeting of the Lords Proprietors of the Province held December 20, 1710, where it was agreed that a seaport town should be erected at Port Royal in Granville County to be called Beaufort Town. An order was passed on June 6, 1717, by the Council of the Province, that any person taking up any of the front lots in the town should be obliged to erect thereon, within two years, a house fifteen feet wide and thirty feet long; those taking up any of the back lots were to build houses of similar dimension within three years from the date of their grants.

A map supposed to be either the original or a copy of the first map of Beaufort is in the Historical Commission at Columbia. The street or space along the water front is not designated by any name on the plan. In the grants and in some deeds giving the boundaries of the front lots this street is called Bay Street, or The Bay, and as such it is known to-day.

In 1785 the commissioners (John Joyner, William Hazzard and Robert Barnwell) are directed by an Act passed March 24, of that year, "to expose to sale in whole or in lots the land commonly known to be common adjoining the town of Beaufort." The funds secured from the sale were to be used for rebuilding the parsonage house on the glebe lands.

The house which was sold to St. Helena's Church as a rectory is in front of the east gate of St. Helena's Church, and is

ST. HELENA'S CHURCH, BEAUFORT, ESTABLISHED 1712
From a hand-colored print

THE RECTORY, ST. HELENA'S, FROM THE CHURCHYARD
Built long before the Revolutionary War

one of the oldest houses in Beaufort. It was the home of John Barnwell, who was called "Tuscarora Jack" from having driven that powerful tribe of Indians out of Carolina. He came to this part of the country in 1701.

BARNWELL HOUSES IN BEAUFORT

At the corner of Washington and Cartaret Streets, on the Point, stand the ruins of the "old tabby house," once owned by John Barnwell, grandson of "Tuscarora Jack." John Barnwell married Sarah Bull, the daughter of General Stephen Bull.

Stephen Bull and John Barnwell were the two most prominent names in the first permanent settlement in the neighborhood of Port Royal, which, having the finest natural harbor in the State, was naturally first selected for settlement. It was so difficult to defend, however, that the first two attempts failed. The annals of Beaufort County during its first century may be said to consist of accounts of these two gentlemen.

The son and grandson of Stephen Bull were both named William, and both were Royal Governors of South Carolina. Stephen Bull had unusually large land grants, and was very wealthy; he endowed and built Sheldon Church, twice laid in ruins (during the Revolution, and again during the Confederate War), and he is buried in a vault under this church.

Colonel John Barnwell founded the town of Beaufort, which at the commencement of the Confederate War was chiefly inhabited by his descendants, in families of Elliott, Stuart, Rhett, Fuller, etc., and he seems to have been the founder of Beaufort Church, near the east end of which he is buried in a vault, only a few bricks of which are visible above the ground.

Up to the time of the Confederate War the old tabby house of the Barnwells occupied two squares; that in front was kept as an open lawn, on which the boys of the town played ball, and the Beaufort artillery drilled. Large oaks festooned with moss were on the side. Directly in front of, and on the sides of the house was a pretty flower garden, and separating it from the yard on the east side of the house was a row of orange trees. In this yard was a two-story servant house, constructed of the same primitive material as the main dwelling, a compound of oyster shell and lime called tabby, as was the two-story carriage house. To the rear of these was the vegetable garden.

The oldest house in the town was built in 1690 at the northeast corner of Mrs. Waterhouse's lot, and it is said that Senator John Barnwell, who fought in the Revolutionary War (a grandson of "Tuscarora Jack"), was born there in 1748. As Mr. Edward Barnwell, a nephew of "General Jack," and father of Mr. Osborne Barnwell, was also born in this house in 1785, and it is probable that the place belonged to the Barnwell family for many years during the early period of the settling of Beaufort. It is so constructed with long piercings in the foundations, that muskets can be aimed in either direction, and underneath them a ledge runs along, on which munitions may be stored. This structure was erected when the Yemassee and Cherokee Indians used to make war on the whites. In those days warning signifying uprisings was sent from island to island by the waving of a red flag.

Mr. Fickling bought the house for a school, but it was afterwards used as a Masonic Hall, when it received its present name of the "Temple of the Sun," the porch with four large columns facing the east. Later the house was bought by Mr. Zealy, whose family occupied it until 1861. It is now the residence of Mr. and Mrs. Richard Van Bray, Jr.

Beaufort district was for many years known as "Indian Land." A discovery was made on Little Island, Beaufort County, of a communal dwelling that could have been built and used only by a people kindred to the Aztecs, to the tribes who owned the stern sway of Powhattan, and to the fierce Iroquois and Hurons—the "Mingos" of Cooper's tales, who differed racially, and probably radically, from the nations of Algonquin stock who inhabited the entire eastern coast from Florida to Canada. There are certain Aboriginal mounds on the coast of South Carolina.

On the Bay in Beaufort is an attractive two-story wooden house with a hipped roof and large chimneys, which was once known as the Calhoun residence, and is now occupied by Mrs. O'Dell, mother of Maude O'Dell, the noted actress. It is perhaps best known as the home of Edward Barnwell; and the fact that he was married three times, and was the father of sixteen children, may account for the substantial wings built to the east and west of the house, and the very large piazza adorning the entire front of this establishment. With such sizeable families it is natural that many other quaint and delightful houses in Beaufort, in addition to the three already mentioned, should have been connected with the historic Barnwell name.

HOMES ON THE POINT

The Paul Hamilton house is rightfully considered one of the handsomest places in Beaufort. It occupies a beautiful situation on "The Point," to distinguish this section from "The Bay," which is noted for its magnificent live-oaks. The house overlooks a slightly terraced garden leading down to the water's edge, with a quaint sea-wall on three sides to prevent the tide from overflowing the flower beds. The building is of the usual square style common to the Sea Island dwellings, which are designed for coolness and airiness. The principal features of this low-country architecture are the wide halls, rooms with high ceilings, and large verandas, all of which make for comfort in these southern latitudes.

The Hamiltons are a distinguished family in South Carolina history. Paul Hamilton, Comptroller of the State from 1799 to 1804, showed that, in time of stress and danger South Carolina had, during the Revolution, contributed more than five million dollars for the general defense. He also possessed a clear and systematic head, and made the first reports on the resources, debits and credits of the State ever compiled. His reports astonished the legislature, as they then for the first time knew their real fiscal condition, and were enabled to deal intelligently with the resources of the State.

From 1804 to 1806 Paul Hamilton was Governor of South Carolina, and became Secretary of the Navy in 1809, which position he occupied until 1813. Another Hamilton, James, occupied the gubernatorial chair from 1830 to 1832, one of the most exciting terms in history, because of the Nullification Movement.

Miss Mary S. Hamilton, a noted educator of Beaufort, and daughter of Colonel Paul Hamilton, now occupies the Hamilton house, and gives the following account of it: "Colonel Hamilton's house on the point was built in 1856, and planned by his wife and himself. We lived there for five years, and when the fleet entered the harbor in November, 1861, left the house until September, 1866. The story of its recovery may be of interest. The United States Government refused to rent any property to a former owner. They sold the homes in Beaufort for taxes and even when they paid the war tax back to the owners they only gave one-half the tax value and five dollars an acre for the land. Our home had been retained by the government for a hospital. I proposed that my uncle (Dr. Gibbes) who was living with us should write and offer to rent it, as the war was over and hospitals no longer required. He did so, and it was rented at once to him, so that in September, 1866, we returned in a wagon drawn by mules, and lying on mattresses, a happy crowd as we reached our old home after an absence of nearly five years.

"In November the house was put up at auction for sale. My father stated to the crowd gathered that it was his wife's and her children's and he would bid it to a million against another bidder who wanted it as a normal school for negroes. It was, however, knocked down to him at fifteen hundred and fifty dollars, a fortune in those days. He asked the court to allow him three days to visit Charleston and sell several lots my mother owned there from her English ancestors. We had no railroads to Beaufort then, only steamers, and it required three days for the round trip. They consented and he went to make the necessary arrangements. On the second day near sunset my brother of ten years came running in to tell us that at sunset the house was going to be sold. I went downtown to see if the Mayor, Colonel William Elliott, could stop the sale. While waiting at his home my uncle came in to announce the good news that Mr. Simpson, the express agent, and Mr.

"THE POINT," THE HAMILTON HOUSE, BEAUFORT

From a print

Holmes, a merchant, had heard of the proposed sale, raised the money among the business men and just before sunset paid for the home in the name of Colonel Hamilton. I had said that I would never shake hands with a Yankee, but that night across the counter I offered mine in thanks to Mr. Holmes. My father was successful and they were repaid on his return the following day. A Frenchman paid for the Edgar Fripp house back of ours, and would not allow the money to be returned, going away and leaving no address.''

The house on the Point now occupied by the Crofuts was built by Dr. Barnwell Sams in the latter part of the fifties, and was taken during the Confederate War for a hospital. The Sams family bought it at the U. S. Tax sale, and sold it to Mr. Wilson the sheriff. It passed through many hands and was bought finally by the Crofuts.

This residence has been selected as a good type of the ante-bellum residence of Beaufort. Its heavy brick column, supporting the flat roof to the galleries, give a rather massive effect to the establishment.

Near the Point also is the Christensen residence, a beautiful type of the conventional house, set upon a high, gracefully arched brick basement. Both up and down stairs the house has large fine piazzas which extend around the building on three sides. The front piazza on the lower story is broken to admit of a flight of steps leading into the garden, which is adorned with many fine trees and shrubs. The house is supposed to have been built by a Mr. Ledbetter, a Methodist minister. It was bought by Stephen Elliott, sold to Dr. Louis DeSaussure (who married for his second wife Miss Jane Hutson) and the house was later acquired by the Christensen family.

HOMES ON THE BAY

Beaufort is a place of many historic memories, one of her proudest being that she had the honor of entertaining General LaFayette on his visit to this country in the early part of the nineteenth century. The town extended to him an invitation which he accepted, and extensive preparations were made for his reception. Upon his arrival, on the evening of March 2,

1805, he was conducted through a bower of roses, attended by the Beaufort Guards. From the balcony of the John Mark Verdier house on Bay Street just opposite the wharf he spoke to the crowd gathered to welcome him. This is one of the oldest houses now left in the town.

A great ball was arranged in his honor to be given in the "Barnwell Castle," which house was used as a Court House after 1866 and accidentally burned about 1879. An authentic account taken from an old letter written by a member of the Barnwell family, who entertained him, reads:

"We went into Beaufort last Thursday evening expecting LaFayette would come there on Friday. We had lent our house to give the ball in. The ball committee requested us to dress the rooms, as he was expected at two o'clock. We were obliged to leave the rooms half dressed, to go down to the bay to see the procession. We had a very good position as we went to McNeston's Balcony where the arch was erected, but all our trouble was in vain, for after waiting there about an hour we returned to our home. We were afraid that he would not come at all. However, at about twelve notice was given that he had come. We were, of course, deserted by the Guards, who went to conduct him to the house. The procession was then so handsome that I scarcely regretted his not coming in the day. All the boys in the town had lights in their hands, which had a beautiful effect, shining on the long, white plumes of the Guards. He stayed just long enough to shake hands all around and eat supper. As it was the first time that LaFayette had entered any place at night at least it had the effect of novelty!"

After the Civil War every house in Beaufort was sold, and the Elliott house on the Bay passed into the possession of Admiral Beardsley, who was stationed near there, and who gave the place the name of the Anchorage. This house was built by one of the Elliotts, Ralph E. Elliott, a brother of William, who married Phoebe Waight. Phoebe and her husband lived at what is now the Anchorage in their younger days, and the two magnolias on each side of the house were planted by the former, Mrs. William Elliott. An obituary notice published in 1855 follows:

246

"THE ANCHORAGE," ON "THE BAY," BEAUFORT

The residence of the widow of Admiral Beardsley, formerly the Elliott house. Further on are to be seen the Edmund Rhett (Maxey) and the Stuart residences

Died in Beaufort (S. C.) on the 1st of June, 1855, Mrs. PHOEBE ELLIOTT, in the 84th year of her age.

This venerable lady, the oldest inhabitant, save one, of her native town, has passed the boundary of "four score years": yet her strength was not "labor and sorrow." Her eye was hardly dim, nor her brow wrinkled. She enjoyed life to its close, actively discharging its relative duties. Her spirit was bouyant; her affections ardent; and her heart filled with kindness towards her fellow-creatures. She walked before God humbly, thankfully, devoutly. She loved His house, and frequented His courts, and not many days before her death, occupied her place at the table of the Lord. A liberal steward of the property God assigned her, she was ready "for every good work," and did her full share in the Missionary efforts of the zealous congregation to which she belonged.

A long line of descendants encircled her with filial love, and three generations gathered around her dying bed. Her body was borne to the tomb by six of her grandsons, and surviving friends rejoice, in their sorrow, that God hath granted her "long life and good days," and grace to "glorify His name," and adorn her Christian profession.

One son, one grandson, and three nephews (including the Bishop of Georgia) are preachers of the everlasting gospel.

Charleston, June, 1855.

One of the Mr. Elliotts abandoned law for the gospel. The history of the law office which he used is remarkable. Its first occupant was the Rev. Dr. Fuller, a distinguished minister of Baltimore, who abandoned a lucrative practice in Beaufort to devote himself to the ministry. Rev. W. Johnson, late rector of a church on Edisto Island, was in this same office, leaving it, with Stephen Elliott, to enter the Theological Seminary in Virginia; and C. C. Pinckney, another law practitioner in that office abandoned law for the gospel. James Elliott, who finally became an Episcopal bishop, was at one time rector of St. Michael's Church in Charleston.

In the year 1790, by William Elliot, Sea Island cotton was said to have been first raised—on the exact spot where Jean Ribault landed the first colonists. In connection with the Elliott family is another place of scientific interest—on Devils Elbow barony. Upon this is found the village or summer settlement of Bluffton, situated on a bluff fronting the River May. It was the scene of much of the botanical work of Stephen Elliott, who frequently refers to it in his "Sketch of the Botany of South Carolina and Georgia," and in later years it was the field for the botanical observations of Dr. James H. Mellichamp.

Stephen Elliott, the botanist, married Miss Habersham, of Georgia, and their child was Stephen Elliott, who afterwards became Bishop of Georgia. This Bishop Elliott had a very distinguished daughter, Sarah Barnwell Elliott, a leader of the suffrage movement in Tennessee, and a well-known writer of to-day, some of her best-known works, among other novels, being "Jerry," "The Durket Sperret," "The Felmers," and "The House on the Marsh." There have been five bishops in the Elliott family, and there have been warriors also, Elliott's torpedoes being a notable contribution to the science of naval warfare.

There is as much discussion about the spelling of the Elliott name as there is about the Simons and the Hazzards. One of the number, at a recent family reunion, dropped into poetry anent the orthography of the name:

> "They have doubled the 'l'
> To make it swell;
> They have added the 't'
> To be odd, you see.
> Some have put a 'y'
> In the place of an 'i,'
> But still it spells
> E-l-i-o-t."

Opposite the Anchorage is the building known for years as the Sea Island Hotel, which was built by Dr. Stoney and occupied for some time by Nathaniel Barnwell Heyward. Immediately behind the hotel, on Craven Street, was the Thomas Rhett house, and immediately behind the Anchorage, on Craven Street, were two other Rhett houses, the one now used as a rectory, and the Edmund Rhett house, which was the old Maxey house, and came into the possession of the Rhett family when Edmund Rhett married the daughter of Mrs. Tom

HOUSE IN BEAUFORT, S. C., FROM THE PIAZZA OF WHICH LAFAYETTE SPOKE

KITCHEN AND WALL MADE OF "TABBY"
The Sams' Home, Beaufort, now the Crofut House

"WOODLANDS," THE RESIDENCE OF W. G. SIMMS, BARNWELL
From an old engraving

Stuart, whose home lay across the street. Mrs. Stuart was a Miss Williamson, and was twice married, first to a Mr. Cuthbert, and then to Dr. Tom Stuart. The grounds on which the Stuart home stood were extremely spacious, extending to the Bay.

The Onthank residence, also on the Bay, is an interesting brick building with a small square portico. Before the Confederate War it was the home of Mr. H. M. Fuller, and was later the dwelling place of the Onthank family. While an interesting structure, it is by no means historic, except as having been connected with the Fuller family.

The history of this family is associated with lands in St. Andrew's Parish, as well as with Beaufort, and the Fullers have married among all the old families of the town, Dr. Thomas Fuller, a well-beloved physician of this community, being the last to reside there. A distinguished Baptist divine of national reputation was also a member of this Fuller family.

At the time of the Civil War the houses in Beaufort were deserted; furniture, silver, priceless paintings and valuables of all descriptions were left to the mercy of the victor. In one case a dinner was left smoking on the table, and was devoured by the incoming army. The old homes were not burned, but the treasures in them were stolen by the negroes and soldiers, and passed into alien hands. During the rest of the struggle the Union forces occupied Beaufort and Port Royal.

At Barnwell, below Beaufort, stands the home of William Gillmore Simms, the noted writer.

CHAPTER XIII

ON THE ROAD TO COLUMBIA AND COLUMBIA AND ITS HOMES

THE WILLSON HOUSE

N the road from Charleston to Columbia about fifteen miles above Carnes Cross Roads, stands a fine old residence of the farm house type. The material used was of cypress and the house has two large brick chimneys at either gable end. It was built by Dr. John Willson, who came to this country from Monaghan, Ireland. He resigned as ship surgeon because he opposed the brutality of the captain toward his men. He landed at Georgetown, went to Indian Town, in Williamsburg District, married there, moved to St. Mark's Parish, Clarendon; and after a few years crossed the river and located at this place and built his home. Dr. John Willson, 2nd, was born there and so was John O. Willson. The building was constructed by slave labor.

Dr. John Willson died in 1856, but was well-known as a Union man. The Northern troops, spared the house from four raids during the Civil War. It seems a little singular that these Union troops should have known his opinion when he had been dead nine years. Dr. John Willson, the 2nd, was distinguished for his remarkable kindness to his slaves and the needy around him and for his public spirit. His son, John O. Willson D. D., says: "The only times I ever saw my father angry were when a patrol punished one of his negroes, and when a school-master severely chided his oldest daughter." This farm property is still in the Willson family and is now owned by John O. Willson D.D., president of Lander College.

John O. Willson Donaldson, a descendant of Dr. John Willson the 2nd, and a grandson of John O. Willson D.D., during his service in France in the World War, seems to have upheld

HOUSE ON THE ROAD TO COLUMBIA
Built just after the Revolution by the grandfather of Rev. John O. Willson

"FORT GRANBY," NEAR COLUMBIA
From an old print

the record of his progenitors. In *Harper's Magazine* for July, 1919, is found an account of Mr. Donaldson's capture by the Germans, his escape from prison, his recapture and second escape, constituting one of those extraordinary narratives in which luck, misfortune and persistent daring have been so artfully ordered by Fate as to seem almost incredible. "John O. Willson Donaldson is the son of Brigadier General T. Q. Donaldson of the Inspector General's Department at Tours, France. He received his instruction in flying at the ground school, Cornell University, then with the Royal Flying Corp at Thanto, with subsequent gunnery practice in Texas. In June, 1918, as a member of the 32nd Royal Flying Corp, Donaldson, Jr., was sent to France, and during the following two months he brought down nine German planes, of which he was officially credited with five (i.e., witnessed by four observers). Lt. Donaldson was awarded the Distinguished Flying Cross by Field Marshal Haig and has received two citations by General Pershing. He has also been recommended for the Distinguished Service Cross."

GRANBY

Granby, a settlement about two miles below Columbia, was a point of departure from the wilderness and into the Cherokee country. In the immediate vicinity of Fort Granby is found a primitive wooden house.

The Reverend Mr. Guignard, whose grandfather surveyed the city of Columbia and who is familiar with this section of the State, having spent many happy days at Granby, declares that the description given of it in Lossing's Field Book of the Revolution and the names of the owners are perfectly correct. Mr. Guignard says that it is safe to use the description of the house as given in Lossing and adds some interesting data, which is included in the following account.

The house of James Cacey, Esq. (pronounced Kazie), the Fort Granby of the Revolutionary War, is two miles below Columbia on the Congaree River. It is a strong frame building, two stories in height and stands upon an eminence near the Charleston Road, within three-fourths of a mile of Friday's

Ferry upon the Congaree. It overlooks ancient Granby, one of the forgotten settlements of the State, and the country round about.

The house itself is of the prevailing type in the up-country, very similar to the Willson place found on the road between Charleston and Columbia and repeated, with slight variations, all over the upper part of the State. It consists of a two-story building with a tall pitched roof and has large chimneys on either gable end, the peculiarity of the chimneys being the enormous flues. The entrance into this establishment is directly from the piazza and a hall running through from front to rear, but upstairs the arrangement is slightly different, the hall being traverse, extending from gable to gable.

Some gentlemen of Pine Tree of Camden constructed this dwelling as a storehouse for cotton and other products of the up-country, which they wished to send down the river upon flat boats to the domestic and foreign market situated at the sea-port towns. When the chain of military posts from Camden to Charleston was established, this building, strategically located for defence, was fortified and called Fort Granby. There a ditch was dug, a strong parapet was raised, bastions were formed, batteries were arranged and an abatis was constructed, all of which transformed the place from a trading station into a military post, first occupied during the Revolutionary War by a garrison of three hundred and fifty men, chiefly Loyalists and a few mounted Hessians, under the command of Major Maxwell.

Such was the importance of this place that Sumter made a demonstration against Fort Granby, but finding it too strong for his small arms, retired. Later Lee arrived in the vicinity on the evening of May 14th, 1781, the day on which Sumter took possession of Orangeburg, and on the edge of a wood within six hundred yards of Fort Granby he began the erection of a battery and a dense fog next morning enabled him not only to complete it but to mount a six-pounder brought by Captain Finley from Fort Motte, before being discovered.

When the fog rolled away Captain Finley discharged his cannon, and, at the same moment, the legion of infantry advanced, took an advantageous position, and opened fire upon the enemy's pickets. This sudden announcement of the presence of an enemy and this imposing display alarmed Maxwell excessively so that he consented to receive an American, Captain Eggleston (the ancestor of the Winnsboro Egglestons), who was sent with a flag to demand the surrender of Fort Granby.

After a brief consultation with his officers, Major Maxwell agreed to surrender the Fort, on condition that private property of every sort, without investigation of title, should be left within the hands of its possessors. This peculiar condition is ascribed by Lee in his Memoirs to Maxwells' desire to fill his purse rather than to gather military laurels. With various other conditions and after waiving of some of the exceptions by Lee (the American commander), capitulation took place, Maxwell surrendered and vacated, and Captain Rudolph raised the American flag on one of the bastions before noon while the captive garrison with its escort marched away.

The house yet bears "honorable scars" made by the bullets of Lee's infantry, for in the gable which points toward the river, between the chimney and a window, is an orifice formed by the passage of a six-pound ball from Finley's fieldpiece, and Mr. Guignard says that, as a little boy during his frequent visits to Granby, the first thing he did was to investigate the cannon-ball hole to make sure that it was still there. Not only is this hole still evident, but in one of the rooms are numerous marks made by an axe, used in cutting up meat for the garrison.

The house is still in the possession of the family of Caceys, whose ancestors, with those of his father-in-law, Mr. Friday, were the only Whigs of that name in the State, and they often suffered insults from their Tory kinsmen. Mr. Friday owned mills at Granby, and the Ferry (Friday's) still bears his name. The British garrison that occupied Fort Granby paid him for the flour, poultry, cattle and other things which it took, so that it is evident that Major Maxwell dealt fairly with him in this matter at least.

Among the interesting possessions of Granby is a picture of Emily Geiger, a kinswoman of the Caceys, and one of the heroines of the Revolution. She lived with her father, John Geiger, at his home at the forks of the Enoree and Broad Rivers. Although her father was a patriot, he was an invalid and unable to bear arms for his country. His daughter who served her country well was as ardent a patriot as himself. General Greene wished a letter to be carried to General Sumter. That no man could be found to volunteer for this duty is due to the fact that Rawdon was approaching the Congaree. Emily Geiger undertook the service, during the execution of which she nearly lost her life. General Greene was delighted by the boldness of this young girl, not over eighteen years old. He accepted her offer of service, but with his usual caution he made her memorize the message, so that if she should be compelled to destroy it, she could repeat it verbally to Sumter.

Mounted upon a strong and fleet horse Emily then took her departure, her aim being to cross the Saluda at Kennely's Ferry, the Congaree at Friday's Ferry and to proceed as directly as possible to General Sumter, who was then on the Wateree River. Nothing of moment happened to her during the first day's journey, but on the evening of the second day, when more than two-thirds of the distance had been safely passed, three men in the British uniform appeared suddenly before her in the road. Being unable to escape she was then arrested by them and carried before Lord Rawdon, whose camp was about a mile distant. His lordship questioned her closely as to where she was from and where she was going. Her answers not being direct, but evasive, did not satisfy his lordship, who ordered that she should be locked up in one of the upper rooms of the guard house. It was fortunate that she was left here alone for a short while, as she had the opportunity, which she embraced, to destroy the dispatch. She tore it into small bits, chewed and swallowed them. The last morsel was scarcely gone when a woman, prepared to search her and her clothing, appeared. But as nothing of a suspicious character was found upon her, Lord Rawdon, as he was in honor bound, permitted her to pursue her journey unmolested.

254

Not only did Rawdon release her, but furnished an escort to the home of one of her friends a few miles distant, where she partook of some refreshments and rested a few hours. Fearful of further delay she set out with a fresh horse and a guide who showed her a shorter and safer way than the one she had intended taking. By riding all night Emily found herself far from the neighborhood of Lord Rawdon and at sunrise the guide left her to pursue her journey alone. On and on she rode steadily, hot as it was, until about three o'clock in the afternoon of the third day when she suddenly came upon a file of soldiers, who from their dress she knew to be her friends. By them she was conducted to General Sumter, to whom she delivered her message.

It may be of interest to know that Emily Geiger afterwards became the wife of Mr. Thurmits, and is very properly regarded for her service as courier to the Continental Army as one of South Carolina's heroines. The picture is justly a source of pride to her relatives who reside at Granby. Another interesting relic of this house is a card table said to have been used by Lord Cornwallis at his camp.

There are several old burying grounds in that neighborhood, but most of them have gone to decay. In the iron gate of one is plainly discernible the name of "Hayne." Upon one of the old graves the inscription gravely rebukes the beholder in the following quaint words:

> "Stranger, what is this to Thee,
> Ask not my name, but as I am
> So shall you be."

The old wooden house at Granby has not only successfully withstood for over one hundred and fifty years the assaults of its natural enemies, time and weather, but has survived the Revolutionary War and escaped in some miraculous way the fate of so many houses in the path of Sherman's army.

COLUMBIA

Columbia is now the capital of the State of South Carolina. Before the Revolutionary War, when the lower part of the State was the most important portion, Charleston occupied that position. Just after the Revolutionary War, by an Act of General Assembly, commissioners were authorized and required "to lay off a tract of land of two miles square, near Friday's Ferry, on the Congaree River, including the plane of the hill whereon Thomas and James Taylor, Esquires, now reside, into lots of half an acre, each." The streets were not to be less than sixty feet wide, with two principal streets running through the center of the town. The old compass used by J. S. Guignard, the surveyor, in laying off the town is now in the possession of Mr. Guignard's great-grandson, Mr. James G. Gibbes.

"Thomas Taylor," writes Mr. Sally, "has been called the 'Father of Columbia,' because of the fact that the greater part of the city was built upon his former plantation. He was born in Amelia County, Virginia, September 10th, 1743, and came with his parents to South Carolina, a few years later; married Ann Wyche. He was a member of the Provincial Congress of South Carolina in 1775, and was a captain of militia until 1780, when he was promoted to colonel; was wounded at the battle of Fishing Creek; was sometime State Senator for the district between the Broad and Catawba Rivers; was a member of the State Convention which adopted the Constitution of the United States; and was one of the Commissioners who laid out Columbia for the capital of the State; died November 16, 1833, in his 91st year."

The modern Thomas Taylor house is found at 1112 Bull Street. It is an exceedingly handsome and luxuriant modern home. This house is Georgian and is constructed of brick. Set in the walls of the western porch is an interesting panel built of the brick and mortar from the original Thomas Taylor home, which was the first house built in Columbia, when the city was a great plantation owned by the Taylor family.

SEIBELS HOUSE

One of the oldest, if not the oldest, house in Columbia, which was built before Columbia's streets were laid out, is the J. J. Seibels house on Richland Street. This home is built entirely of hand-hewn timber and was erected by A. M. Hale,

ONE OF THE KINARD HOUSES, RICHLAND STREET, COLUMBIA

Now the Seibel residence

and bought some years later by Captain Benjamin Elmore and later purchased by the grandfather of the present owner. In the cellar of this house was found a beam, hand-hewn, and on it the date, 1796, carved, the evident date of the erection of this mansion. Concerning this place, *The State* says, in an article written by Miss Alice E. Wilson, a brilliant Columbia writer: "The house is largely colonial and reminds one strongly of Mount Vernon in its general outline, with its wide rambling spaciousness, and its succession of slender white columns. Around three sides of the house, these columns support a low, outstanding roof above a quaint paving of Old English tile laid on a level with the street.

"When Columbia was laid out in streets, it was found that the piazza trespassed on the sidewalk, but Capt. Elmore applied to the town for permission to lower the floors of the piazza to the street level and leave them open. A pavement and colonade connect the quaint little brick kitchen with the house. The porch on the front is of the very wide old-fashioned type and is broken at both ends by steps leading to the tile pavement from the rooms which are slightly elevated.

"The rooms are built on the old square plan, two on either end of the hall, 12 by 15. The front rooms, with very high corniced ceilings are about 24 feet square. Upstairs the plan is about the same. The colonial note is adhered to in its furnishings."

The attic of this delightful house has lived up to attic expectations. Three quaint little dormer windows serve to break the line of its "barn roof." In this attic, among various other curios, was hidden for years a sword of General Beauregard's presented to an aunt of Mr. Seibels, who was a personal friend of the general. A still more ancient treasure found there was a yellowed document, dated 1786, which was a land deed to Mr. Seibels from Richmond and Wade Hampton, for the sum of four hundred pounds sterling.

The Seibels house, in its perfect state of preservation stands as a landmark in Columbia. It is a wonderfully artistic and beautiful house and one that does credit to both its builder and owner.

BOYLESTON HOUSE

Another old and interesting house in Columbia is that of S. S. Boyleston, at 829 Richland Street. The date of the building of this home is unknown, but its style indicates that it was built some time in the early eighteen hundreds. Its first owner and builder was Jack Caldwell, a merchant prince of old days, and the father of the well-known Caldwell of Hampton's Cavalry. The house was bought during the Ku Klux days by the Misses Hampton, and was later acquired by Mrs. Cotton Smith, from whom it was conveyed to the present owner, Mr. S. S. Boyleston.

The house has three floors, including the basement, in which are to be found the billiard and breakfast rooms. The drawing-rooms, a dining-room and a guest-room are found on the second floor, which in common with many other Columbia houses, constitutes the entrance floor. The hall runs the entire length of the house, and is broken at the rear by a rather unusual stairway, which reverses the stairs found in some houses of its period; these generally start in a double flight and coalesce on the half-way landing and finally reach the floor above in one flight, but the stairway in this house reverses this order; starting in the center of the hall, it branches at the landing and reaches the floor above in two flights.

The cornicings in this house are conventional dentil design, which originated with the Greeks. The chandeliers swing from good specimens of bas-relief moulding on the ceilings. One chandelier worthy of particular mention is in the dining-room, which is finished in white and red velvet and forms a fitting setting for the handsome crystal chandelier and its countless irridescent pendants.

This handsome old home is one of the finest specimens of Greek Renaissance architecture in Columbia, the columns being especially notable.

CRAWFORD HOUSE

Many curious legends and interesting family stories cluster around the Crawford house, which is situated on Blanding

Street and was saved by faithful guards of soldiers during the burning of Columbia. It was built by John A. Crawford, eighty-three years ago, who was then president of the Commercial Bank. The premises formerly occupied a full half square with its gardens and greenhouse famous for rare and foreign plants, of which two South American jujube trees still stand.

The house has a high brick basement and is square. It is famous for its closets, which are built in most unexpected places; the most interesting one is high in the wall over the steps. This is accounted for by the fact that there is no attic to this house, the roof being flat and covered with copper. The house is built of hand-hewn "heart" timber and is reached from the street by a flight of wooden steps. A small entrance is formed by a portico with square columns, the lower half of which are of glass, used for displaying plants.

The hall is a veritable ballroom, 12 by 60, which runs the length of the house, broken only by the ascending stairway to the upper floor. Flanking this hall on the outside and opening from it by large French windows is a piazza running the length of the house and decorated by iron railings with brass knobs. Above are two attractive balconies with similar decorations. On the left side of the house is a succession of three rooms leading one into the other. All are twenty feet square, and have beautiful corniced work and elaborate hand carving above the massive mahogany doors which join these rooms. The original hand-stenciled wall-paper can still be seen on the walls of these large rooms and the bronze chandeliers hang from moisaic decorations in delicate shades. At one end of the center room are tall mirrors, which are so arranged as to give the effect of open windows with panes of glass.

The quaint old-fashioned style of furnishing and decoration is artistically carried out by heavy, richly colored draperies suspended from elaborately carved gilt cornices. Brass andirons and old-fashioned bellows are found in the fireplaces; these with their handsome black marble mantels carrying out the scheme of dignity and repose. Colonial furniture and china and other possessions are still in the house, over all of

259

which look down from the walls portraits of dead and gone Crawfords, among them the original owner, John A. Crawford.

MARSHALL HOUSE

A two-story brick building constructed about 1820 by Jesse DeBruhl, now the Marshall house, was designed, it is believed, by Robert Mills, the architect who is responsible for many handsome buildings in South Carolina. This house was for many years the home of the late Col. J. Q. Marshall, and is now in the hands of his daughter, Mrs. James Hammond. It is situated on the northeast corner of Laurel and Marion Streets and is one of the most imposing residences in the City of Columbia. (See frontispiece).

The wide spacious piazza does not extend the entire length of the house, as it did in many of the houses of that date, but its massive columns that reach to the gabled roof lend an air of dignity to this old brick mansion. An artistic fan-shaped transom above the large front doorway furnishes ample light for the wide hall running the entire length of the house. Unlike the houses of that period, the staircase was hidden from view, being concealed in a small back room, known as the staircase room, but of late years this staircase has been removed and one is now to be seen in the rear end of the hall. The halls, both upstairs and down, are flanked on either side by two big square rooms, with high ceilings and deeply recessed windows.

It was in this home that the Confederate general, James A. Johnstone, made his headquarters in 1865. When it was vacated by Johnstone, it seemed good to General Sherman's soldiers as fuel for their extensive conflagration and was about to be set in flames when Mrs. Wiley, who was a very young and beautiful woman, appeared on the scene and begged that her home be spared. The soldier's heart softened and he ordered that guards be placed around the house. Thus we have left to-day one of the most artistic productions of the nineteenth century.

MOORE HOUSE

Closely related to the Marshall house because of its similarity of architecture and because of the date of its con-

THE "TOM WILSON" HOUSE, COLUMBIA

struction, is the Moore house at 1409 Gervais Street. There have been some modern improvements made on the house in the past few years. The large ell at the back was added for sleeping porches. Charm is given to this old home by its large piazzas, both upstairs and down, in the rear and in front. It was here that LaFayette was entertained and a large ball was given in his honor.

In later years the house was used as Colonel Stone's headquarters, and because of this fact it was spared from the treacherous flames of General Sherman's army. Prof. Yates Snowden, says that it was from the porches of this house, that he as a little boy watched the progress of Sherman's army as it marched down Gervais Street in February, 1865.

The place has passed through many hands, having at one time been the home of Dr. Leland of the Presbyterian Theological Seminary, and after various other owners was acquired by Governor John Lide Wilson, and is now in possession of R. L. Moore, of Columbia.

DESAUSSURE HOUSE

The residence, 1421 Gervais Street, now owned by W. J. Powers was built over a hundred years ago by Chancellor DeSaussure and was his home for some years. The house has passed through many hands. From Mr. DeSaussure it went to Judge William Martin, who built the little brick house in the yard and used it for his law office. Col. Robert Hart Goodwin then acquired it and later sold it to the Bauskette family, by whom many brilliant balls and other entertainments were given. During the Reconstruction period it was bought by Judge Willard, a Northern lawyer, who lived there for some time in great style. It then passed through the hands of Captain Stamley, the Condit family, and Mr. M. C. Heath, of Columbia, and is now occupied by Mr. W. J. Powers.

This home, though simple in style and appearance, has many stories of interest and bits of tradition connected with it. The house stands in the midst of a garden filled with rare plants and shrubs. The little brick structure at the rear is famous in spring for the clambering wisteria that completely covers it. The house itself is a typical square colonial building with its long, wide halls from which two rooms open on either side. The lower hall is divided by an arch, behind which a massive square stairway leads to the floor above.

The double verandas are supported by large, square columns. These verandas stretch the length of the house and lend an air of hospitality so characteristic of the Southern homes of that period. The massive front doorway is an especially fine piece of architecture.

The most interesting bit of history connected with this home is that when LaFayette made his memorable visit to Columbia and was entertained at the Moore house next door, it is said that the house was not large enough to accommodate his entire suite, so the latter were entertained elaborately at the DeSaussure residence. The fences were taken down between the two premises so as to give convenient access to the two homes.

PRESTON HOUSE

The land upon which Chicora College for Women is now located passed from the commissioners to Judge Thomas Waites, and by him was sold to Ainsley Hall, a prominent Columbia merchant, who came to America from England in 1800, settled in South Carolina and married a Miss Hopkins. Mr. Hall, with the assistance of Robert Mills, the architect, built a handsome home upon his newly purchased property. The exquisite white marble mantel in the east drawing-room and the weather-beaten fountain in the old gardens reflect the talent of one of the greatest sculptors of that day, Hiram Powers.

The house is mostly colonial in style, set on a high brick basement, with a broad marble-tiled porch flanking its entire front. The corniced roof is supported by beautiful Doric columns. At either end, as well as in the middle of the porch, steps are found leading into the garden. The entrance faces the middle steps and leads into a walk which enters from the street between massive iron gates.

The hall within is divided by a beautiful arch, beneath which a fine circular staircase leads to the floor above. On either side of the front hall are the east and west drawing-rooms which are reached by wide swinging doors. These doors, with the large French windows, high ceilings and good floor space, produce an air of spaciousness that characterizes the old Southern homes. The entire front could be thrown into one room, and such a house lends itself readily to magnificent entertainments.

In the year 1826 or 1828 the property was bought by General Wade Hampton, of Revolutionary fame. General Hampton was the father of Colonel Wade Hampton, who served as aide to General Jackson in the battle of New Orleans, and grandfather of Governor Wade Hampton, who has endeared himself to the hearts of every South Carolinian. General Hampton's wife (his third wife), who was, before her marriage, Miss Mary Cantey, devoted the remainder of her life to the maintenance of the property. The beautiful English walks were laid out under her direction, and a landscape gardener was employed to beautify the grounds. She imported and planted rare trees of every description; a greenhouse was built and filled with the choicest plants; hedges of boxwood bordered the walks and flowers bloomed at every turn. It was an earthly paradise.

Upon General Hampton's death the property was inherited by Mrs. Sally Hampton Preston, the wife of John S. Preston. In these days the place was a scene of splendid Southern hospitality. Fashionable ladies and courtly gentlemen danced in the big parlors, promenaded up and down the broad portico and sipped tea in the garden under the trees. "A Diary from Dixie," telling of one of the balls held at this mansion, gives the following description of the mistress of the house: "Mrs. Preston was resplendent in diamonds, point lace and velvet. There is a gentle dignity about her that is very attractive. Her voice is low and sweet, and her will is iron, quiet, retiring and reserved. She has chiseled regularity of features, a majestic figure, perfectly moulded." Some of those entertained in the

Preston home were Winfield Scott, Daniel Webster, Henry Clay, Millard Filmore and Franklin Pierce.

During the Federal occupation of Columbia General John A. Logan and his troops used the house for headquarters. In February, 1865, when Sherman was giving orders for the destruction of the Hampton home, the interview was overheard by a nun, who reported the news to her Mother Superior. In the meantime the convent had been destroyed and the nuns were promised instead any building left standing in the city. As the Hamptons and Prestons had been true friends of the Mother Superior, she immediately resolved to occupy the mansion. She notified Sherman of her plans, and regardless of the fact that it was Logan's headquarters, moved over immediately and took possession. The house owes its preservation to its beauty. When the troops came to set fire to it, one of the Sisters who longed to save the establishment from the merciless flames, caught sight of a face in the crowd, which gave her inspiration. The expression on it provided new courage and urged her to ask: "Is there no lover of beautiful architecture, no admirer of Southern furnishings among you?"

The owner of the face, finely cultured and sweet, set on very young shoulders, slipped beside the Sister. He was a mere boy, perhaps a bugler. The Sister never knew. To the guard she said: "Let this boy come with me and see the lovely rooms. He shall tell you if there is anything worth saving. Then you may burn the place."

For some unheard-of reason the men agreed to this suggestion, laughing and jeering all the while. They desired to humor the boy. No harm could possibly be done. It was only a matter of time when they should consign the house to flames. Why not let him go in?

Silently the big door closed. And quite as the Sister expected the boy was entranced. He had never seen so wonderful a mantel, as broad a staircase, nor such lofty ceilings.

"My, it is shameful to burn this house. But there's no stopping those men; they are determined," he said.

264

THE PRESTON PLACE, OR " AINSLEY HALL," COLUMBIA

"If I could only do something," sighed the desperate Sister; "get word to General Ewing."

A generous impulse filled the boy. Perhaps 'twas pity. Fate guided him. "I'll go," he cried, and shortly afterwards the Sister bolted back the doors again. He was gone. Just how long it took the boy to find General Ewing no one ever guessed. It seemed an eternity.

Then after an age made interminable by shouts and screams and glaring flashes of firelight, a heavy knock was distinguished above the din. Hesitatingly the Sister reopened the door, and to her surprise there stood General Ewing. To the drunken soldiers who were bent on burning the house he simply said, "General Sherman orders those fires out!" Then he went.

Quietly the men slunk away and shortly the streets were dark again. The gardens grew greyly mysterious once more. But for the golden glimmer of the hall candle, Preston Manse was wrapped in total darkness. The Sister, kneeling, told her beads; and the boy somewhere in his tent compared a veil of darkness to a scarf of flames. "So Preston Manse was saved."

In 1889 the building was sold to Rev. W. R. Atkinson for a Presbyterian College for Women. Afterwards it flourished under the presidency of Dr. Atkinson, Dr. Pell and Miss McClintock, and in 1914 it passed into the hands of the Presbyterian Synod and was consolidated with Chicora College, Dr. S. C. Byrd becoming president. The building is used as the administration building and is being kept in perfect preservation by the authorities of the institution.

KINARD HOUSE

The Kinard house at 1400 Lady Street was the wooden court-house erected about 1716 in Saxe-Gotha, a settlement on the opposite side of the Congaree River from the present city of Columbia. Later this building was taken down, brought to Columbia and erected as a Presbyterian Church. Subsequently it was moved across the street to the present site, and used as a Theological School.

When Mr. Niersee came to Columbia, about 1830, to build the State Capitol, he bought and remodeled the old school into a home and lived in this house during the construction of the Capitol. It was then purchased by Captain John Waites, who in turn sold it to John Kinard, in whose family it has since remained. The exterior of the house is not unusual in appearance, being rectangular in shape, with old-type piazzas. The chief characteristic of the interior is its wide, airy hall with square stairway at the rear. This front hall is intersected at its center by a small lengthwise hall, which divides the front and back rooms on one side of the house and opens on the side into a narrow balcony. At the intersection of these halls is a high, very beautiful arch, which with the lofty ceilings, elaborate and delicate cornice work, give the house an imposing and dignified atmosphere. This inside work is said to have been done by old negro slaves. The hall chandelier is of wrought iron, with a plaster decoration above, in the design of an inverted lily. In olden time many slaves were expert workmen in interior decoration and the cornicing in the two drawing-rooms on either side of the hall is quite heavy. In one room they are in the old Greek design of the oak leaf, but the opposite room contains beautiful bas-reliefs on walls and ceiling, in a garland rose design, bordered with mouldings of gold. Long, old-fashioned, gilt-bordered mirrors and antique furniture complete the harmonious interior of this house.

BLANTON DUNCAN HOUSE

Another Columbia house that escaped the general conflagration of the Federal Army was the Blanton Duncan house. Information taken from an official deposition of Wm. Tecumseh Sherman says, "I assisted Mr. Simons, who married a Miss Wragg of my acquaintance, to move his family and effects from the threatened house up to my own, which was the house of Blanton Duncan, then contractor for the manufacture of Confederate money." Many claim for the DeBruhl house this doubtful honor of having been Mr. Sherman's Headquarters. Mrs. Chestnut in her book, "A Diary from Dixie," calls Blanton Duncan "A thoroughly free and easy Western man, handsome and clever, more audacious than either, perhaps."

General Wood's Headquarters were Mrs. Lucy P. Green's house, while General Howard's Headquarters were Mrs. Louisa S. McCord's house opposite South Carolina College grounds.

The Federal Army was encamped on the south side of Gervais Street in the fields belonging at that time to Col. Theodore Stark, just opposite to Mrs. Walker's residence, and where "Shandon" is now. The Walkers lived on Gervais Street, just east of the bridge on the Charlotte Railroad that crosses that street, which bridge was popularly known as the "tin bridge."

General Logan's Headquarters, as has already been stated, were established at the Preston house, from which he removed when the Sisters took possession.

CHAPTER XIV

THE OLD CHERAWS, LAURENS, LANCASTER, AND NEWBERRY

PRINCIPAL STAGE ROUTES THROUGH SOUTH CAROLINA

(According to " The Geography of South Carolina," by William Gilmore Simms, dated 1843.)

From Columbia by Camden to Cheraw, 88 miles, daily.

From Columbia by Lexington C. H. to Augusta, Ga., 76 miles, daily.

From Marion C. H. by Leesville to Fayetteville, N. C., 77 miles, daily.

From Marion C. H. by China Grove to Georgetown, 60 miles, daily.

From Georgetown to Charleston, 60 miles, daily.

From Charleston by Jacksonboro to Savannah, 111 miles, daily.

From Cheraw by Montpelier to Fayetteville, 66 miles, daily.

From Charleston by the South Carolina Railroad to Augusta, 135 miles, daily.

From Charleston to Columbia by Railroad, via Branchville & Orangeburg, 124 miles, daily.

From Yorkville by Laurensville to Abbeville, 104 miles, three times a week.

From Abbeville by Petersburg, Ga., to Milledgeville, 115 miles, three times a week.

From Charleston by Pineville to Camden, 141 miles, twice a week.

From Columbia by Laurensville to Greenville, 115 miles, twice a week.

From Greenville by Merrittsville to Ashville, N. C., 62 miles, twice a week.

From Greenville by Abbeville to Augusta, Ga., 150 miles, twice a week.

From Columbia by Winnsboro to Yorkville, 79 miles, twice a week.

From Cheraw by Wadesboro, N. C., to Salisbury, 84 miles, twice a week.

From Abbeville to Edgefield C. H. to Cooker's Spring, 63 miles, twice a week.

From Pendleton by Carnesville, Ga., Bushville and Gillsville, 78 miles, once a week.

THE CRAIG HOUSE

THE Craig house in Chesterfield District is a valuable contribution from the little known section of our State.

In Gregg's "History of the Old Cheraws," the statement is made that many of the records of Chesterfield County remain in a good state of preservation, but few are to be found in the public offices of Marlboro. Unfortunately for the history of justice as administered in the Cheraws District, all the Circuit Court records, with those of Darlington County, were destroyed with the burning of the Court House about 1804.

The Court House of Marlboro was first located near Gardner's Bluff, afterwards removed lower down on the main river road above Crooked Creek, and there continued until the extreme unhealthiness of the locality rendered a change necessary, when finally Marlboro Court House was located at the present seat, Bennettsville. For Chesterfield the site of the present Court House was chosen, and for Darlington also, after a great deal of discussion, the present site was selected.

The District of Cheraws was divided by the celebrated County Court Act of 1785 and the Cheraws District became the three counties enumerated, which three counties are supposed to have been named in honor of the Duke of Marlboro, Colonel Darlington, who distinguished himself in the War of the Revolution, and the Earl of Chesterfield.

So sparse were the settlements in the neighborhood that a few years before nothing but an old Indian trail led from this point to Camden. It has been an interesting task to locate an authentic house connected with the history of these primitive days and sparse settlements, and this has been successfully accomplished through the kindness of W. D. Craig, of Chesterfield, S. C. Further search in history but confirms his statements.

In the history of the old Cheraws, the name of Alexander Craig appears in the records of Chesterfield during the Revolutionary War. He was elected County Judge for Chesterfield in 1793 and we find him as late as 1798 appearing in connection with the establishing of the boundary line, according to Gregg.

The Craig House in Chesterfield was built in 1798 by John Craig, a Revolutionary soldier and the younger of three brothers. Gregg's History states that he was still a young man at the time of the Revolutionary War and was long after known as a worthy man and a useful citizen, having been connected for many years with the Court of Common Pleas and Ordinary for that district.

The history of the family so far as ascertainable is that three brothers, James, Alexander and John, came from the Upsher part of Ireland about 1770. They settled in Chesterfield County, Virginia, between Richmond and Petersburg. John and Alexander moved from there to Cheraws District; they lost connection with James, supposing that he either died or was killed during the Revolutionary War. John and Alexander Craig, with others, organized Chesterfield County, S. C., as has been previously stated.

In 1795 John Craig married Sarah Chapman, whose people had emigrated from Westmoreland, Va., and whose brother, Captain John Chapman, of Revolutionary fame, lived in this old home until his death. They reared a large family and their descendants yet reside in Chesterfield.

It was this John Craig who built the old Craig homestead, which still stands, a fourteen-room house with a basement under the whole foundation. This house was one of a half dozen family residences that made up the village of Chesterfield and is the only one left standing to-day. There were no hotels in this little village in those days and this Craig house entertained all the great men who visited there. Chesterfield being the county seat, many of the most distinguishd men of the state stayed under the roof of this house.

Under the old régime a review was held once a year, called the Governor's Review, at which the Governor or one of his

CHANCELLOR JOHNSON'S HOME NEAR MAR'S BLUFF OLD CHERAW

staff inspected the military organizations at the county-seat. The great folk were entertained at the Craig place. This general muster far exceeded Christmas or the Fourth of July in excitement, for the house was filled from attic to cellar and everyone on the plantation, white or colored, was worked to the utmost to get ready for this great day.

In the kitchen, the old Dutch oven, which held half of a beef and half a dozen turkeys at one time, was cleaned out and filled to the full with good things to eat. The cattle and horses were taken away to make room for the equipments of the military aides.

Court time was hardly less exciting and one room in this old house is still known as "The Judge's room," because it was reserved for the chancellors and judges. The room across from this room possesses peculiar interest, it is known as "McDuffie's room." A tradition that does not accord with the general accepted story of George McDuffie's life has it that McDuffie was not born but came up one morning like "Topsy" on the old Camden Road near Sugar Loaf Mountain in this county, at a spot that is still pointed out by the older citizens as the place where McDuffie was discovered by a philanthropic gentleman going from Cheraw to Camden in his carriage.

The story goes that he saw McDuffie sitting by the road crying and finding out that McDuffie had an aspiration to be "somebody," questioned him. He found that McDuffie's tears were caused because he was hedged about by so many obstacles. The gentleman decided that he had found a good instrument for some of his surplus dollars, so he decided to interest himself in this young man and he started George McDuffie on his way to an education. McDuffie's struggles for means with which to finish his education at the South Carolina College brought him to this old house and here he stopped and occupied a room while he taught school in Chesterfield.

There are many things to support this tradition, among them being the fact that James McDuffie who was raised in this same section, claimed and was acknowledged to be George McDuffie's nephew. He (James) belonged to the Eighth South Carolina Regiment and was killed in the battles around Richmond. His widow was on the Confederate pension roll until her death a few years ago.

From this old house have gone soldiers for every war since the Revolution and they seem to have adopted the Spartan Mother's Motto, either "To bring back the shield or to be brought back on it."

After the death of John Craig and of his wife, Sarah Chapman, this house came into the possession of their youngest son, W. E. Craig. We learn that W. E. Craig married a Miss Parke, whose brother, Dr. James Parke, having just finished his education as a surgeon in Ireland, went from this house to the Mexican War in 1846–48 and was killed. Later on in the Civil War another brother of Mrs. Craig, R. D. Parke, having had small-pox while studying medicine in Dublin, was put in charge of the small-pox hospital in Charlotte, N. C.

Another warrior connected with this house was General Blakeney, a nephew of John Craig and also of his wife. He had spent a good part of his boyhood days in this house. He was a captain in the Mexican War. The name Blakeney is still found in Kershaw County.

To continue the war record—the morning of April 13th, 1861, was a memorable time for this household. The news came that Fort Sumter had been fired upon. M. J. and J. M. Hough (who had been boarding at this house for a considerable time) and T. P. Craig (oldest son of the household) proceeded at once to Charleston where J. A. Craig (another son) was a student at the Citadel Academy. This cadet corps was soon to engage in action.

In 1864 J. A. Craig and W. D. Craig (sons of W. E. Craig) after being in service on the Carolina coast, went to Virginia not knowing where they would be assigned. This led to a peculiar gathering together of the threads of family ties. Upon getting off the train at Walthall Junction, the two brothers went immediately into a hot skirmish in which W. D. Craig received a flesh wound, the scar of which he still bears and strangely enough this happened almost on the threshold of the old Craig home in Virginia from whence his grandparents had departed about a century before. This old Virginia house was then occupied by a Craig family, supposed to be descendants of James Craig, the missing brother. Hagood in Memoirs of the War of Secession, mentions this old Craig house in Virginia.

The two Craig brothers did their part and on May 16th, 1864, J. A. Craig was killed and W. D. Craig received a wound inflicted by three minnie balls, again this fatality occurred on home ground, happening almost on the Craig farm in Chesterfield County, Va.

The war record continues, for James Craig, who was born and reared in this house, was captain of one of the companies in the Fourth South Carolina Cavalry.

A curious detail of life connected with the Craig homestead concerns London, a colored boy about five years old. Discovered in a huckleberry patch and brought to the village to be taken care of, he was bound to W. E. Craig and lived there as houseboy until he was old enough to join the United States Army. He is supposed to be the first colored man from this section to join the United States Army.

The final history of the house is that the only daughter of W. E. Craig married W. J. Hanna, and came into possession after the death of her mother. Her two sons, W. J., Jr., and J. W. Hanna, volunteered and served through the Spanish-American War. W. J. Hanna did service during the World War.

The picture of the Craig house shows in the foreground an old tree, quite the most ancient and historic in the county. The dwelling is an interesting type of a two-story house, evidently built of primitive materials, the wood being cut upon the holdings of the builder. No doubt in its day this place constituted a mansion. It is evident that the planters evolved their own style of architecture for all over the up-country is found the same general type of home. Evidently the two-story house with hall running through it, and piazzas in front, with kitchen in the ell at the rear, was found best adapted for the living needs of the family, slaves not being so ordinary to the up-country people as to the big rice planters in the low-country.

LAURENS—TOWN AND COUNTY

It was in the village of Laurens, S. C., that at one time Andrew Johnson worked at the tailor's trade. His residence and tailor's shop with signboard have been pointed out with much interest to curious visitors. He came to Laurens in 1827, from Raleigh, N. C., where he was born, and remained there as a journeyman tailor for two years. During that time he became engaged to a young lady in the neighborhood, but told one of his friends that he saw by her mother's manner that he was not favorably looked upon, the mother having told Johnson that her daughter should not marry a tailor. He was so mortified by the rebuff that he left Laurens the next day.

His father (town constable in Raleigh, messenger of the bank, and sexton of the church) died when the son Andrew was two years old. The boy never went to school a day in his life, and after his marriage he was taught by his wife to read and cipher. He continued as a tailor, going from Laurens to Greenville, S. C., and thence to Greenville, Tennessee, where he married Miss McCarthy of that town.

Step by step he ascended the political ladder; first elected to town council, then as mayor, in a few years he was elected to Legislature. State Senator, Congressman and Governor of the State he became in turn, then rose to United States Senator, Military Governor of Tennessee by President Lincoln, and Vice-President under the same, at whose death he assumed the Presidency of the country, the highest office in the land.

MUSGROVE'S MILL

Laurens County, so called for Henry Laurens, is rich in history. On the Enoree River, near the town of Laurens, stands Musgrove's Mill, now owned by the Thornwell Orphanage. This was the scene, during the Revolution, of a spirited action, "one of the hardest fought with small arms." McCrady, in his "South Carolina in the Revolution" says: "It is remarkable that few American historians have at all noticed this important and hard-fought battle. Hill in his narrative (Sumter MSS) complains that none of the historians who have

written of the Revolution in the State have mentioned it.''
Captain Hammond's account appears in Johnson's ''Traditions of the Revolution,'' and it is briefly described by McCall
in his ''History of Georgia''; Draper gives a full and particular account of it in ''King's Mountain and Its Heroes.'' In
none of the accounts, however, is ''Dicey's Ride'' mentioned,
yet Dicey was as great a heroine as our country produced, and
her deed deserves recognition.

An old mill once stood at Milton, in the long ago; a most
important spot during stage-coach days, and we might say
especially interesting as it was just off this old stage road that
the little band of patriots was massacred by ''Bloody Bill''
(Cunningham). This spot is recorded as Hay's Station, but is
near Milton. The old stone or rock building still stands.

''Another old mill over one hundred years old, and still at
work, is near Clinton. In that time it has not passed out of
the same family.'' This description probably refers to Musgrove's Mill, already mentioned; it is given by a resident
of Clinton.

McCrady says:

''In 1780 . . . after the battle at the Old Iron Works, or
second battle of Cedar Springs, on the 8th of April, Colonel
Ferguson sent his wounded to Musgrove's Mills on the south
side of the Enoree River, in what is now Laurens County.
. . . Ferguson set out (after receiving an express from Colonel Turnbull) . . . pushed on, and marched to Colonel
Winn's plantation about eight miles west of Winnsboro, where
he halted and lay, awaiting news from Camden.''

On the American side, McDowell, having been kept well
informed of Ferguson's movements, and having learned that
a party of loyalists were stationed at Musgrove's Mills, he
conceived the idea that, as the road was open, the post vulnerable, and the term of enlistment of Col. Shelby's men about
to expire, a pressing motive presented itself to embrace this
opportunity of striking the British another blow.

Colonels Shelby and Clark were appointed to lead, and with
them were Captains James McCall and Samuel Hammond.
The day before the expedition started these men were joined

by a Virginian, Colonel James Williams, who was rough, rash and fearless, whose ambition for glory led him to the use of means not overscrupulous in the accomplishment of his ends, but whose fearlessness led him into the thick of the fight, and who here freely poured out his blood and yielded up his life for his country. Colonel Brandon, Colonel James Stein and Major McJunkin joined the party, and recruited the strength of the mountain men with a few followers. Shelby attributed the valor and persistency of the battle to the great number of officers who were with him as volunteers.

Colonel Innes and Major Fraser, the British officers, had their headquarters at Edward Musgrove's residence. The Americans, by a clever ruse, drew the British from their post of vantage to a rude breastwork they had erected, and although the battle was hard fought the British lost 63 killed, 90 wounded, and 70 prisoners, while the Americans made good their escape. During an advance of forty, and a retreat of fifty miles, the Americans never stopped to eat, but made use of peaches and green corn for their support. In less than three days this party of two hundred marched 100 miles, fought a battle and brought off with them 70 prisoners.

ROSEMONT

In Laurens County there are possibly three or four old houses of sufficient note to warrant consideration. The first is "Rosemont," the ancestral home of the Cunninghams, a singular feature being that though the family were Tories during the Revolution, a later member of the family, Miss Ann Pamela Cunningham, was the originator of the idea to buy Mt. Vernon and was made the first regent of the Mt. Vernon Association.

The ignorance in regard to Mt. Vernon, the home of Washington, is deplorable. It is not generally known that the women of America bought Mt. Vernon in 1858, and have restored and maintained it ever since without a penny from the

United States or from any State. This great accomplishment is strong evidence of woman's administrative and executive ability, and the men of America should give recognition and acknowledgement to the great fact.

George Washington died December 14, 1799, and for half a century Mount Vernon seemed neglected and forgotten. In 1854 John Augustine Washington, owner of the estate, made repeated efforts to sell the property to the United States and to the State of Virginia. Every effort failed.

At last a noble and patriotic spirited woman of South Carolina, Miss Ann Pamela Cunningham, seeing the advertisements in a newspaper, was seized with the desire to stimulate the women of America into acquiring and restoring Mount Vernon.

Miss Cunningham was a daughter of Captain Robert Cunningham, of Laurens District, a distinguished soldier of the War of 1812, and was educated at Brahamville Academy near Columbia by Julia Pierpont, of Vermont (then Mrs. Marks), at the celebrated school founded by her husband and herself at this place, where so many Southern women of culture and refinement received their early education, among others the mother of President Roosevelt. Miss Cunningham carried her ideas concerning Washington's Home into effect after the most Herculean efforts. She finally founded "The Mount Vernon Ladies' Association of the Union" and became the first regent. She appointed as vice-regents one lady from each State.

The immediate object of this first woman's society was to raise funds for the purchase of two hundred acres of the Mount Vernon estate, including the mansion and the tomb wherein repose the mortal remains of General Washington. The ultimate design was to teach the people of the United States to remember Washington and his great achievements.

The association appealed to the country for $200,000, the price demanded for this portion of Mount Vernon. The pledge given was the preservation and restoration of the home of Washington. The money was raised by the women of that time, their greatest help being the orator of that day, Edward Everett, who by his lectures on Washington raised $70,000.

Miss Cunningham lost her health so completely in her great effort of going from place to place, interviewing Senators and men of public affairs that she finally was carried about upon an invalid's air-bed from which she used only to address influential gatherings which might assist in her patriotic enterprise.

It is needless here to recount the disasters and discouragements which attended the initiative efforts of this small band of devoted women. One formidable cause of opposition, scarce credible in our day, was the prejudice then prevailing against women as workers in any public affairs. But inspired by the enthusiasm of Miss Cunningham the feat was finally accomplished, and although the Civil War halted the work of the association, no vandal hand was raised against this shrine of a nation. After the Civil War friends arose on every side, material aid flowed in, not only in money, building materials, fertilizers, food for the stock, but assistance came in all shapes. The press throughout the land stood by the association. The Masonic lodges responded to the call to save the great Mason's home from destruction. Wall Street's brokers' board sent money, while little children clubbed together to rebuild a gate. Others to rebuild the colonnades. The work progressed steadily year by year.

The necessary repairs accomplished, then came the task of restoration. In the mansion the replacement of such furniture as was owned by Washington has been accomplished where possible; when this was not obtainable, furniture of historic value and of the past century style has been placed in the rooms. The bedstead on which General Washington died stands in his room, mirrors are restored to their former positions. Nellie Custis' piano stands in the music room again and Washington's flute lies upon it. Clocks are returned to their mantels, chairs, tables and a sideboard have resumed their places. The large silver-mounted plateau, used at Washington's state dinners, is now returned to Mount Vernon, a recent gift from a vice regent, herself a great-granddaughter of Martha Washington.

There are also many other historic and valuable relics of Washington and his time. The garden is as he left it, with

278

the quaint box-wood hedges and borders. The old-time roses, pinks, lilies, mignonette, sweet William, lilacs, magnolia trees, and acacias, and even the greenhouses and servants' quarters are restored and are as Washington saw them. The lawns he loved, the trees he planted, all are there, silent but eloquent.

The dream of the enthusiastic founder of the Mount Vernon Association is realized. The home of Washington is restored, and has become the shrine of liberty-loving pilgrims from home and foreign lands, and left as a heritage to Americans as is shown in this extract from the farewell address of the founder of the association to her women associates, given after twenty years of service, on June 1, 1874:

"Ladies, the home of Washington is in your charge; see to it that you keep it the home of Washington. Let no irreverent hand change it; no vandal hands desecrate it with the fingers of progress!

"Those who go to the home in which he lived and died, wish to see in what he lived and died!

"Let one spot in this grand country of ours be saved from change.

"Upon you rests this duty."

Miss Cunningham's own home, "Rosemont," is located in the western part of Laurens County, S. C., five miles southwest of Cross Hill, on the east bank of the Saluda River. It is the best-known residence in upper South Carolina, and was the home of the Cunningham family. It has been said that the brick was brought from England, and the inside woodwork was of English oak, also brought over from the old country, but this is an error, as Mr. A. S. Salley shows in quoting from a journal kept by an old school teacher in the "Up Country," Reuben Pylis, who says that about the year 1790, while a school boy in his teens, "I went to a Stephen Herd, who taught on Saluda River. Boarded at Patrick Cunningham's, where my father was working on a fine new house."

This "fine new house" had decorated fireplaces. Much of the old furniture is still there, including a handsome secretary and large mahogany table, while rare paintings adorn the walls of the living-room. In the state drawing-room mirrors are let into panels between the deep-set windows, and these dim old looking-glasses give the low-ceilinged room a curious air of mystery and enchantment hard to describe—an eerie sense of forgotten presences hard to convey in words. A brother of Miss Pamela's, Clarence Cunningham, a classmate of President Wilson at Princeton, lives there alone in this shadowy old home of long ago, hidden away in Laurens County, but worthy to become a South Carolina shrine in memory of Miss Pamela Cunningham and her great work at Mount Vernon.

STONEY POINT

Although Rosemont is in Laurens County it is nearer Greenwood, S. C., than to the town of Laurens, and not many miles from Rosemont, in Greenwood County, so Mr. H. L. Watson, the editor of *The Index-Journal,* of Greenwood, says, "is Stoney Point, home of the Smiths, into which family former Congressman Aiken married, and I think also former Governor Aiken, 1844–1846."

EDEN HALL

Mr. Watson is also authority for the interesting information that "in the lower section of the county is a fine old mansion, Eden Hall, built by the late Dr. Wm. Hearst. He was a very wealthy man and benefactor of Erskine College. W. R. Hearst, the newspaper publisher, belongs to this family; his great-grandfather moved from that section to Missouri and his father from there to California."

TUMBLING SHOALS

Another interesting place is the Tumbling Shoals residence in Laurens County, 13 miles east of the town. According to the account of Captain William D. Sullivan, Sr., of Gray Court, John and William Arnold built a house for themselves and a primitive mill, which they erected at Tumbling Shoals about 1800. This house is still standing in a good state of preservation, and is used as a dwelling place for an operator in the modern power plant which has superseded the mill. The hand-hewn shingles and weather-boards were "home-made," no doubt cut out with a whip saw operated by the Arnolds in true pioneer style, while the nails with which the shingles and weather boards were attached to the frame were made of wrought iron by the neighboring blacksmith.

In 1820 Joseph Sullivan, father of Wm. D. Sullivan, moved from Greenville district to Tumbling Shoals. He bought the mill and water power from Henry Barrow, 45 acres of land for $1200, and another tract of land containing 1000 acres for $500.

In 1837 he built a large flour and grist mill, also a saw mill and cotton gin, which were operated until sold to the Reedy River power plant about ten years ago. The following year (1838) he constructed a two-story dwelling house on the east side of Reedy River, in which house Wm. D. Sullivan was born, who has lived there for 82 years.

Within two miles of Mr. Sullivan's house is the Friend-ship Presbyterian Church, which is situated on a high, dry ridge between the waters of Reedy River and South Rabun Creek, ten miles east of Laurens Court House. It was organized by Colonel Samuel Levers in 1820 as a Presbyterian Congregation, calling itself Friendship Presbyterian Church. James Dorroh (who died in 1820) donated the land on which to build the church. This was first a Union Church, having been organized in 1809 by the Baptists and Presbyterians jointly, and being used by both denominations for eleven years, during which time it was known as Rabun Church. In 1820 the Baptists sold their interests and withdrew, organizing Rabun Church a few miles further north. In 1859 the Presbyterians replaced this first structure with the church that is now standing, and which was used for a centennial celebration in 1920. Prominent Scotch-Irish family names are found on the church rolls, among them Dorrohs, Simpsons, Averys, McKnights, Morgans, Sullivans and Cunningham, who built the church.

BELFAST

Another house of some historic interest in this section is on the Laurens side of the road that separates Newberry from

Laurens. It was built in the early years of the nineteenth century, and is of brick, two stories and a half high, with exceptionally large rooms. Tradition has it that the brick, like the builder, came from Ireland. Colonel John W. Simpson came over to this country from Ireland near Belfast, and named his home Belfast in memory of that place. He was the father of William D. Simpson, who was elected Lieutenant-Governor when Wade Hampton was elected Governor in 1878; became Governor when Hampton went to the Senate; and was later made Chief Justice of the Supreme Court.

The house passed into other hands, and in 1851 or 1852 was bought by John Wallace from a Mr. Eichelberger; it belongs now to Robert G. Wallace. The building contains four large rooms, about 22 by 28, two small ones, and, in the half-story, a long "garret" which seems to be intended for "old plunder." The present owner has added a wooden dining-room and kitchen. The plastering on walls and ceilings is what is known as "hard finish" and is without crack, despite the earthquake of 1866; the mantels are high and their facings quite ornamental. In the large rooms an elaborate cornice follows a curved pattern in several layers on the ceilings; the side walls are exceptionally thick. No nails are used in the flooring boards, but round pegs very similar to those used in decking a ship, which leads to the belief that Col. John W. Simpson may have been a sea-faring man.

For so large a house the piazza is quite small, but the grounds are extensive, including the Wallace family burying ground with monuments and tablets. Nearby is Hay's Mountain, where a massacre of the Whigs by the Tories took place during the Revolutionary War, and in olden times when mail was carried by postillions on horseback this house was the only post-office between Laurens and Newberry. A famous Rock Spring is found on the grounds.

The present owners are of a distinguished up-country family, one of which is W. H. Wallace, father of Professor Wallace, of Wafford University, and the well-known editor of the *Newberry Observer*. Although the original builders, the Simpson family, no longer reside at Belfast, yet it is represented in the State by Henry Y. Simpson, of the Laurens bar, grandson of the first owner, and son of the late Chief Justice Simpson, who was born at Belfast.

THE SIMS HOUSE, LANCASTER

James Marion Sims, according to Joseph Wardlaw's "Genealogy of the Witherspoon Family," was the son of Col. John Sims and Mahala Mackey. He was born in January, 1813, graduated at South Carolina College in 1832, at Jefferson Medical College, Philadelphia, 1835, and in 1836 married Eliza Theresa Jones, daughter of Dr. Bartlett Jones, a skilful physician and a man of renown, decided intelligence and great popularity. This marriage influenced his life greatly. A few facts about Dr. Jones are not amiss.

Dr. Bartlett Jones was born in Prince William County, Virginia, in 1787, graduated as M. D. in Philadelphia in 1806, and settled at Lancaster, S. C., in 1808. Here, in 1810, he married Eliza Jane Dunlap, a daughter of Dr. Samuel F. Dunlap and Mary Crawford (daughter of Major Robert Crawford). After his marriage he built a house at the southeast corner of Main, or Brown and Arch Streets. The house itself was typical of the "up country," being a square two-story building with its main entrance opening directly from the piazza into the hallway which bisected the establishment. There is nothing architecturally great to render this house worthy of notice in a volume of Historic Houses, but the fact that there the great physician, Marion Sims, first received his inspiration and love for medicine from his father-in-law, and there first engaged in that practice of medicine destined to revolutionize modern surgery.

Many authorities give illuminating glimpses of the early struggle of Sims which can be read at leisure, but after moving around from "pillar to post" his love of healing prevailed, and he set himself to map out new fields of endeavor in his chosen profession.

Gen. E. McCrady, in an address dealing with the history of the South Carolina Medical College says:

"It happened there was sitting on the benches of this first class under the new organization of the college a youth from the Waxsaws, the native place of Andrew Jackson, who was to do more good in his generation than his great compatriot, and to surpass even the great French physician and biologist, Ravenel, as well in his fame as in his kindness and beneficence to the poor and suffering. This was Dr. J. Marion Sims, whose name you will find on the roll of the class of 1834. It was my fortune to know Dr. Sims, and to know him somewhat intimately, and I can bear testimony that amidst all his professional triumphs, in the full tide of his fame, having the decorations of the governments of France, Italy, Germany, Spain, Portugal and Belgium as a great benefactor of mankind, he looked back with pleasure and affection, and loved to talk of the old days when he studied medicine in the college with his friend Sparkman, and 'dear old Dick Baker' as he used to speak of that excellent physician, Dr. C. R. F. Baker, of Clarendon, who died just before him. Let me speak a word of Dr. Sims to you, young gentlemen, and before this Charleston audience, for the applause of strangers, and the honors bestowed by Royalty and Courts were not so dear to him as the fact that he was a Southerner and a South Carolinian.

"He was a bold pioneer, opening new pathways; original and with creative genius, he discovered for himself, and *made his discoveries a gift to the profession.* Truly he did so. As his writings have been translated into every modern European language, so the instruments of inventions of which it would require much space to give even a list are found in the consulting rooms of every surgeon in the civilized world; but no royalty or tribute did he ever ask for them. He took no toll upon his inventions for the relief of suffering. He took out no patent upon the instruments he invented for the benefit of humanity.

"Eventually Dr. Sims' search led him to Montgomery, Alabama, where he established a small private hospital for negro women; the prototype of the great Woman's Hospital in New York. That grand institution is a monument to a South Carolinian on the Atlantic. On the Pacific another Carolina physician has left his monument in the Toland Institute.

"In 1853 Dr. Sims removed from Montgomery, Ala., to New York where during the following year he founded the Woman's Hospital, the first institution of the kind on this continent; as it has been well said: 'If Sims had done nothing else, the energy and determination displayed in placing this institution in a proper working condition would be sufficient to entitle him to the gratitude of the public, and to establish his claim as a wise philanthropist.'

"Dr. Toner, in his biographical sketch of Dr. Sims, recalls the account given by the New York newspapers of a 'Lecture,' as Dr. Sims called it, in which he first presented to the public his scheme for a Woman's Hospital in 1854, and cites the *Tribune* as saying:

" 'He aimed, by the history of a Southern institution with which he had been connected, and its results, to show how much might be done in this city, and how great was our need.'

"The story of Sims is the story of a *Man Who Triumphed*. Many men whose minds have carried them as near to great things have failed because unable to climb the path they saw so well! The flesh will not always do the work the mind conceives. Fortunately for humanity it was not so with Dr. Sims. When he saw that suffering could be relieved it lay on him as a call from God. He had a mission, a calling to fulfill, which neither weariness, nor sickness, nor poverty could prevent. In reading the story you will admire the genius, but you will love the man who devoted himself to the task.

"Failure followed failure, but Sims did not doubt the result. Money, labor, health, all he poured into his work, while friends and relations pressed him to desist, and appealed to him to remember his wife and children, if he cared nothing for himself. But in vain, till they began to do as the boys of old did to Columbus as he walked the streets filled with the vision of the New World, touching their heads significantly as they passed him. At last, however, success came. As he was walking home one evening, dejected, not because he doubted his discovery, but fearing his health and means would all go before he could demonstrate it, a little piece of wire on the ground struck his eye; and he took it up scarcely thinking of what he was doing. That little piece of wire solved the problem, and Sims is famous to-day because he found the use of a silver suture and modern methods of surgery were made possible.

"The death of Dr. J. Marion Sims carried profound grief to the American profession. Not only in this country, but abroad, in whatever land true medicine lives, his departure was mourned. Surely South Carolina may well be proud of this son, who not only became a great public benefactor, but is among the rare instances of those who have given discoveries and inventions of immense value to the world without price or reward ."

NEWBERRY
"COATESWOOD"

Newberry is one of the old settlements in the upper part of the State, but the history of these counties has never been written in detail and few records are obtainable, although South Carolina is as proud of her sons of the hills as she is of her sons of the sea and the dwellers along the rivers.

One of the oldest public buildings in Newberry is a beautiful piece of architecture, marred only by a flight of steps which breaks the harmony and destroys the unity of this gem carved and set in the early days of Newberry. A bas-relief on the façade of the old court house has an interesting story says Mr. W. H. Wallace, editor of the *Newberry Observer*. In 1876, just after the redemption of the State, Mr. O. Wells was given the contract to make repairs on the building, which had become shabby under radical régimes. In finishing the façade he conceived the idea of making an allegory of the State's downfall and its redemption, so that he who ran might read, in the fallen palmetto tree with a game-cock standing on its roots crowing defiantly, and the American eagle with extended wings grasping the top of the tree in the attempt to lift it upright, the story of a "prostrate State."

The most historic house in Newberry is that of the late Chancellor Johnstone, who died some fifty years ago. The house is still in the family, and is occupied by his daughters, Mrs. Clara McCrary and Miss Fannie Johnstone. Senator Alan Johnstone is a son of the late Chancellor. Sketches of Chancellor Johnstone are found in the "Annals of Newberry," O'Neall and Chapman, second part; in Carwile's "Reminiscences of Newberry," and in N. R. Brooks' "Bench and Bar." In quoting from a sketch of the house written by Mrs. McCrary, a great many of the facts of which were taken from the above-named sources, it is stated that

"Coateswood, the home of Chancellor Job Johnstone at Newberry, S. C., was built by him about the year 1835. The plan of the building is that of an English basement house. It contains twelve rooms and two additional garret rooms, making four stories. The first story is of brick finished with stucco, the two upper stories and attic are of frame. The brick wall of the first story is solid and is twenty inches thick. The interior woodwork (mouldings, framings of doors and windows, mantels, etc.) is exceedingly tasteful. The carving was all done by hand and was the work of the contractor and builder, Phillip Schoppert, a citizen of Newberry. His handiwork is to be seen in many of the older homes of Newberry.

"The brick in the house was all made upon the place and the lumber used was made from timber grown in Newberry County. The lime for mortar and plastering was imported and brought by wagon from Charleston. In the rear of the house and separated from it is the long brick kitchen, having a large open fireplace with crane. Another feature which dates far back is the Sun Dial between the house and kitchen. The house is located on the crest of the hill, which situation shows to advantage the good points of the establishment."

Chancellor Job Johnstone was of Scotch-Irish descent, his parents, John Johnstone and Mary Caldwell, emigrating to this country and settling in Fairfield District, South Carolina, about three miles below Winn's Bridge on Little River. He was named for his maternal grandfather, Job Caldwell, of Londonderry, Ireland, who was in his day a distinguished physician. His early life was spent in Fairfield, Chester and Newberry Districts. Graduating at a very early age from the South Carolina College in 1810 he studied and practiced medicine for a short time, reading with Dr. Davis, of Columbia, and graduating at the College of Physicians and Surgeons, New York, in 1815. Finding that profession unsuited to his tastes he turned to the law, for which he had always a leaning and to which he had previously given some study in the law offices of Mr. John Hooker at York and Mr. Clark at Winnsboro. In 1817 he entered the office of John Belton O'Neall at Newberry, and in the winter of 1818 was admitted to the Courts of Law and Equity, and formed a partnership with Mr. O'Neall. This partnership existed until 1828. He had in the meantime, in November, 1826, been elected Clerk of the Senate, serving until November 3, 1830, when he was elected Chancellor. In 1847 he was made presiding Judge of the Equity Court of Appeals. This office he filled through all the changes in the Judiciary until 1859 when he was elected Associate Judge of the Court of

Appeals. This last position he accepted, and discharged most ably its duties until his death in 1862. Mr. O'Neall, his partner at law and life-long friend, his senior by less than two months was closely connected with him again when each was elevated to the Supreme Bench as Chief Justice and Associate Justice. It may not be amiss in this connection to say that Chief Justice O'Neall survived him by little more than a year, his death occurring on December 27th, 1863.

In the War of 1812 Job Johnstone was appointed and commissioned Quartermaster to the 36th Regiment, Eastern Division, May 26th, 1812, aged nineteen years.

In 1832 he was a member of the celebrated Nullification Convention, and it is said that he assisted in drawing up the ordinance of nullification adopted by that body. He took an active part in organizing Aveleigh (Presbyterian) Church at Newberry and was made one of its elders. In compliment to him the name Aveleigh was given to the church, as that had been the name of the church of his forefathers in England. He was Commissioner to the first General Assembly of the Southern Presbyterian Church which met in Augusta, Ga., December 4th, 1861, at which time the Southern Church formally withdrew from the Northern.

In closing this sketch of the life of Chancellor Job Johnstone and the description of his home, it is well to conclude with the tribute paid to him by his alma mater in a brief résumé of his life, "It has been said that during twenty-one years of his administration no one lost his right or his estate through the maladministration of Job Johnston."

CHAPTER XV

JOSEPH McCULLOUGH HOUSE, FORT HILL, LOWTHER HALL, TOMASSEE AND THE BURT HOUSE IN ABBEVILLE

THE JOSEPH McCULLOUGH HOUSE

HE Joseph McCullough house was built nearly a hundred years ago, on the old stage-coach road running from Greenville, in the northwestern part of the state, to Augusta, Ga. The house, which is of brick, is set on a slight terrace formed by a stone coping, the building itself being placed about twenty feet back from the road, and privacy being insured by a row of fine old cedar trees. Although the material from which the house is constructed is brick, there is a most curious use of plaster to simulate a vari-colored stone. The plaster is applied to the bricks in blocks about two by three feet square, giving a beautiful, mellow effect, as the colors used are soft blue, pink, and granite, while the blocks are outlined with a narrow white edging.

Originally the house had a shed room at the rear, as well as an upstairs piazza on the front. Each end of this piazza was enclosed to form a small room. These details are given in order to show how it was possible for this establishment to house so many people.

In the days when there were no railroads in upper South Carolina all freight was handled on wagons, and all travel was by private conveyance, thus this homestead, which stands in the extreme lower corner of Greenville County, was used not only as a family residence, but as a public inn, by Joseph Mc-Cullough, who was a large landholder, a merchant, and a shrewd trader in all kinds of stock. The two latter avocations he was able to pursue to advantage by reason of the strategic position he had selected for his home. In those days of heavy travel from the seacoast to the mountains there was great necessity for accommodations for man and beast, including the hogs, mules, horses and other cattle that were driven on foot from Tennessee and Kentucky to the markets of Carolina. These creatures, as well as the traders and drovers accompanying them, had to be furnished with food and lodgings, and Joseph McCullough prospered by providing them for all concerned. Thus the old house was, at one time, very much in demand as a public inn.

Upon approaching the house from the road a traveler ascends the weather-beaten stone steps leading from the road to the terrace, and traverses the remains of an interesting looking formal garden to the piazza, which is reached by one granite step, and from which immediate entrance is had to the house. At each gable end of the old place a massive chimney is found, and at the left side is a long wing, while just a few feet from the side steps of this wing is an old-fashioned well with the sweep and bucket.

J. W. McCullough, a grandson of the original owner, was raised at the old home, but had, he said, like most children, paid little attention to its history; all that he remembered was that the house was built by contract, of brick plastered over, and when finished the keys were handed over to his grandfather.

Another relative, Mrs. T. S. McKittrick, of Toney Creek neighborhood, whose grandmother was a niece of the original owner, Joseph McCullough, writes of the relationship, stating that the elder Mr. McCullough was instrumental in bringing her grandparents to this country. She says, in speaking of the old inn: "My earliest recollection of the place is when it was a well-kept home with many beautiful outdoor shrubs and flowers, having also a well-furnished conservatory. To my childish mind the beautiful hothouse flowers were things of wonder."

Still another member of the family is Mr. W. D. Sullivan, of Gray's Court, an old gentleman over eighty years of age, who takes much interest in such matters, and has written a great deal of historical data dealing with this section. His

THE JOSEPH McCULLOUGH HOUSE, ABOVE GREENVILLE

sister married one of the McCulloughs, and thus became lady of the house. Although still owned by the original family, it is no longer occupied by them; from the writer's personal visit to the place, however, and from letters of relatives the history of the old house has been compiled, the narratives of several widely separated people agreeing as to names and dates.

Mr. Sullivan supplies an interesting story about the house itself in the following account: "In about 1850 I was at John Robinson's circus at McCullough. We took care of the whole outfit. The manager made a great impression on me and I now call to mind that he had all the show people registered and assigned to rooms just like a hotel. All the rooms of the house were numbered, with signs tacked on the doors on white papers."

Other interesting anecdotes are told concerning this house and its inhabitants. As one of the writers naïvely says: "Old Joseph McCullough, from some of the things I have heard of him, was not a religious man." His characteristic as a shrewd trader is evidenced in a story told of his having packed a grindstone in a bale of cotton to increase its weight, and sending it to Atlanta to be sold. However, "chickens come home to roost," said the narrator of this incident, "and some time afterwards my grandfather was at the store when old Uncle Joe opened a barrel of sugar and there was the stone, which had come back to him. He called his cousin and partner, 'Oh, Read, come here,' and holding up the grindstone remarked, 'it looks ——— familiar, doesn't it!' "

It seems that old Colonel James McCullough, who inherited the house upon the death of his father, Joseph McCullough, was an officer in the Confederate Army, being Colonel of the 16th South Carolina Volunteers. He was also a big planter, ran a general store, and ginned for the public. He and his wife, who was a Miss Sullivan, had no children, but they seemed to have loved young people, and to have been open-hearted, as they raised a dozen or more nieces and nephews.

The original owner had other children than Colonel James McCullough, as we glean from the fact that J. W. McCullough, a grandson of Joseph (the first), is still living, although the house did not remain with him in the direct family line, but passed to the adopted son of Colonel James McCullough, Hon. Joseph A. McCullough, formerly of Greenville, but now of Baltimore, Md. This latter is a prominent and well-known lawyer, in whose hands the old place now remains.

Stirring times indeed must have been witnessed by this ancient structure, and one feels that the house and the owner thereof fit in very well with the spirit of the poem which says:

"Let me live in a house by the side of the road
Where the race of men go by——"

FORT HILL, CALHOUN'S HOME

"Fort Hill" is best known as the home of John C. Calhoun. The oldest part of the building was erected by Rev. James McElhenny, who was called to the pastorate of the "Old Stone Church" in the present county of Oconee, about 1807. He named the place "Old Clergy Hall" and used it as a rectory because he and his son-in-law, the Rev. James Archibald Murphy lived there together. The Rev. McElhenny was twice married, his first wife was Miss Jane Moore, of York District, but the second time he married a widow, a Mrs. Wilkinson, of John's Island, who was originally a Miss Smith, of Charleston. One of the daughters of this marriage married Lieutenant Hamilton Hayne, U. S. N., and her son was Paul Hamilton Hayne, the poet. That singer of rare and beautiful songs, so little known, was born in Charleston, S. C., in the house now standing on Ashley Avenue on the western side (one door north of Bull Street), now occupied by Mr. Gibson, superintendent of the Charleston Water Works.

When Clergy Hall passed into the hands of the Calhoun family the name was changed from "Clergy Hall" to "Fort Hill," and it is evident that at this time the wings to the house were added. The house is erected on a gentle slope in sight of the Seneca River. It is one of the characteristics of the colonial buildings, that when a view is to be commanded the house is placed flat on the ground, and this house is no exception. The building faces southwest and has a porch on that

292

"FORT HILL," RESIDENCE OF JOHN C. CALHOUN, CLEMSON COLLEGE

JOHN EWING CALHOUN HOME, NEAR CLEMSON COLLEGE
Built by a Harrison, now a residence of the Ravenel family

side, but there are also porches on the north and south sides of the house. The present owners, nieces of John C. Calhoun, use the north porch as an entrance, but when the house was in the possession of John C. Calhoun he used the porch that faces east. Much attention is given to these porches because they are the best architectural feature of the house. Their columns are of brick, plastered over, and the flooring is paved with blue and white flagstones. The wood used in the construction of the house is probably cedar, because it is very prevalent on the estate. The inside woodwork is of red cedar. Formerly in the large rooms were a number of pictures that are now in the Clemson College library. There are now a great many relics in one of the rooms, some very handsome pieces of furniture; among them a broad sofa, on which is carved a large eagle. It is said that the design of the eagle on the silver dollar was taken from this old sofa. The dining table of John C. Calhoun is another piece of furniture of interest in this house and an interesting chair, also Calhoun's piano complete the list.

John C. Calhoun married his cousin, Floride Calhoun. In the following extract from a letter of Mrs. Calhoun, Floride's mother, to Andrew Pickens, Jr., an interesting reference is made to this young girl who afterwards married John C. Calhoun. The letter is dated September 2nd, 1800, and post-marked at Newport, September 4th.

"I had the happiness to find my family well and my mind relieved of a great deal of anxiety occasioned by a foolish report which prevail'd in Charleston, that Floride was engaged to be married, and indeed so far as to say that the event had taken place, but there was not the least foundation for such a report . . . what anxiety a Daughter who is growing up occasions a Parent, but I have every reason to hope that she will be a comfort to me as few girls of her age conduct themselves with more propriety."

When at Fort Hill, Calhoun arose at daybreak and walked over the hills that made up his plantation. His keen eyes took in at a glance the condition of the fields and of the crops. At half-past seven he again entered his home and sat down to breakfast. Then he worked steadily in his office until three o'clock. The writing of long letters on public questions kept him busy. After dinner he read history and books of travel or carried on conversation with distinguished visitors of whom he had many.

It is interesting to note that John C. Calhoun inherited many of the characteristics of his pioneer progenitors, as will be found in an amusing anecdote of his father, Patrick Calhoun, told by Judge O'Neal:

"In the debate of a law in the legislature of the colony to give a premium of so many shillings for a Wolf's scalp, Patrick Calhoun (who settled in 1756 on Lory Cane, Abbeville County, the founder in South Carolina of the Calhoun family) is represented as saying he would much rather 'gie a poond for a lawyer's scalp.' He was the same who, in 1765, was called Captain Calhoun, and who at the head of a company of rangers, was directed to escort the palatines to their settlement called Londonerry. His wife was Martha, sister to John Caldwell, who was an eminent surveyor and located much of the land in Newberry District."

John Caldwell Calhoun, after a final speech on nullification, died on the last day of March. He was the most prominent advocate of State sovereignty, was noted for his keen logic, his clear statements and demonstrations of facts, and his profound earnestness. Webster said concerning him that he had "the indisputable basis of high character, unspotted integrity, and honor unimpeached. Nothing grovelling, low, or mean or selfish came near his head." His sarcophagus is found in the western cemetery of St. Philip's Churchyard, Charleston, and a large monument stands on Marion Square.

A painting in the City Hall at Charleston of John C. Calhoun, executed by Healy, an American artist, is a much admired one. It represents Calhoun in his characteristic attitude of addressing the Senate, with his left hand, beautifully feminine in appearance, upon his breast. On the canvas in the background are several faces depicted, said to be of his contemporaries. The painting is the masterpiece of Healy's art.

After Mr. Calhoun's death in 1850, Mr. Thomas C. Clemson, who married Calhoun's daughter, Anna Maria, sold his farm in Edgefield County and moved to Pendleton, his wife's childhood home. By will, Mr. Clemson gave to the State of South Carolina, a portion of that property in Pendleton for the purpose of establishing an agricultural college. On this property stands Clemson Agricultural College, which is now one of the largest colleges for men in the South. It is located on the dividing line between Pickens and Oconee Counties in the picturesque foothills of the Blue Ridge Mountains. It has an elevation of about nine hundred feet and commands an excellent view of the mountains. The climate is invigorating and healthful, and the surroundings are in every way favorable to the best physical and mental development.

One of the most interesting sidelights thrown upon the character of John C. Calhoun, is furnished in a book written by the late Mr. George W. Williams, describing the behavior of Calhoun—a visitor at Nacoochee, the Williams' Georgia Estate—when news was received that South Carolina had "nullified." Mr. Williams tells of how Mr. Calhoun remained silent for several hours and betrayed the utmost agitation, walking swiftly up and down the corridor of the house with his hands behind his back. He knew the price the South would have to pay for the Doctrine of States Rights.

LOWTHER HALL, PENDLETON

Pendleton District Records concerning old homes have all been destroyed, although the county boasts a handsome Court House which is a beautiful piece of architecture, and which was formerly the "Farmers' Hall," now used as a Post Office. This building has been the scene of many historic gatherings. A visitor will be attracted by the old sun dial and the cannon in front called the "Red Shirt" cannon—"Red Shirts" being the name by which Hampton's men were known during the reconstruction days.

Although the subject matter does not relate directly to Pendleton, it is of interest to know of a scene which transpired in old Oconee, formerly part of the Pendleton District, when Hampton was electioneering. One of the men who witnessed it, Mr. Charles Russell, now in his eighties, said that when Hampton spoke at Walhalla he stood on a little balcony outside of the hotel, the crowd being so large that no hall would contain it. The dramatic moment arrived when Hampton raised his right hand, leaned forward, and said to those rude mountain men to whom he was appealing for support in the coming election intended to redeem South Carolina from Radical Rule, "Gentlemen, if I am elected to rule in this high office, by the Living God I *will* rule!" The crowd went wild. Hampton was afterwards elected, and the mountain men flashed the news from peak to peak; as in the old days of Grecian history, they signaled by fire.

In speaking of the absence of records, Miss Annie Sloan, of Charleston, a descendant of the Sloan family long identified with the Pendleton district and whose ancestor built and operated probably the oldest mill in consecutive use in South Carolina, said that at one time she visited a house bought by people without any regard for history and arrived just after papers relating to the Blockade Runners had been burnt. At another time her brother, Earl Sloan, rescued the manuscript notes of some of the celebrated German chemist, Lieber's, documents which were being similarly disposed of.

The Reverend C. C. Pinckney, at one time rector of the Episcopal Church built in 1820, spoke of his congregation—then composed of Earls, Calhouns, Hugers, Sloans, Hanckels and others—as being representative of the greatest collection of wealth and culture in the State.

An interesting story connected with Pendleton concerns "Tommy Dawson," who dwelt with his daughter in a pretty little place right by the village of Pendleton. His garden was so beautiful that it led to the discovery of his story, which was that he had been a drummer-boy in the English army in the Battle of Waterloo, and afterwards became one of Queen Victoria's gardeners.

There are some old homes in and around Pendleton, but as no records can be found, and few dates and little data of any special significance the history of this interesting section will have to be rather meagre. Tradition says that Lowther Hall is the oldest house in the town of Pendleton, but no one knows

"LOWTHER HALL," THE TRESCOTT HOUSE, PENDLETON

beyond the fact that there really was a Lord Lowther, and that he built or occupied as a hunting lodge the house now retaining his name. Lord Lowther was an Englishman and loved to roam. It is said that he perished at sea on his way back to America from England. Lowther Hall has been added to and almost entirely rebuilt in some parts. It is now in the possession of Edward A. Trescot.

The original lodge was built of logs in one day, the foundation, sills, and all structural timber being of the same material. When the house was undergoing repairs the carpenters called attention to the massive timber of solid tree trunks roughly adzed on four sides by hand, and in as perfect condition and as strong and fine as when first cut. The house was never nailed together, but mortised with foot-long oaken pegs.

The present owner, Mr. Edward Trescot, says that the original lodge was said to have been a small two-room house, one up and one down, and was built by one of the Sloans, who afterwards went to England, taking with him a water color view of the Blue Ridge Mountains as seen from the rear of the house. Having used up all of his money, Mr. Sloan showed the picture to Lord Lowther, who was so much taken with it that he said he would buy the house as a hunting lodge.

Whether the foregoing is really true is hard to ascertain. But a friend of the Trescot family who was connected with the Foreign Office in London made, about 1895, somewhat of an investigation of this tradition, and as a result was more than inclined to believe that Lord Lowther had owned and used the house as a hunting lodge. His letter to Mr. Trescot's father bearing on the subject perished in a fire which destroyed the Trescot country home near Pendleton.

From November, 1768, to January, 1772, there appeared in the *Public Advertiser* in London the celebrated "Junius Letters." Later these were published separately in two volumes. The identity of "Junius" has remained forever a mystery. It is said that a man named Miller, who assisted in the printing of these letters, was forced or induced to leave England in order to keep this secret. It is also said that part of his pay was the printing outfit on which these political volumes were set up. Whether this latter is true or not, it is certain that Miller landed in Charleston with a printing outfit, located later at Pendleton, and there issued, from Lowther Hall, *The Pendleton Messenger*. It is a curious coincidence that one of the first sets of volumes of the "Junius Letters" found a resting place at Lowther Hall, where Miller first put up the printing press after issuing the letters in London, these volumes having been sent to Edward Trescot, great-grandfather of Edward Trescot, the present owner.

The Trescot family were originally from Charleston and were wealthy and cultured people. Studying the Abstract of Titles will reveal the fact that they possessed, among other pieces of property, land in Hampstead, and on East Bay at the corner of Broad Street, where the Carolina Savings Bank now stands. The will of Edward Trescot, dated in 1818, states that he has four sons, John, George, Henry and William, and names his grandchildren, Edward, Henry and Elizabeth, children of his late son William. Space does not permit of tracing the ramifications of this family, the most distinguished member of which is William Henry Trescot, born in Charleston, S. C., 1822, died in Pendleton, S. C., 1898. After graduation at the College of Charleston he studied law in the office of his uncle, Edward McCrady. Soon after his admission to the bar he married Eliza Natalia Cuthbert and settled as a planter on Barnwell Island, an island on the coast which came down to his wife by Royal Grant of George III, where he lived until the plantation was occupied by Federal troops during the Civil War. At thirty years of age, in 1852, he was appointed Secretary of the Legation at London, served two years, returned to Charleston, occupying the house where his law office was, and reëntered upon the practice of law, diplomatic and international subjects. As early as 1857 in *Russell's Magazine* it was said of him:

"Our readers, we take it, will scarcely need to be told that among the younger prose-writers of the South, Mr. Trescot is one of the most vigorous, thoughtful and matured. His two elaborate works upon the Diplomacy of the Revolution, and the Diplomatic History of the Administrations of Washington and Adams, have earned for him a wide and deserved reputation."

Mr. Trescot became Assistant Secretary of State in 1860; during the Civil War not only served in the Legislature of South Carolina, but was on the staff of General Roswell S. Ripley. Of this period of his life Mrs. Chestnut says in her "Diary from Dixie": "Trescot is too clever ever to be a bore. . . . Calls himself 'Ex-Secretary of State of the United States,' 'Nothing in Particular' of South Carolina or now the Confederate States."

A less facetious pen, that of Governor McGraw, deals more justly with Mr. Trescot's perceptions and sentiments, saying that with the election of a Republican President, March 4, 1861, to use the terse and expressive language of Trescot, "a circle was to be drawn around the South beyond which institutions should not grow, and within which it was the expressed desire of an all powerful Government that they should gradually perish, and that it should stand, like one of its own oaks, rung for slow but certain destruction."

Mr. Trescot was assistant to the Hon. James L. Petigru in codifying the laws of South Carolina. In 1877 he was Consul for the United States before the Halifax Fishery Commission, and in 1880 he was Commissioner to China to negotiate a treaty, which he succeeded in signing. A list of the offices he held includes Special Envoy Extraordinary and Minister Plenipotentiary to Chili in 1881, Commissioner to negotiate a commercial treaty with Mexico in 1882, and Delegate to the Pan-American Conference in 1889.

Mr. Trescot was an able writer. His principal published works relate to diplomacy, upon which subject he is universally regarded as the highest authority in the South. He is the author of "Diplomacy of the Revolution," Appleton & Co., 1852 ; "Diplomatic History of the Administrations of Washington and Adams," Little, Brown & Co., 1857; "An American View of the Eastern Question," John Russell, 1854; "Address Before South Carolina Historical Society"; "Eulogy on Gen. Stephen Elliott before South Carolina Legislature," 1866; "Memorial of Gen. Johnston Pettigrew," 1870.

In writing of his death which occurred in 1898, LeRoy F. Youmans calls him the "Greatest American Diplomat," and pays a tribute to Mr. Trescot in the *News and Courier* which cannot be quoted on account of its length, but which is illuminating and instructive. Edward Trescot has this to say of his father's death: "At the time of my father's death he had, I feel confident, been sent on more diplomatic missions than any other man. He was buried in the churchyard of St. Paul's Episcopal Church here, and upon the monument which marks his grave is a quotation from an address of his before the South Carolina Historical Association at Charleston in May, 1859. It reads as follows: 'South Carolina . . . she will soothe the hours of that long twilight when we will creep gladly to her bosom, there to rest forever.' "

TOMASSEE

"Tomassee," the home of General Andrew Pickens, is of interest to the people of South Carolina not because of its beautiful architecture and costly equipment, but because it was the home of one of the most noted sons of our State. In the hills of South Carolina can be found the home that in many respects reflects the character of this noted statesman, soldier and scholar.

In 1752, Andrew Pickens, a boy of thirteen years, was brought to the Piedmont section of South Carolina by his parents, who were in search of a milder climate than that of the States farther north from whence they came. As years passed on his strong character and undaunted courage made him a leader among men. At twenty-one years of age we find him a colonel in the expedition against the Cherokee Indians. In 1765 he married Miss Rebecca Calhoun, a daughter of Ezekiel Calhoun, a prominent man of the Piedmont section.

Historians have neglected to emphasize General Pickens' service to his country. He was widely known all through upper South Carolina for his piety and fearless bravery, and when he declared against George III men everywhere flocked to the patriot standard. Gen. Pickens never drew a cent of pay for his Revolutionary services, he felt his reward in the love of his country. Aside from many other honors bestowed upon him he was a member of the convention which formed the State

OLD STONE CHURCH, PENDLETON, BUILT 1790
From an old print

Constitution. In 1794 he became a member of Congress, which then sat in Philadelphia. The following is quoted from a book concerning the Old Stone Church of Oconee County.

"At that time there were neither railroads nor stage coaches. . . . All travel was done on horseback. Picture to yourself a man who was approaching his three score years, of martial figure and dignified demeanor, mounted on a spirited milk-white Andalusian steed, whip in hand, and hostlers filled with a brace of pistols, the silver mountings of which glittered in the sunlight; a three-cornered hat, from beneath the silvery gray hair, put smoothly back, and tied in a queue, and undress military coat, ruffled shirt, fair top boots, with handsome silver spurs; following at a little distance, on a stout draft house, is his African attendant, Pompey, in livery of blue, with scarlet facings, carrying a portmanteau, with a consequential and dignified air showing in every movement the pride of a body-servant to his revered master. Paint this in your mind's eye, and you have before you a gentleman of the Eighteenth Century, with his servant on his way to Congress; such was General Andrew Pickens, as he passed through to Philadelphia in 1794."

After refusing reëlection to Congress, General Pickens retired to his old home, "Tomassee," where he died in peace and quiet on the 11th of August, 1871. In the cemetery of the Old Stone Church on the road between Pendleton and Fort Hill can be found on a simple tombstone this inscription: "General Andrew Pickens was born 13th, September, 1739, and died 11th August 1817. He was a Christian, a Patriot and Soldier. His character and action are incorporated with the history of his country. Filial affection and respect raises this stone to his memory."

The Daughters of the American Revolution have converted Tomassee into a school for the mountain children, and it stands as a memorial to its owner. Pickens' library, which is very complete, is being used in this school. Near Tomassee stands a colonial fort, once garrisoned by the British, called Oconee Station.

A little may be said here of General Pickens' younger son, Andrew, who afterwards became Governor of South Carolina. He was elected just before the breaking out of the Civil War, rendered distinguished service in the legislature, in Congress, at the Court of St. Petersburg and in the executive chair of the State. Governor Pickens' home stands in Charleston at the northeast corner of Smith and Beaufain Streets. Governor Pickens' son, Francis, was also Governor of South Carolina, thus we find that this family has been well represented in the political history of the State.

The family later became identified with the history of Edgefield County and in the town of Edgefield is to be found a large old rambling wooden house, built and occupied by the Pickens family.

One of the most interesting of the family was the daughter of the lovely Lucy Holcome, of Texas, and the Andrew Pickens who was the Ambassador to Russia—her name being "Duscha."

Duscha Pickens is said to have been the most fascinating woman of upper South Carolina. Although she was not beautiful, she had made, so it is said, a study of man and his moods, and could subjugate at a moment's glance the most doughty flirt of the opposite sex, and one of her descendants who now resides near Washington, D. C., is said to have inherited this peculiar quality of fascination.

THE BURT HOUSE IN ABBEVILLE

The house in Abbeville, S. C., known as the Burt house was built by Mr. David Leslie about the year 1850. The house was bought by Rev. T. Hoyt, a Presbyterian minister, who left Abbeville. Mr. Andrew Simonds was the next owner of this property. He was the president of the First National Bank of Abbeville. He married Sarah Calhoun, and with his wife later moved to Charleston, being connected with the First National Bank of Charleston. It is to be remarked that his two sons, John and Louis, now occupy the positions of President and Vice President of this establishment.

The Simonds' home in Abbeville came into the possession of Mr. Armistead Burt, who was an intimate friend of Gen. George McDuffie, also of John C. Calhoun, and was the associate of Mr. Calhoun for years in Congress, being his nephew

THE BURT HOUSE, ABBEVILLE, BUILT BY A CALHOUN

At this house was held the last meeting of the Confederate Cabinet

by marriage. Mr. Burt occupied this place during the Confederate War, and in this house, on the sixth of May, 1865, was held the last cabinet meeting of the Confederacy, only three members being present in addition to President Davis.

It may be asked how so strange an historical coincidence came to pass, that in Abbeville in the Burt house, was performed the last official act of the Confederacy, while hardly a stone's throw from the spot was Secession Hill, where four years previous was held the first of the Secession meetings, at which Judge Wardlaw of Abbeville vainly pleaded for some other way to be found for the South to secure her political rights than by secession. It may be said in answer that Armistead Burt had been in the House of Representatives while Davis (afterwards President) was in the Senate, and a warm personal friendship had sprung up between these two men. It is only reasonable to suppose that when President Davis, his cabinet and escort, were retreating through South Carolina, after leaving the hospitable home of General M. W. Gary in Cokesbury because pursued by Federal forces, the thoughts of President Davis should turn to his friend Armistead Burt, and that he should seek shelter under his hospitable roof, there to hold the last meeting of his cabinet.

Tradition states that when the last official document had been signed and the official seal of the Confederacy impressed by Secretary of State Judah P. Benjamin, the great seal of the Confederacy was thrown into a well on the premises. Thus do we touch upon one of the great mysteries of Southern history, the fate of the Great Seal of a Nation that perished.

The following afternoon, hearing again the Federal forces were only a few miles off, it was deemed expedient for the President's party to push on and across the Savannah river, and endeavor to escape into Georgia. About midnight, therefore, the order was given, slowly and wearily the soldiers went out of the town. As President Davis was captured and incarcerated soon after leaving the Burt house, this place has a peculiar significance in Southern history.

ADDITIONAL HOUSES OF HISTORIC INTEREST IN SOUTH CAROLINA

Below are given names of houses not included in the present volume for lack of space. These include the most important.

A   Abbeville—Town and County.
Cheves Homestead (County).
Wardlaw Home (Town).

B   Barnwell—Town and County.
Aldrich Homestead (Town).
Hagood Residence (Town).
Hagood Homestead (County).
The Brabham House at Ehrhardt, S. C., Barnwell Co.
The Ford House (County).

C   Camden.
Tom Kirkland's House (County).
The Boykin Home (County).

                     Old Cheraw—Town, County, District.
Kollock (County).
Duval (Town).
House near Easterling's Mill where Gen. Winfield Scott stayed.
Hartwell Edward's Home—Mar's Bluff.
J. W. Wallace's Home near Mar's Bluff.
Old Houses at Society Hill (Old Cheraw District).
Pegues (Town).

                     Chester—Town and County.
Davie Homestead—Langford Section (County).
"Red Bank"—The Eberhardt Home, Chester County.
Arthur Gaston's Residence (Town).

D   Darlington.
James Homestead (Town).
E. M. Williamson House (Darlington County). Built in 1812 by Jordan Sanders.

E   Edgefield.
Hammond Houses near Hamburg (Old Edgefield District).
The Bettiss, Bouknight Place (County).
The Pickens' Home (Town).

G   Georgetown.
" Chantilly," Alston Place (County).
House from which Major James escaped.

M   Marion.

Jacob Brawler's Primitive Home (Marion County).
Gen. G. N. Evans' House (Marion Town).
"Pierre Haven"—Home of Judge C. A. Woods (Town).

O   Orangeburg.

The John Cart Home (Town).
The Bull Residence (Town).
Salley Residences (County).

S   Sumter.

The Colcalough Homestead.
The Dick Homestead.

W   Winnsboro.

The MacMaster Homes, Winnsboro (Town).
The James Kincaid House, Winnsboro (Town).
Cornwallis' Headquarters, Winnsboro.

Y   York.

The Bratton House (Scene of Huck's defeat).
The Bratton Homestead (Town).

It has not been considered needful to include in this list the houses in Charleston, S. C., which have received such adequate treatment in the "Dwelling Houses of Charleston," by Miss Alice Smith and her father, Mr. D. E. Huger Smith.

INDEX

INDEX

INDEX

INDEX

INDEX

317

INDEX